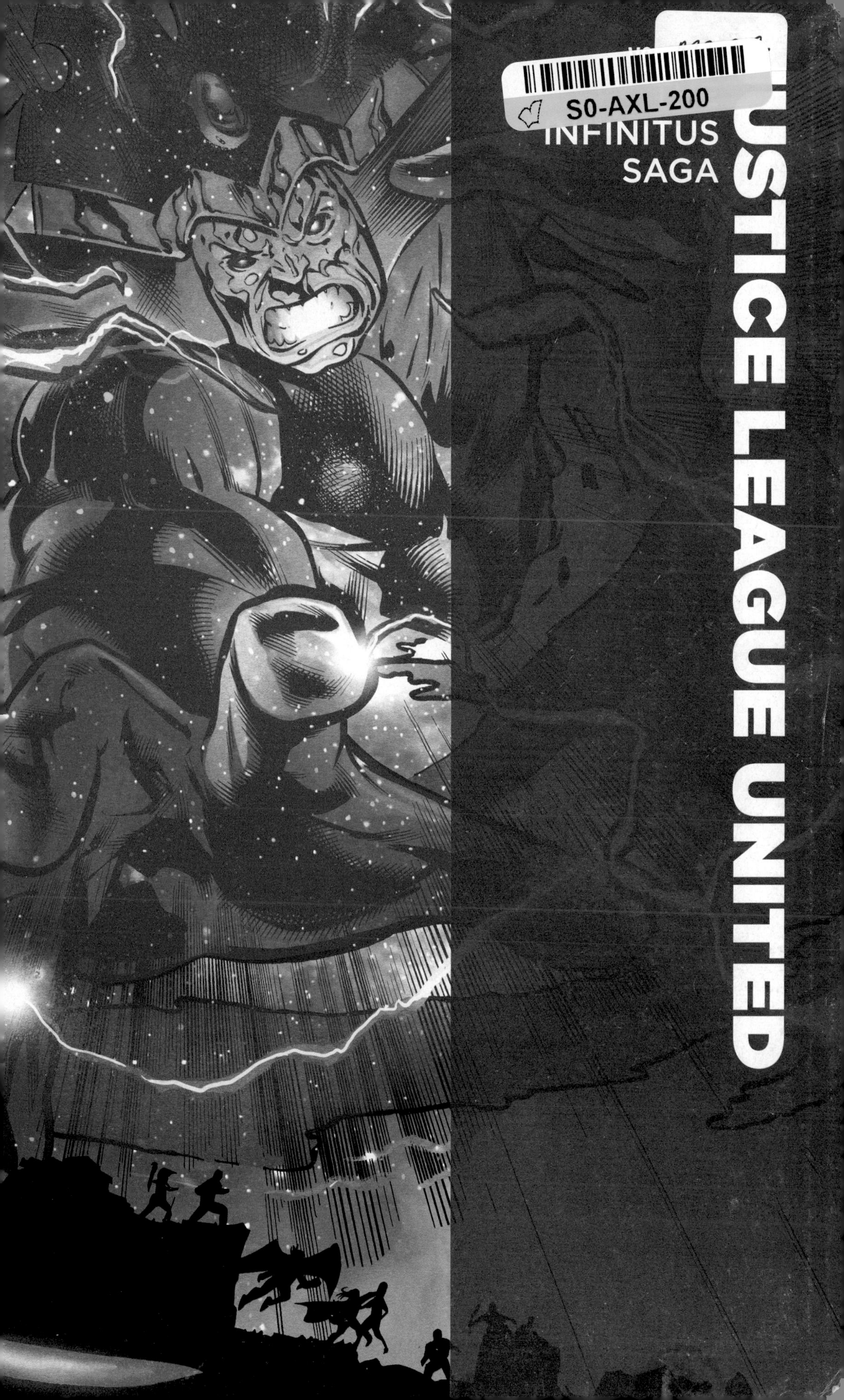
JUSTICE LEAGUE UNITED
INFINITUS
SAGA

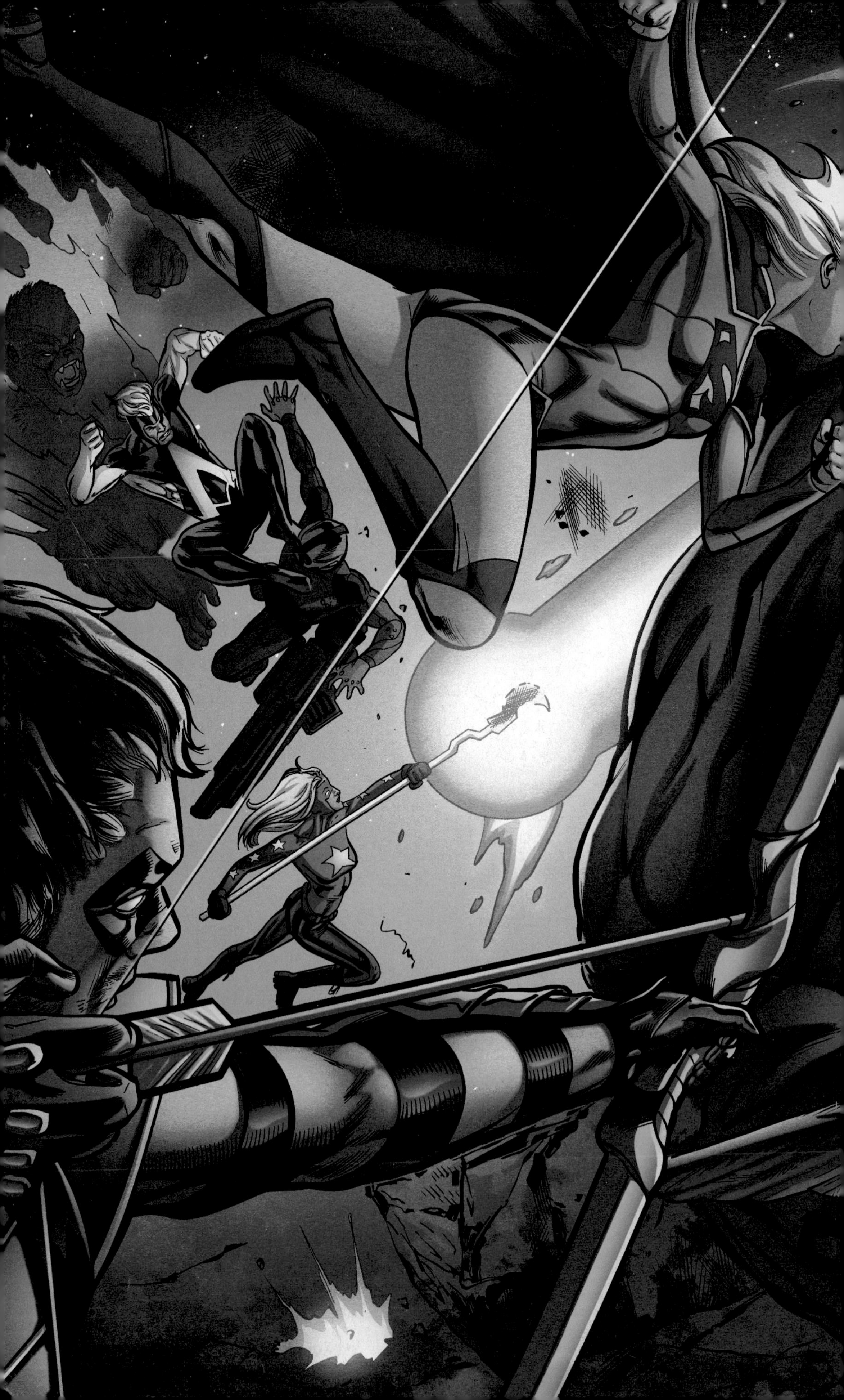

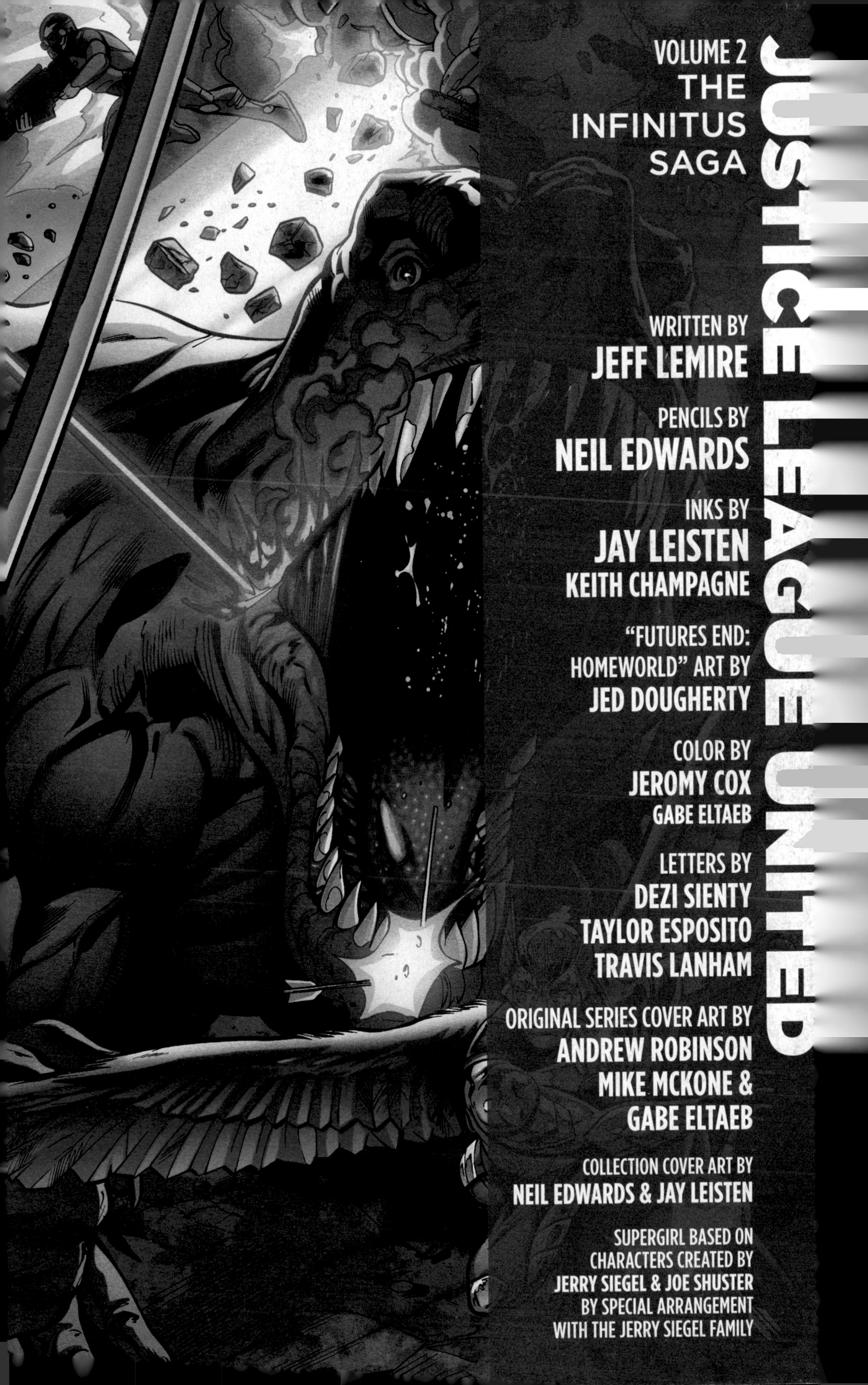

JUSTICE LEAGUE UNITED

VOLUME 2
THE INFINITUS SAGA

WRITTEN BY
JEFF LEMIRE

PENCILS BY
NEIL EDWARDS

INKS BY
JAY LEISTEN
KEITH CHAMPAGNE

"FUTURES END: HOMEWORLD" ART BY
JED DOUGHERTY

COLOR BY
JEROMY COX
GABE ELTAEB

LETTERS BY
DEZI SIENTY
TAYLOR ESPOSITO
TRAVIS LANHAM

ORIGINAL SERIES COVER ART BY
ANDREW ROBINSON
MIKE MCKONE &
GABE ELTAEB

COLLECTION COVER ART BY
NEIL EDWARDS & JAY LEISTEN

SUPERGIRL BASED ON
CHARACTERS CREATED BY
JERRY SIEGEL & JOE SHUSTER
BY SPECIAL ARRANGEMENT
WITH THE JERRY SIEGEL FAMILY

JUSTICE LEAGUE UNITED VOLUME 2: THE INFINITUS SAGA

Published by DC Comics. Compilation and all new material copyright © 2015 DC Comics. All Rights Reserved.
Originally published in single magazine form in JUSTICE LEAGUE UNITED 6-10, JUSTICE LEAGUE UNITED ANNUAL 1,
JUSTICE LEAGUE: FUTURES END 1, JUSTICE LEAGUE UNITED: FUTURES END 1 © 2014, 2015 DC Comics. All Rights Reserved.
All characters, their distinctive likenesses and related elements featured in this publication are trademarks of DC Comics.
The stories, characters and incidents featured in this publication are entirely fictional.
DC Comics does not read or accept unsolicited ideas, stories or artwork.

DC Comics, 2900 West Alameda Avenue, Burbank, CA 91505
Printed by RR Donnelley, Salem, VA, USA. 9/9/16.
ISBN: 978-1-4012-7035-3
First Printing.

Library of Congress Cataloging-in-Publication Data

Lemire, Jeff, author.
Justice League United. Volume 2, The infinitus saga / Jeff Lemire, writer ; Neil Edwards, artist.
pages cm
ISBN 978-1-4012-7035-3
1. Graphic novels. I. Edwards, Neil (Comic artist), illustrator. II. Title. III. Title: Infinitus saga.
PN6728.J87L56 2015
741.5'973—dc23
2015031186

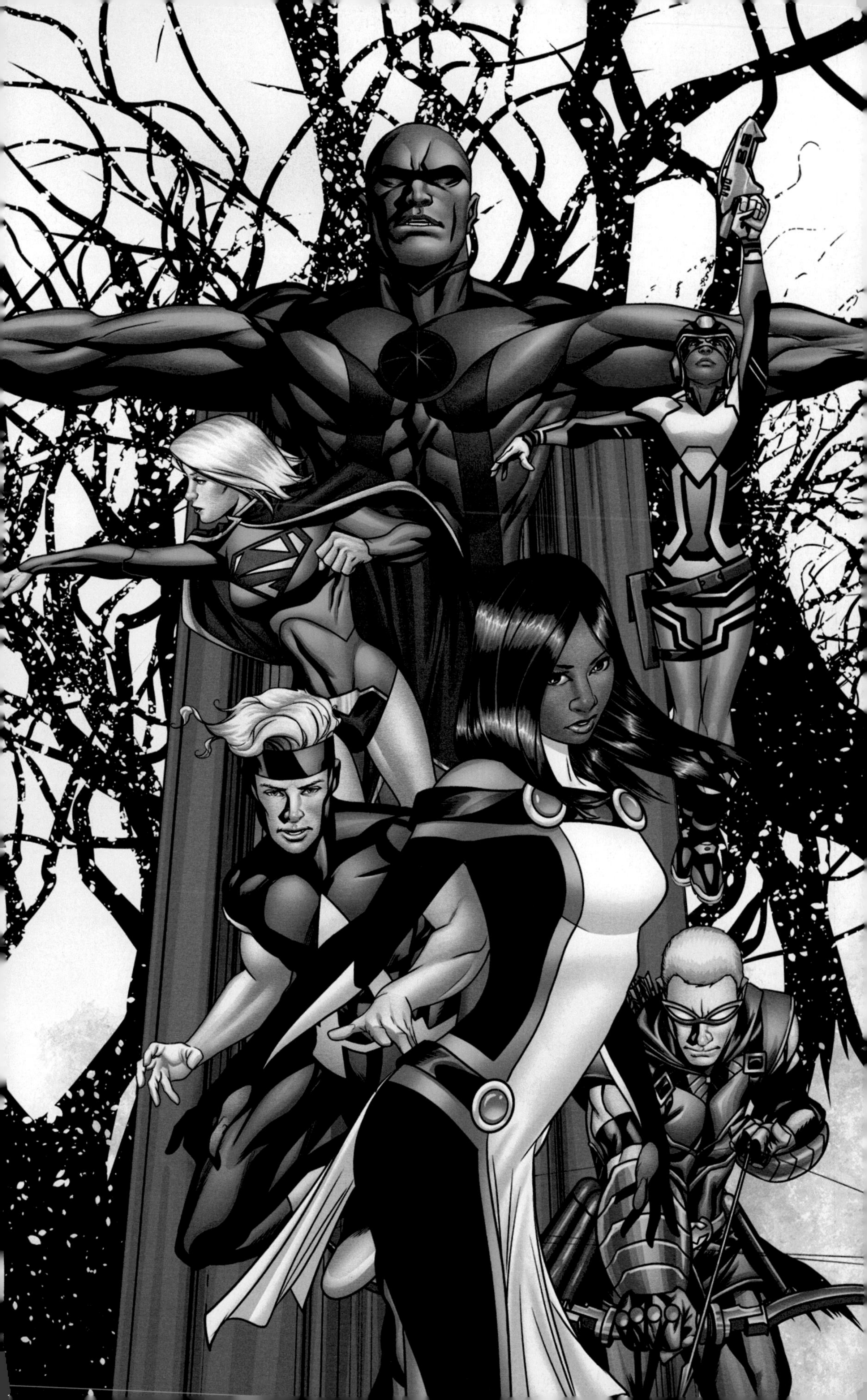

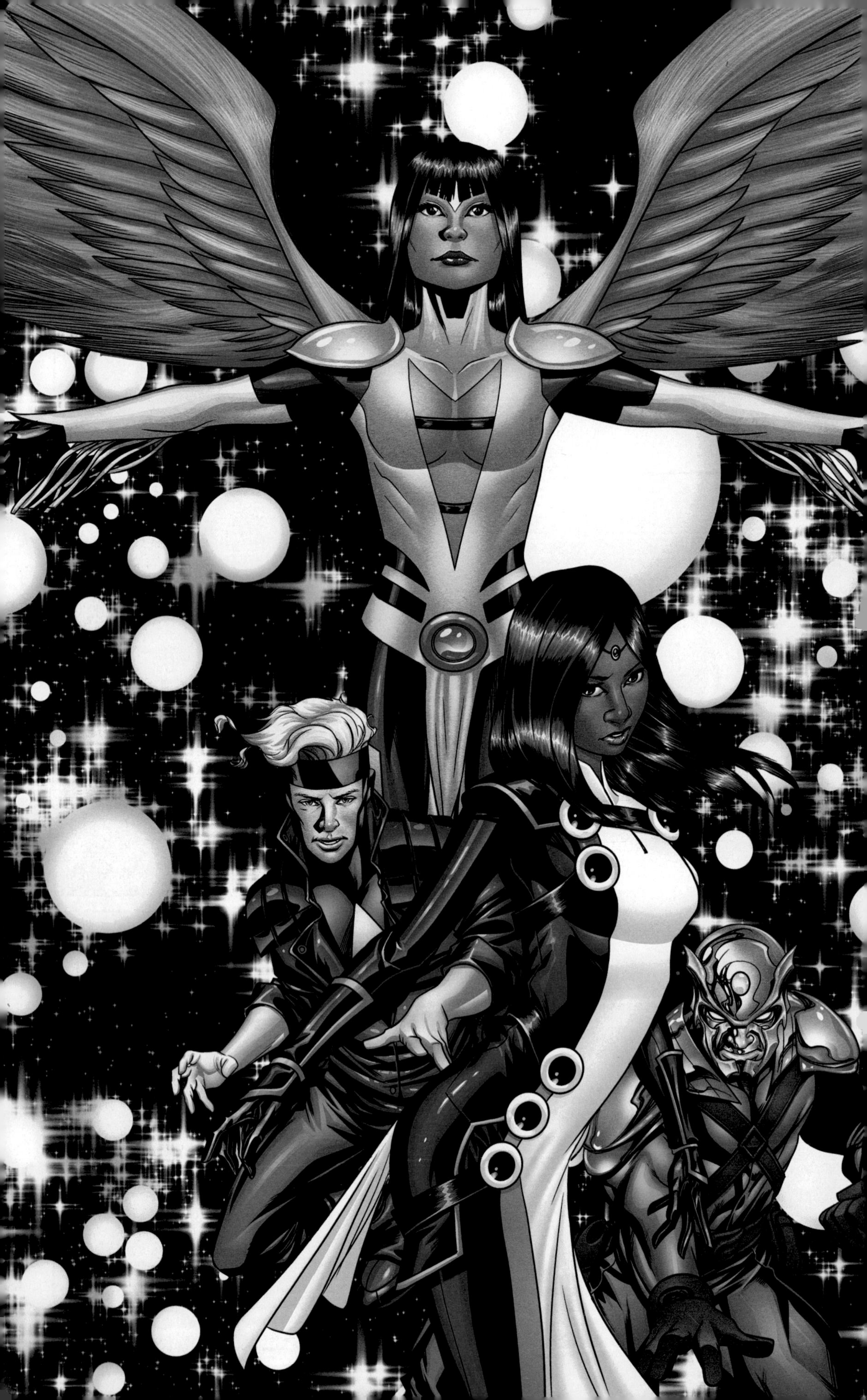

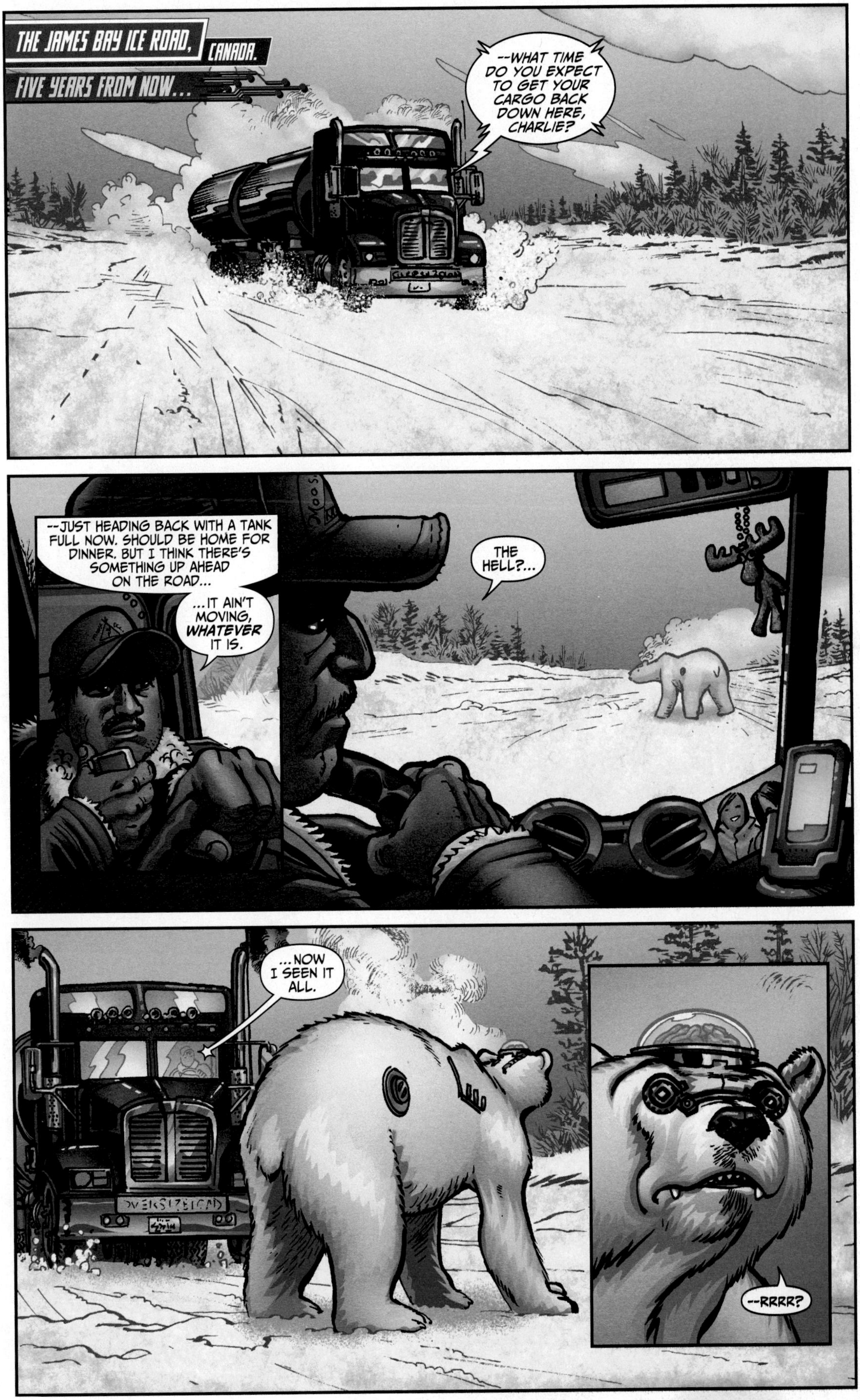
THE JAMES BAY ICE ROAD, CANADA.
FIVE YEARS FROM NOW...
--WHAT TIME DO YOU EXPECT TO GET YOUR CARGO BACK DOWN HERE, CHARLIE?
--JUST HEADING BACK WITH A TANK FULL NOW. SHOULD BE HOME FOR DINNER. BUT I THINK THERE'S SOMETHING UP AHEAD ON THE ROAD...
...IT AIN'T MOVING, WHATEVER IT IS.
THE HELL?...
...NOW I SEEN IT ALL.
--RRRR?

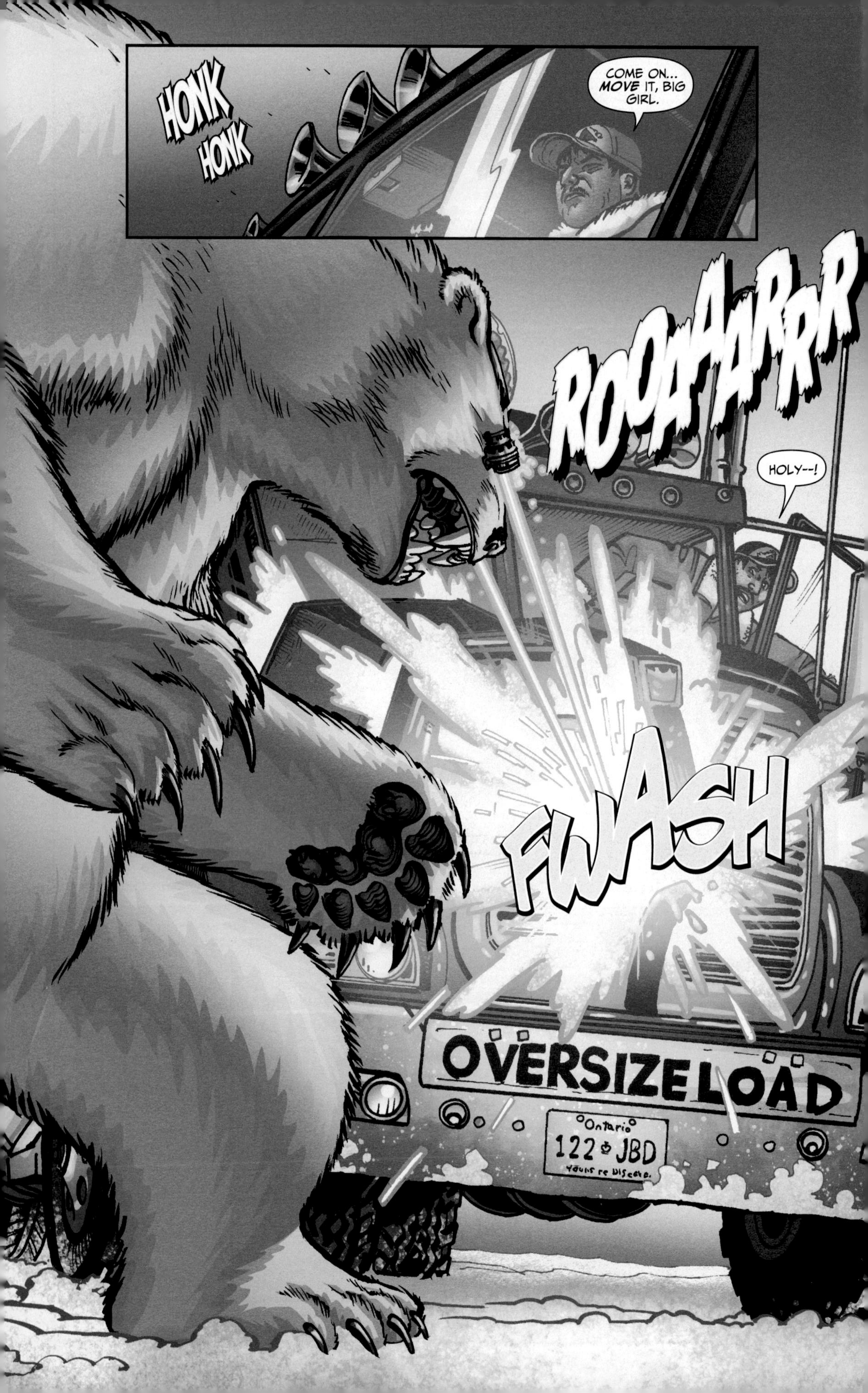
HONK
HONK
COME ON... MOVE IT, BIG GIRL.
ROOAARRR
HOLY--!
FWASH
OVERSIZE LOAD
Ontario
122 JBD

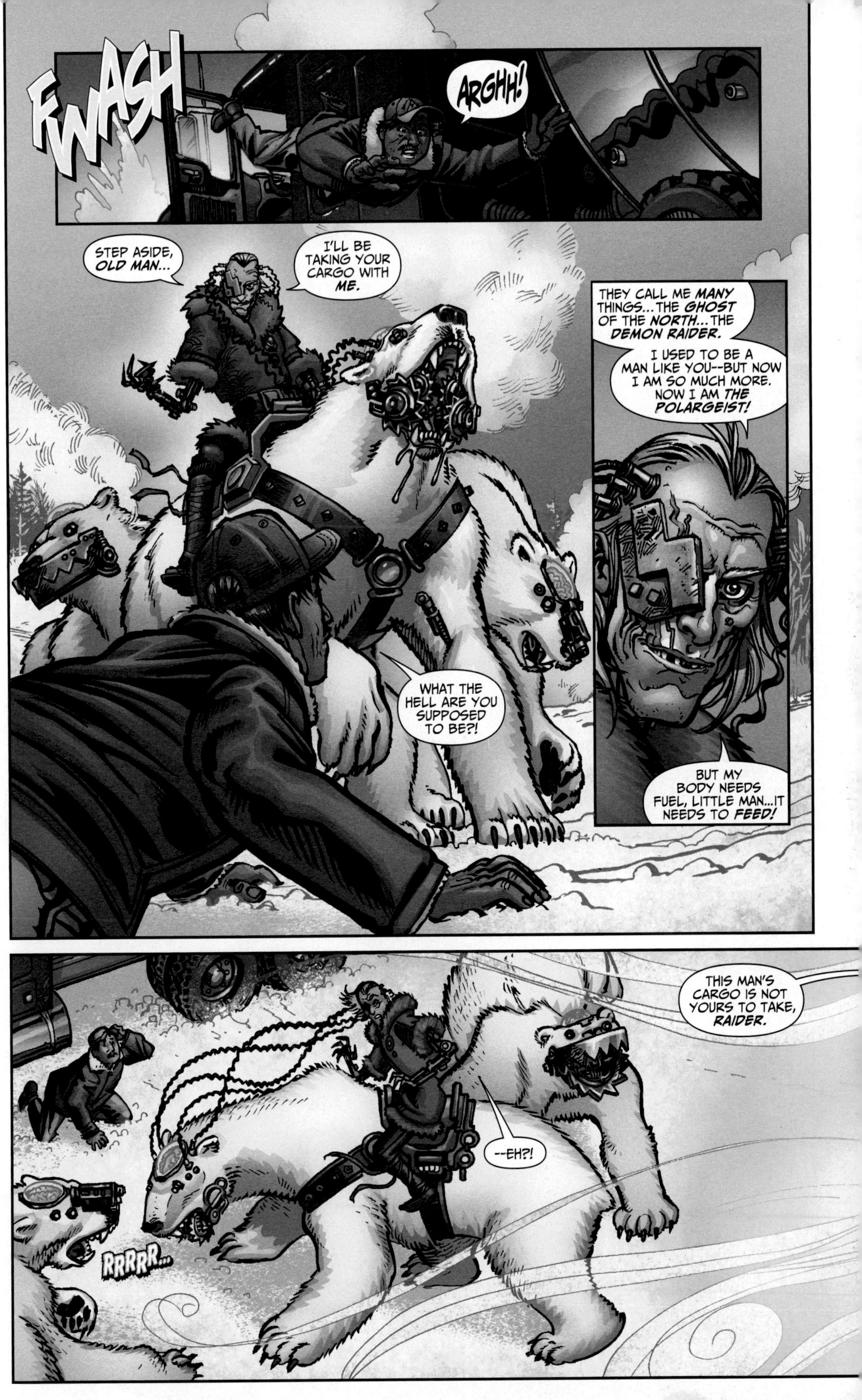
FWASH
ARGHH!
STEP ASIDE, OLD MAN...
I'LL BE TAKING YOUR CARGO WITH ME.
WHAT THE HELL ARE YOU SUPPOSED TO BE?!
THEY CALL ME MANY THINGS...THE GHOST OF THE NORTH...THE DEMON RAIDER.
I USED TO BE A MAN LIKE YOU--BUT NOW I AM SO MUCH MORE. NOW I AM THE POLARGEIST!
BUT MY BODY NEEDS FUEL, LITTLE MAN...IT NEEDS TO FEED!
THIS MAN'S CARGO IS NOT YOURS TO TAKE, RAIDER.
--EH?!
RRRRR...

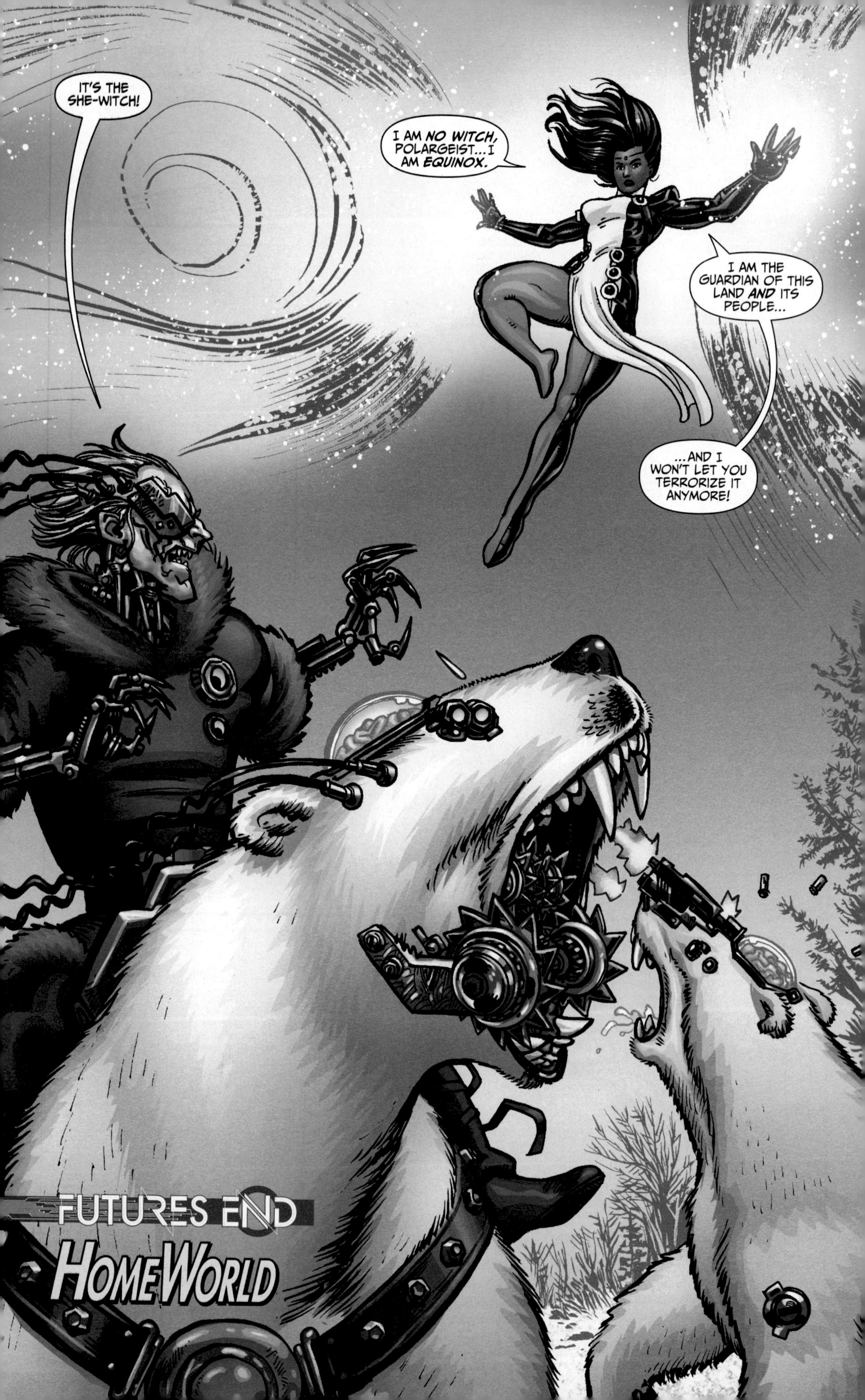
IT'S THE SHE-WITCH!
I AM NO WITCH, POLARGEIST...I AM EQUINOX.
I AM THE GUARDIAN OF THIS LAND AND ITS PEOPLE...
...AND I WON'T LET YOU TERRORIZE IT ANYMORE!
FUTURES END
HOMEWORLD

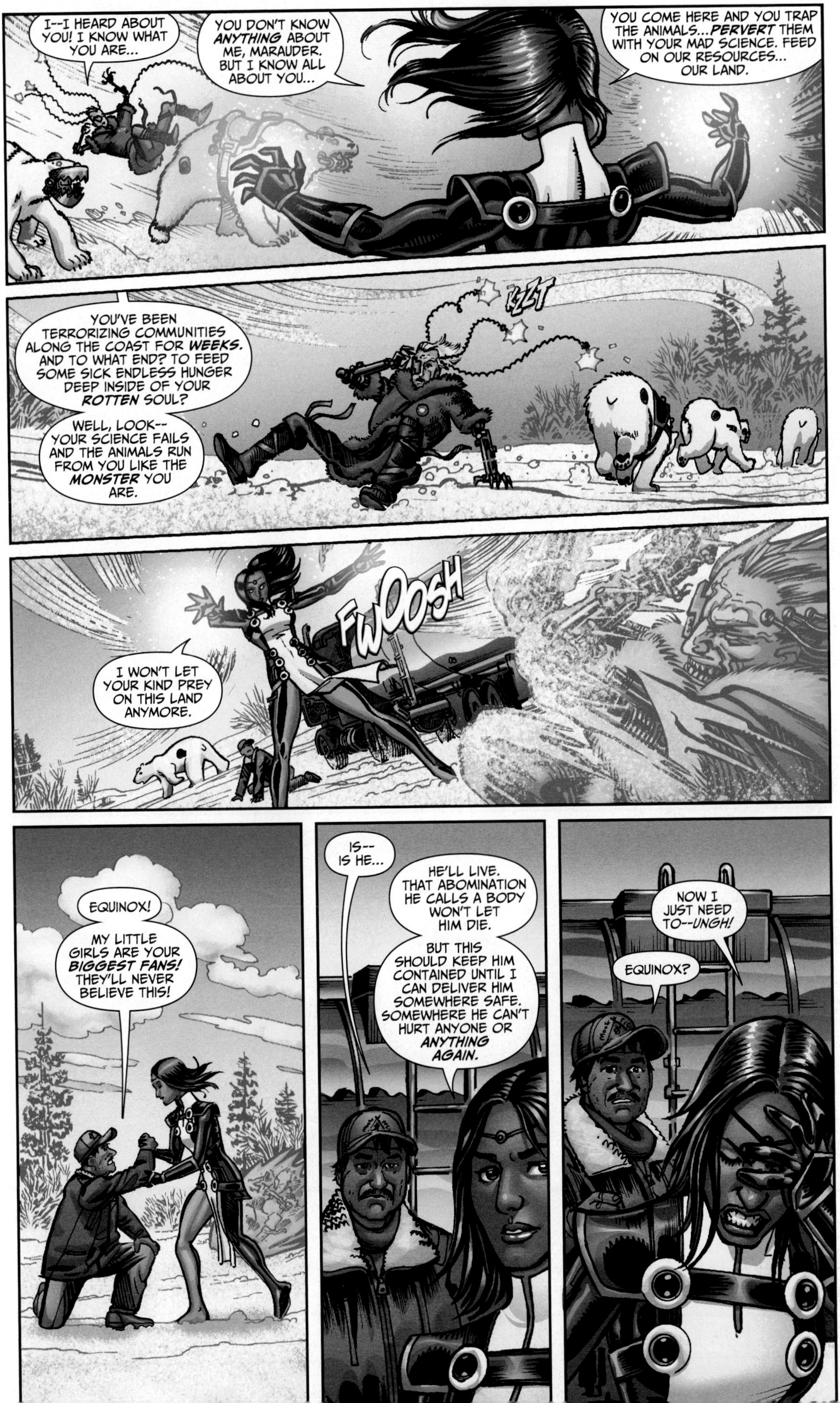
I--I HEARD ABOUT YOU! I KNOW WHAT YOU ARE...
YOU DON'T KNOW *ANYTHING* ABOUT ME, MARAUDER. BUT I KNOW ALL ABOUT YOU...
YOU COME HERE AND YOU TRAP THE ANIMALS...*PERVERT* THEM WITH YOUR MAD SCIENCE. FEED ON OUR RESOURCES... OUR LAND.
KZZT
YOU'VE BEEN TERRORIZING COMMUNITIES ALONG THE COAST FOR *WEEKS.* AND TO WHAT END? TO FEED SOME SICK ENDLESS HUNGER DEEP INSIDE OF YOUR *ROTTEN* SOUL?
WELL, LOOK-- YOUR SCIENCE FAILS AND THE ANIMALS RUN FROM YOU LIKE THE *MONSTER* YOU ARE.
FWOOSH
I WON'T LET YOUR KIND PREY ON THIS LAND ANYMORE.
EQUINOX!
MY LITTLE GIRLS ARE YOUR *BIGGEST FANS!* THEY'LL NEVER BELIEVE THIS!
IS-- IS HE...
HE'LL LIVE. THAT ABOMINATION HE CALLS A BODY WON'T LET HIM DIE.
BUT THIS SHOULD KEEP HIM CONTAINED UNTIL I CAN DELIVER HIM SOMEWHERE SAFE. SOMEWHERE HE CAN'T HURT ANYONE OR *ANYTHING AGAIN.*
NOW I JUST NEED TO--*UNGH!*
EQUINOX?

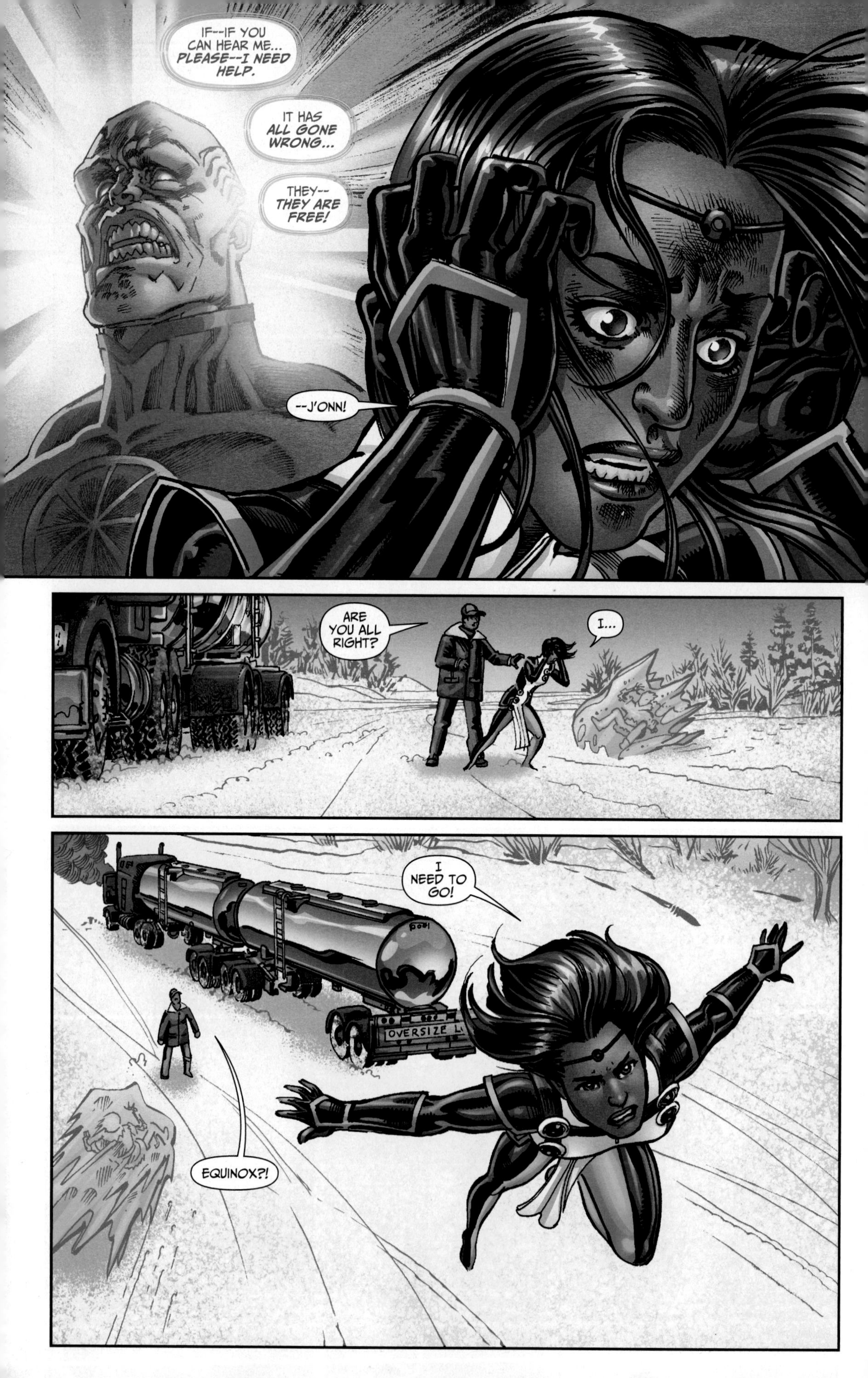
IF--IF YOU CAN HEAR ME... PLEASE--I NEED HELP.
IT HAS ALL GONE WRONG...
THEY-- THEY ARE FREE!
--J'ONN!
ARE YOU ALL RIGHT?
I...
I NEED TO GO!
OVERSIZE L
EQUINOX?!

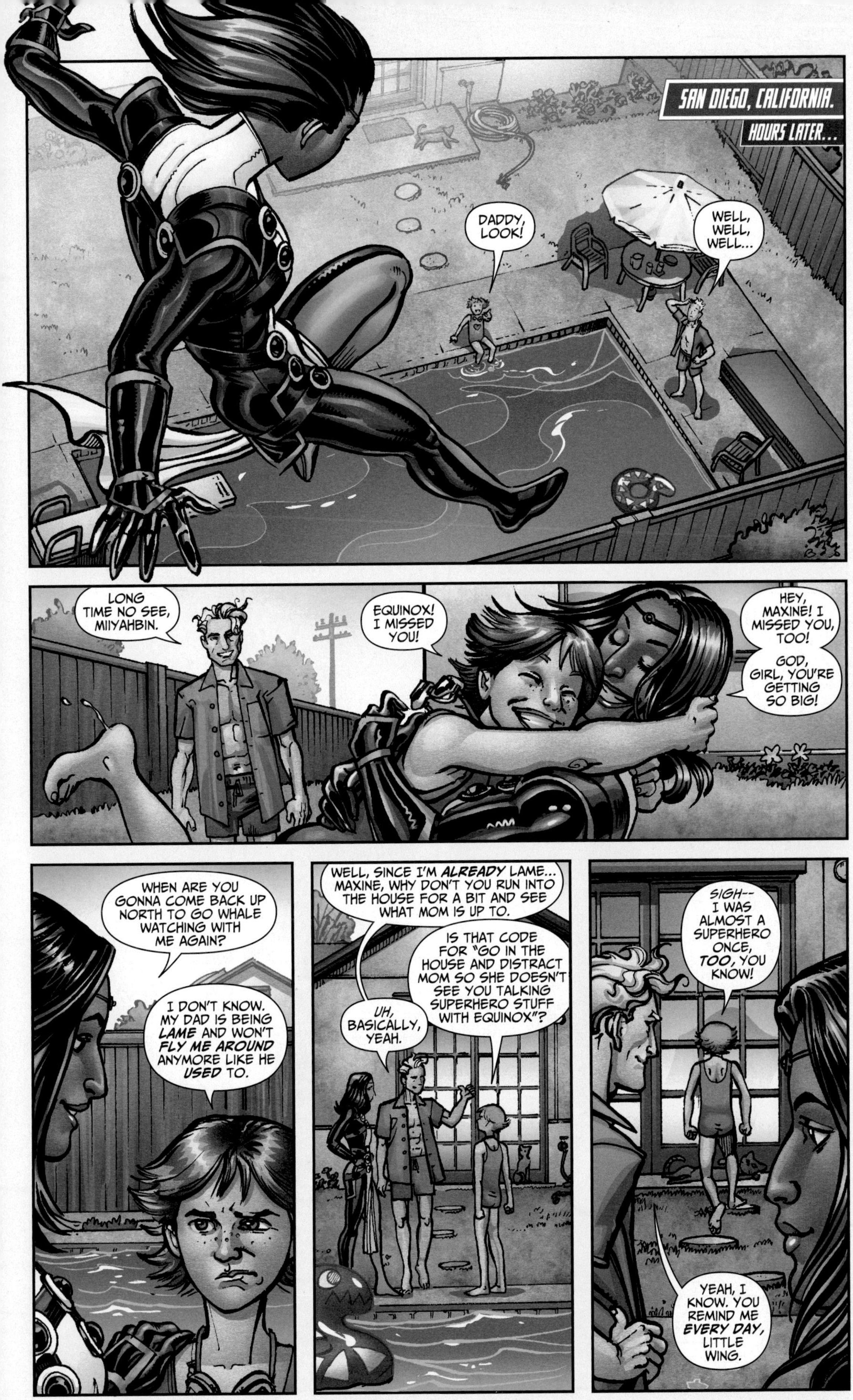
SAN DIEGO, CALIFORNIA.
HOURS LATER...
DADDY, LOOK!
WELL, WELL, WELL...
LONG TIME NO SEE, MIIYAHBIN.
EQUINOX! I MISSED YOU!
HEY, MAXINE! I MISSED YOU, TOO!
GOD, GIRL, YOU'RE GETTING SO BIG!
WHEN ARE YOU GONNA COME BACK UP NORTH TO GO WHALE WATCHING WITH ME AGAIN?
I DON'T KNOW. MY DAD IS BEING LAME AND WON'T FLY ME AROUND ANYMORE LIKE HE USED TO.
WELL, SINCE I'M ALREADY LAME... MAXINE, WHY DON'T YOU RUN INTO THE HOUSE FOR A BIT AND SEE WHAT MOM IS UP TO.
IS THAT CODE FOR "GO IN THE HOUSE AND DISTRACT MOM SO SHE DOESN'T SEE YOU TALKING SUPERHERO STUFF WITH EQUINOX"?
UH, BASICALLY, YEAH.
SIGH-- I WAS ALMOST A SUPERHERO ONCE, TOO, YOU KNOW!
YEAH, I KNOW. YOU REMIND ME EVERY DAY, LITTLE WING.

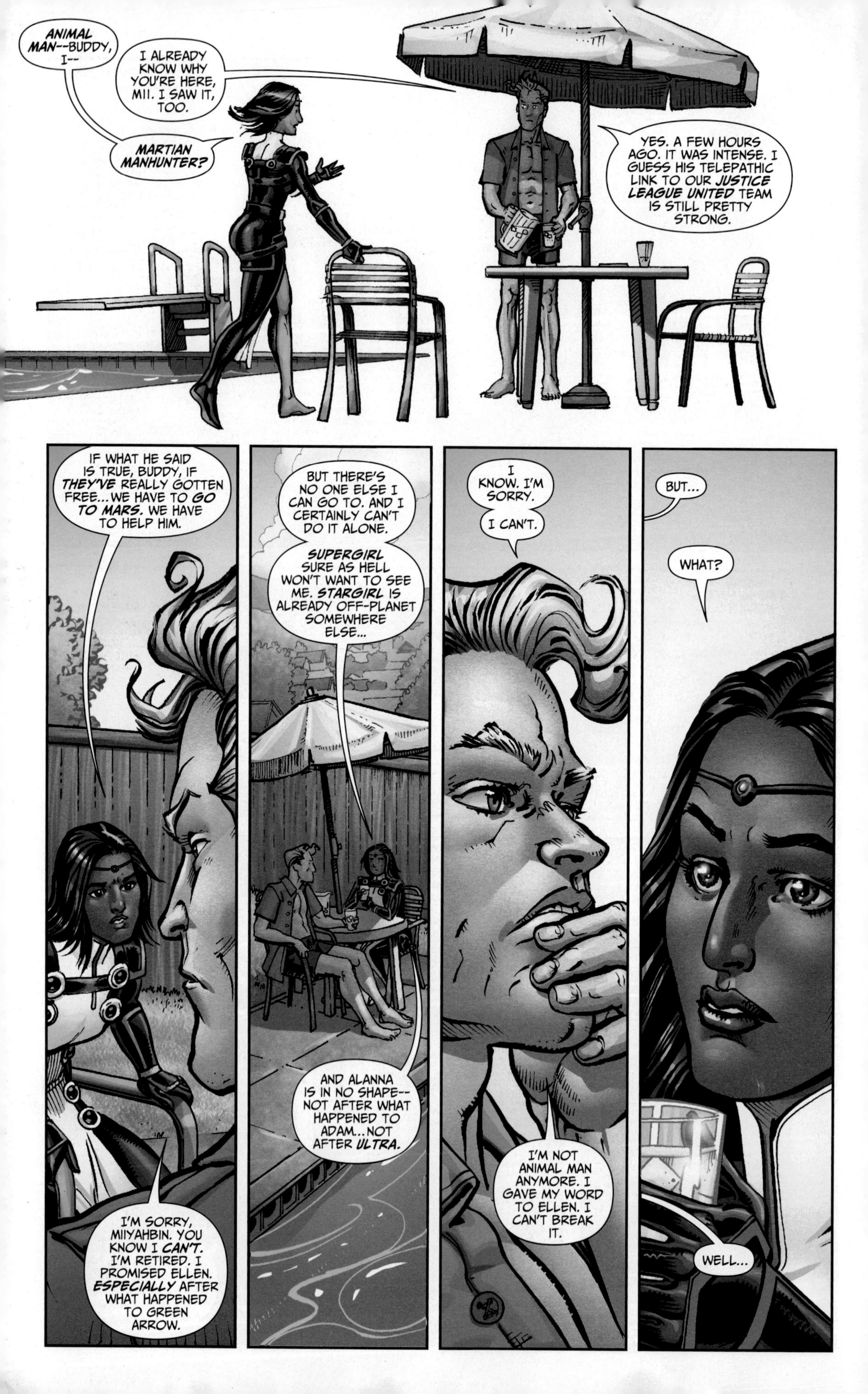
ANIMAL MAN--BUDDY, I--
I ALREADY KNOW WHY YOU'RE HERE, MII. I SAW IT, TOO.
MARTIAN MANHUNTER?
YES. A FEW HOURS AGO. IT WAS INTENSE. I GUESS HIS TELEPATHIC LINK TO OUR JUSTICE LEAGUE UNITED TEAM IS STILL PRETTY STRONG.
IF WHAT HE SAID IS TRUE, BUDDY, IF THEY'VE REALLY GOTTEN FREE...WE HAVE TO GO TO MARS. WE HAVE TO HELP HIM.
I'M SORRY, MIIYAHBIN. YOU KNOW I CAN'T. I'M RETIRED. I PROMISED ELLEN. ESPECIALLY AFTER WHAT HAPPENED TO GREEN ARROW.
BUT THERE'S NO ONE ELSE I CAN GO TO. AND I CERTAINLY CAN'T DO IT ALONE.
SUPERGIRL SURE AS HELL WON'T WANT TO SEE ME. STARGIRL IS ALREADY OFF-PLANET SOMEWHERE ELSE...
AND ALANNA IS IN NO SHAPE--NOT AFTER WHAT HAPPENED TO ADAM...NOT AFTER ULTRA.
I KNOW. I'M SORRY.
I CAN'T.
I'M NOT ANIMAL MAN ANYMORE. I GAVE MY WORD TO ELLEN. I CAN'T BREAK IT.
BUT...
WHAT?
WELL...

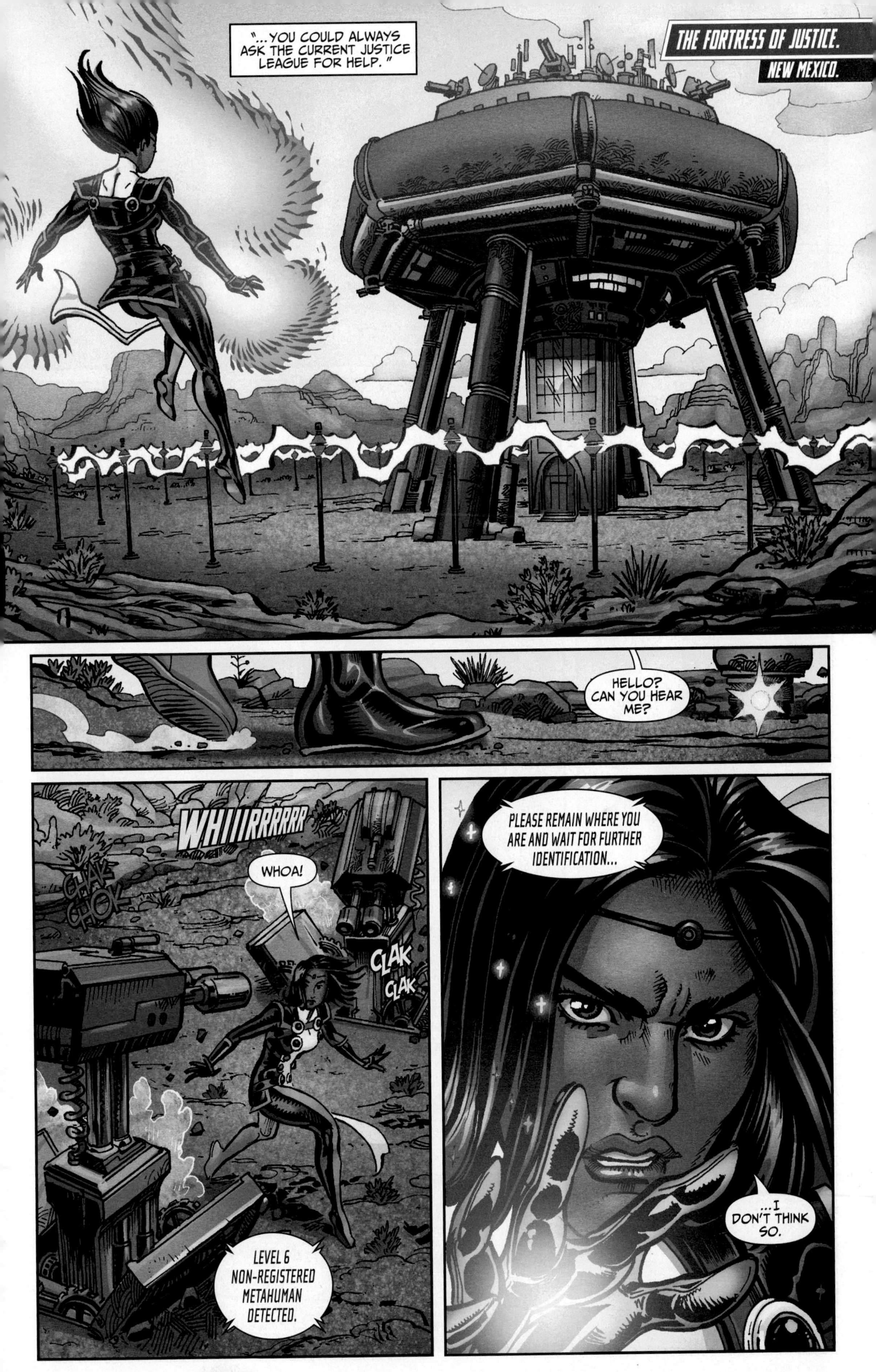
"...YOU COULD ALWAYS ASK THE CURRENT JUSTICE LEAGUE FOR HELP."
THE FORTRESS OF JUSTICE.
NEW MEXICO.
HELLO? CAN YOU HEAR ME?
WHIIIRRRRR
CHAK CHOK
WHOA!
CLAK CLAK
LEVEL 6 NON-REGISTERED METAHUMAN DETECTED.
PLEASE REMAIN WHERE YOU ARE AND WAIT FOR FURTHER IDENTIFICATION...
...I DON'T THINK SO.

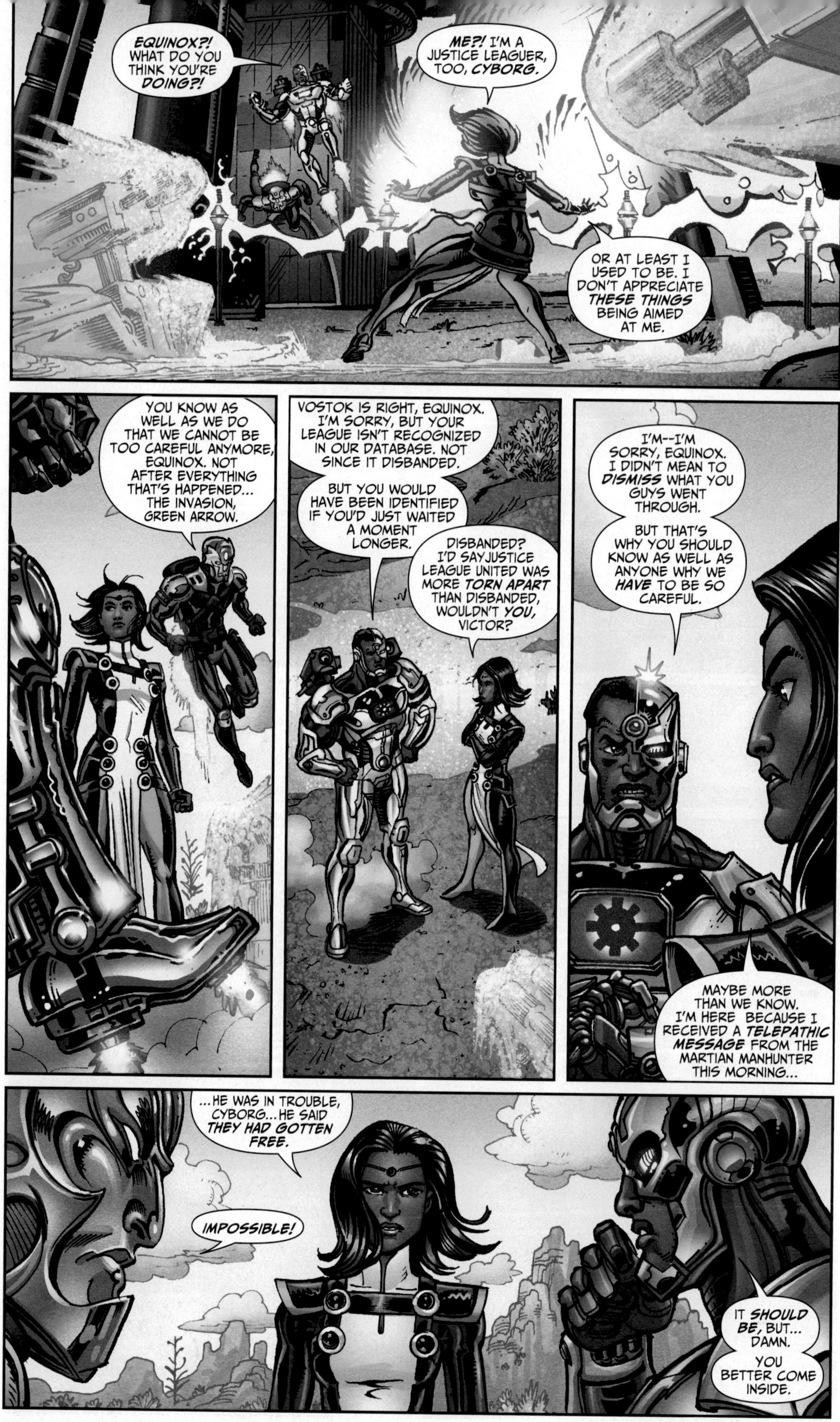

EQUINOX?! WHAT DO YOU THINK YOU'RE DOING?!
ME?! I'M A JUSTICE LEAGUER, TOO, CYBORG.
OR AT LEAST I USED TO BE. I DON'T APPRECIATE THESE THINGS BEING AIMED AT ME.
YOU KNOW AS WELL AS WE DO THAT WE CANNOT BE TOO CAREFUL ANYMORE, EQUINOX. NOT AFTER EVERYTHING THAT'S HAPPENED... THE INVASION, GREEN ARROW.
VOSTOK IS RIGHT, EQUINOX. I'M SORRY, BUT YOUR LEAGUE ISN'T RECOGNIZED IN OUR DATABASE. NOT SINCE IT DISBANDED.
BUT YOU WOULD HAVE BEEN IDENTIFIED IF YOU'D JUST WAITED A MOMENT LONGER.
DISBANDED? I'D SAYJUSTICE LEAGUE UNITED WAS MORE TORN APART THAN DISBANDED, WOULDN'T YOU, VICTOR?
I'M--I'M SORRY, EQUINOX. I DIDN'T MEAN TO DISMISS WHAT YOU GUYS WENT THROUGH.
BUT THAT'S WHY YOU SHOULD KNOW AS WELL AS ANYONE WHY WE HAVE TO BE SO CAREFUL.
MAYBE MORE THAN WE KNOW. I'M HERE BECAUSE I RECEIVED A TELEPATHIC MESSAGE FROM THE MARTIAN MANHUNTER THIS MORNING...
...HE WAS IN TROUBLE, CYBORG...HE SAID THEY HAD GOTTEN FREE.
IMPOSSIBLE!
IT SHOULD BE, BUT... DAMN.
YOU BETTER COME INSIDE.

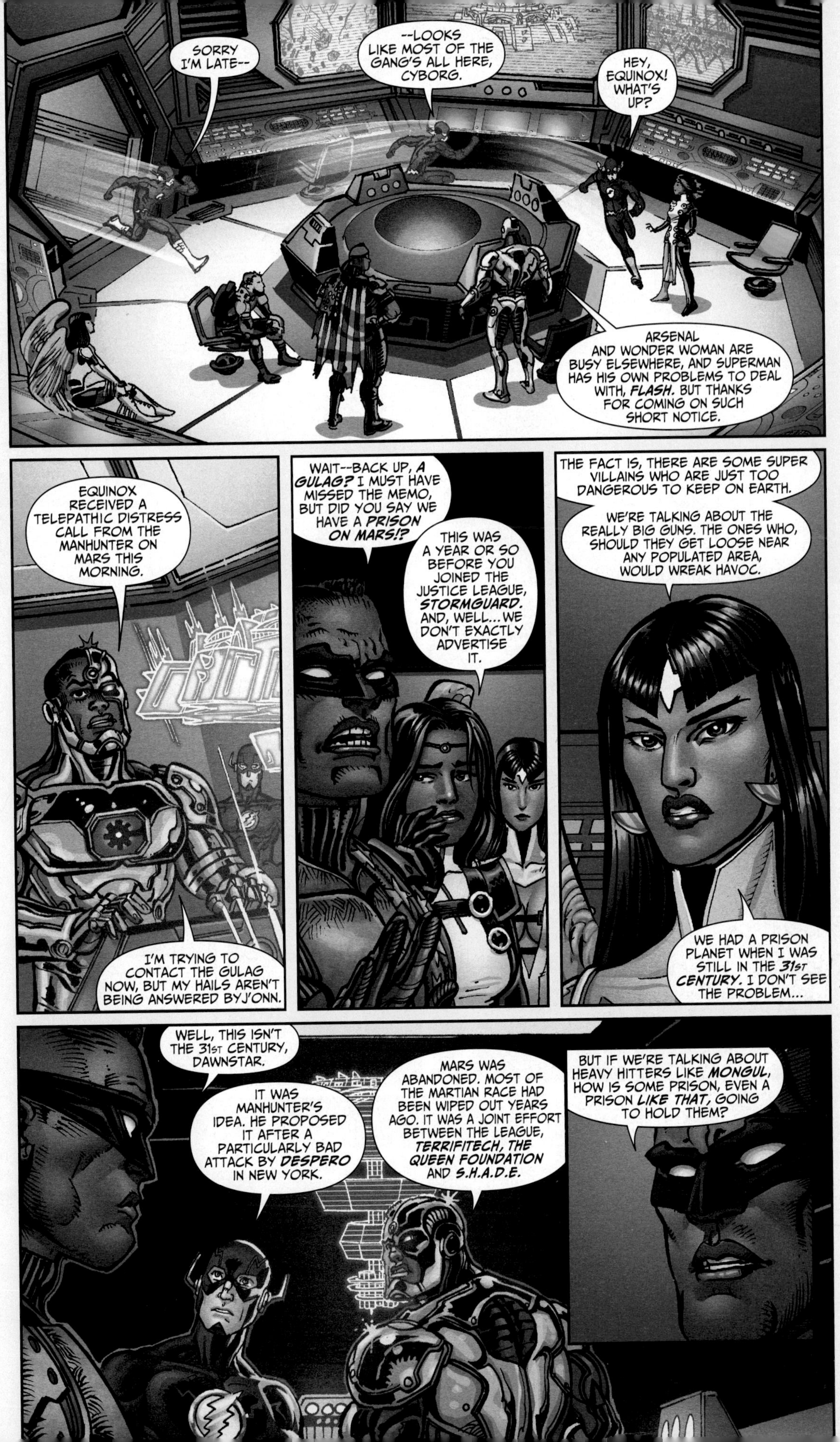
SORRY I'M LATE--
--LOOKS LIKE MOST OF THE GANG'S ALL HERE, CYBORG.
HEY, EQUINOX! WHAT'S UP?
ARSENAL AND WONDER WOMAN ARE BUSY ELSEWHERE, AND SUPERMAN HAS HIS OWN PROBLEMS TO DEAL WITH, FLASH. BUT THANKS FOR COMING ON SUCH SHORT NOTICE.
EQUINOX RECEIVED A TELEPATHIC DISTRESS CALL FROM THE MANHUNTER ON MARS THIS MORNING.
I'M TRYING TO CONTACT THE GULAG NOW, BUT MY HAILS AREN'T BEING ANSWERED BY J'ONN.
WAIT--BACK UP, A GULAG? I MUST HAVE MISSED THE MEMO, BUT DID YOU SAY WE HAVE A PRISON ON MARS!?
THIS WAS A YEAR OR SO BEFORE YOU JOINED THE JUSTICE LEAGUE, STORMGUARD. AND, WELL... WE DON'T EXACTLY ADVERTISE IT.
THE FACT IS, THERE ARE SOME SUPER VILLAINS WHO ARE JUST TOO DANGEROUS TO KEEP ON EARTH.
WE'RE TALKING ABOUT THE REALLY BIG GUNS. THE ONES WHO, SHOULD THEY GET LOOSE NEAR ANY POPULATED AREA, WOULD WREAK HAVOC.
WE HAD A PRISON PLANET WHEN I WAS STILL IN THE 31ST CENTURY. I DON'T SEE THE PROBLEM...
WELL, THIS ISN'T THE 31ST CENTURY, DAWNSTAR.
IT WAS MANHUNTER'S IDEA. HE PROPOSED IT AFTER A PARTICULARLY BAD ATTACK BY DESPERO IN NEW YORK.
MARS WAS ABANDONED. MOST OF THE MARTIAN RACE HAD BEEN WIPED OUT YEARS AGO. IT WAS A JOINT EFFORT BETWEEN THE LEAGUE, TERRIFITECH, THE QUEEN FOUNDATION AND S.H.A.D.E.
BUT IF WE'RE TALKING ABOUT HEAVY HITTERS LIKE MONGUL, HOW IS SOME PRISON, EVEN A PRISON LIKE THAT, GOING TO HOLD THEM?

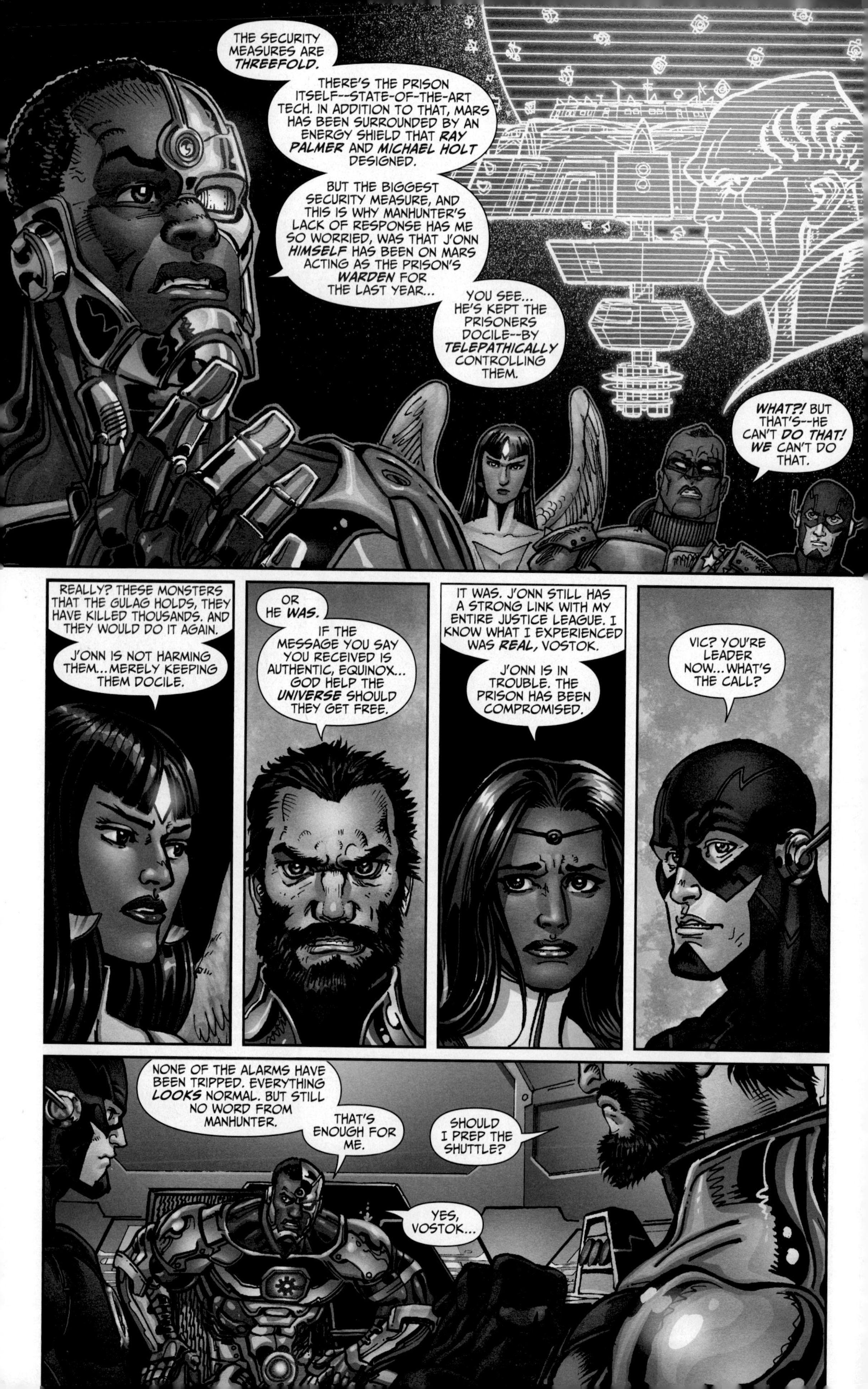
THE SECURITY MEASURES ARE THREEFOLD.
THERE'S THE PRISON ITSELF--STATE-OF-THE-ART TECH. IN ADDITION TO THAT, MARS HAS BEEN SURROUNDED BY AN ENERGY SHIELD THAT RAY PALMER AND MICHAEL HOLT DESIGNED.
BUT THE BIGGEST SECURITY MEASURE, AND THIS IS WHY MANHUNTER'S LACK OF RESPONSE HAS ME SO WORRIED, WAS THAT J'ONN HIMSELF HAS BEEN ON MARS ACTING AS THE PRISON'S WARDEN FOR THE LAST YEAR...
YOU SEE... HE'S KEPT THE PRISONERS DOCILE--BY TELEPATHICALLY CONTROLLING THEM.
WHAT?! BUT THAT'S--HE CAN'T DO THAT! WE CAN'T DO THAT.
REALLY? THESE MONSTERS THAT THE GULAG HOLDS, THEY HAVE KILLED THOUSANDS. AND THEY WOULD DO IT AGAIN.
J'ONN IS NOT HARMING THEM...MERELY KEEPING THEM DOCILE.
OR HE WAS.
IF THE MESSAGE YOU SAY YOU RECEIVED IS AUTHENTIC, EQUINOX... GOD HELP THE UNIVERSE SHOULD THEY GET FREE.
IT WAS. J'ONN STILL HAS A STRONG LINK WITH MY ENTIRE JUSTICE LEAGUE. I KNOW WHAT I EXPERIENCED WAS REAL, VOSTOK.
J'ONN IS IN TROUBLE. THE PRISON HAS BEEN COMPROMISED.
VIC? YOU'RE LEADER NOW...WHAT'S THE CALL?
NONE OF THE ALARMS HAVE BEEN TRIPPED. EVERYTHING LOOKS NORMAL. BUT STILL NO WORD FROM MANHUNTER.
THAT'S ENOUGH FOR ME.
SHOULD I PREP THE SHUTTLE?
YES, VOSTOK...

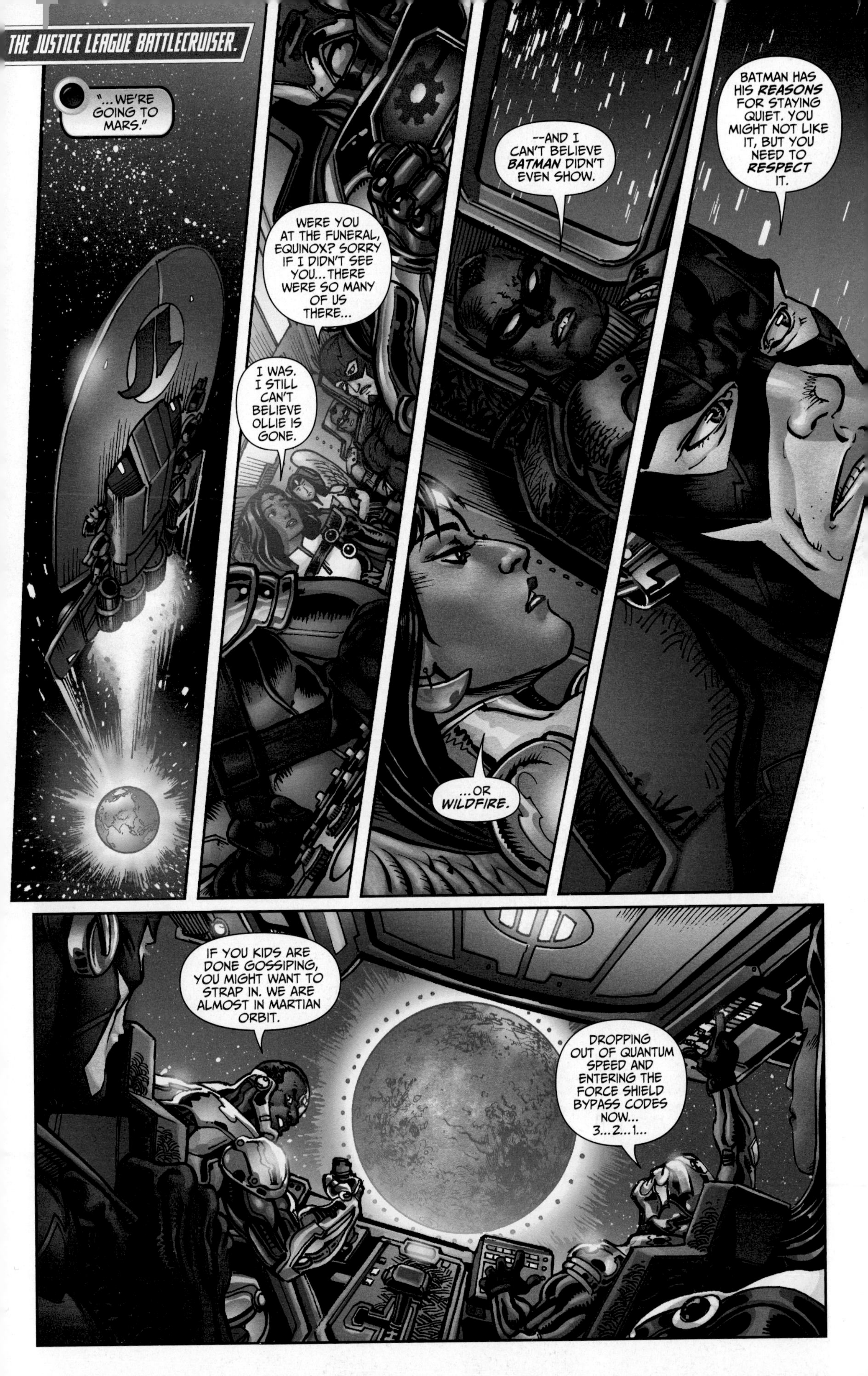
THE JUSTICE LEAGUE BATTLECRUISER.
"...WE'RE GOING TO MARS."
WERE YOU AT THE FUNERAL, EQUINOX? SORRY IF I DIDN'T SEE YOU...THERE WERE SO MANY OF US THERE...
I WAS. I STILL CAN'T BELIEVE OLLIE IS GONE.
--AND I CAN'T BELIEVE BATMAN DIDN'T EVEN SHOW.
...OR WILDFIRE.
BATMAN HAS HIS REASONS FOR STAYING QUIET. YOU MIGHT NOT LIKE IT, BUT YOU NEED TO RESPECT IT.
IF YOU KIDS ARE DONE GOSSIPING, YOU MIGHT WANT TO STRAP IN. WE ARE ALMOST IN MARTIAN ORBIT.
DROPPING OUT OF QUANTUM SPEED AND ENTERING THE FORCE SHIELD BYPASS CODES NOW... 3...2...1...

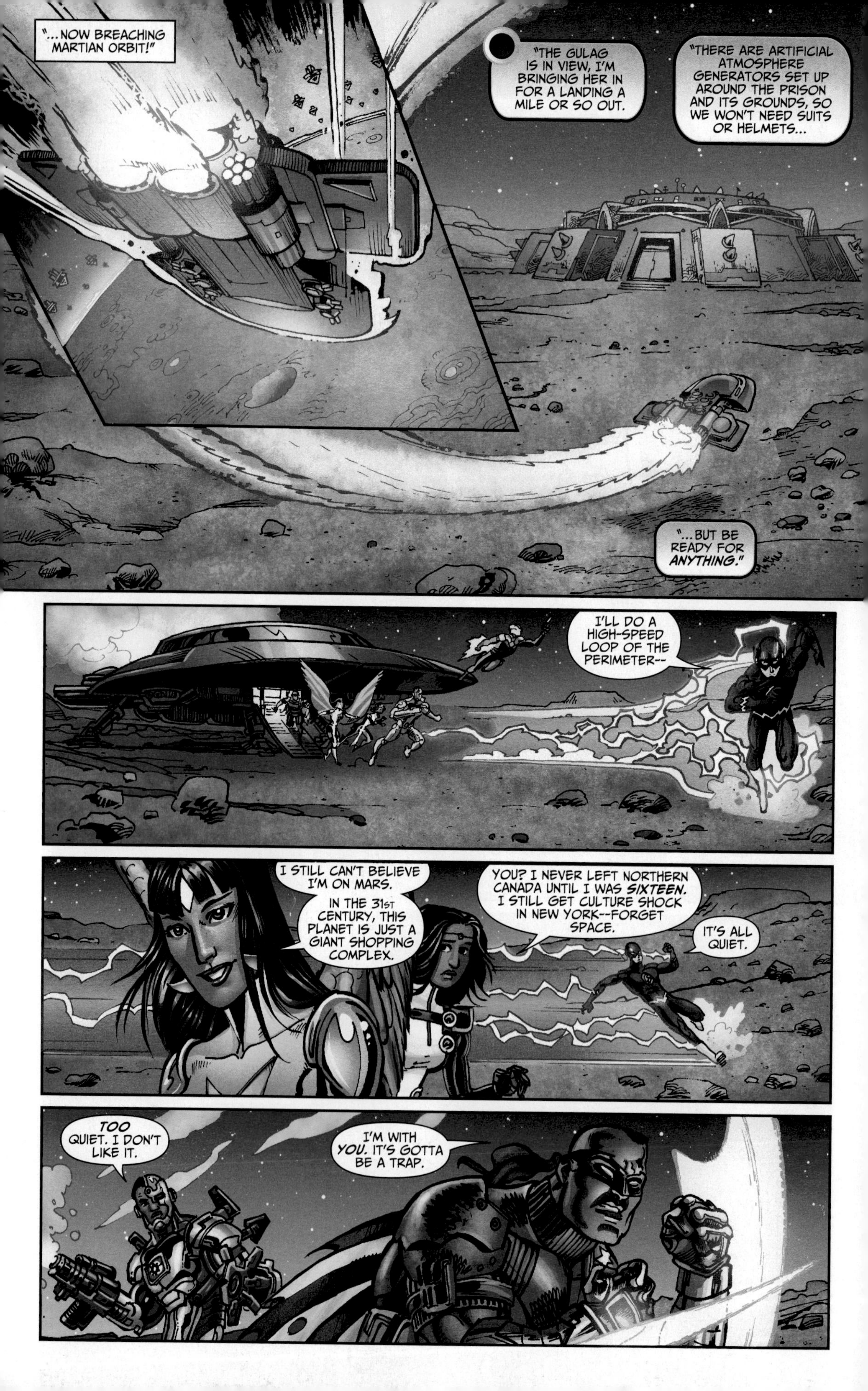
"...NOW BREACHING MARTIAN ORBIT!"
"THE GULAG IS IN VIEW, I'M BRINGING HER IN FOR A LANDING A MILE OR SO OUT.
"THERE ARE ARTIFICIAL ATMOSPHERE GENERATORS SET UP AROUND THE PRISON AND ITS GROUNDS, SO WE WON'T NEED SUITS OR HELMETS...
"...BUT BE READY FOR *ANYTHING.*"
I'LL DO A HIGH-SPEED LOOP OF THE PERIMETER--
I STILL CAN'T BELIEVE I'M ON MARS.
IN THE 31ST CENTURY, THIS PLANET IS JUST A GIANT SHOPPING COMPLEX.
YOU? I NEVER LEFT NORTHERN CANADA UNTIL I WAS *SIXTEEN.* I STILL GET CULTURE SHOCK IN NEW YORK--FORGET SPACE.
IT'S ALL QUIET.
TOO QUIET. I DON'T LIKE IT.
I'M WITH *YOU.* IT'S GOTTA BE A TRAP.

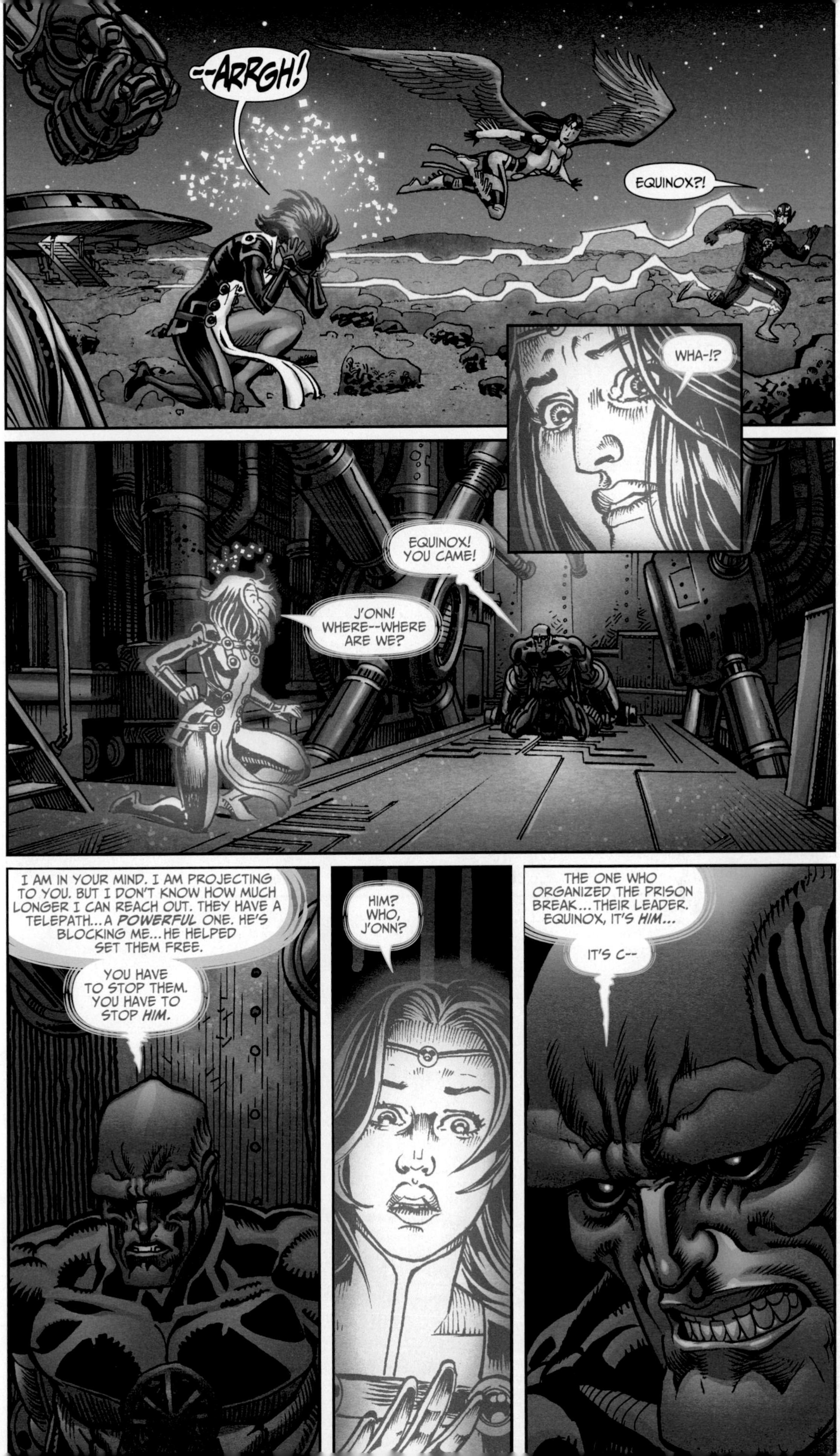
--ARRGH!
EQUINOX?!
WHA-!?
EQUINOX! YOU CAME!
J'ONN! WHERE--WHERE ARE WE?
I AM IN YOUR MIND. I AM PROJECTING TO YOU. BUT I DON'T KNOW HOW MUCH LONGER I CAN REACH OUT. THEY HAVE A TELEPATH...A POWERFUL ONE. HE'S BLOCKING ME...HE HELPED SET THEM FREE.
YOU HAVE TO STOP THEM. YOU HAVE TO STOP HIM.
HIM? WHO, J'ONN?
THE ONE WHO ORGANIZED THE PRISON BREAK...THEIR LEADER. EQUINOX, IT'S HIM...
IT'S C--

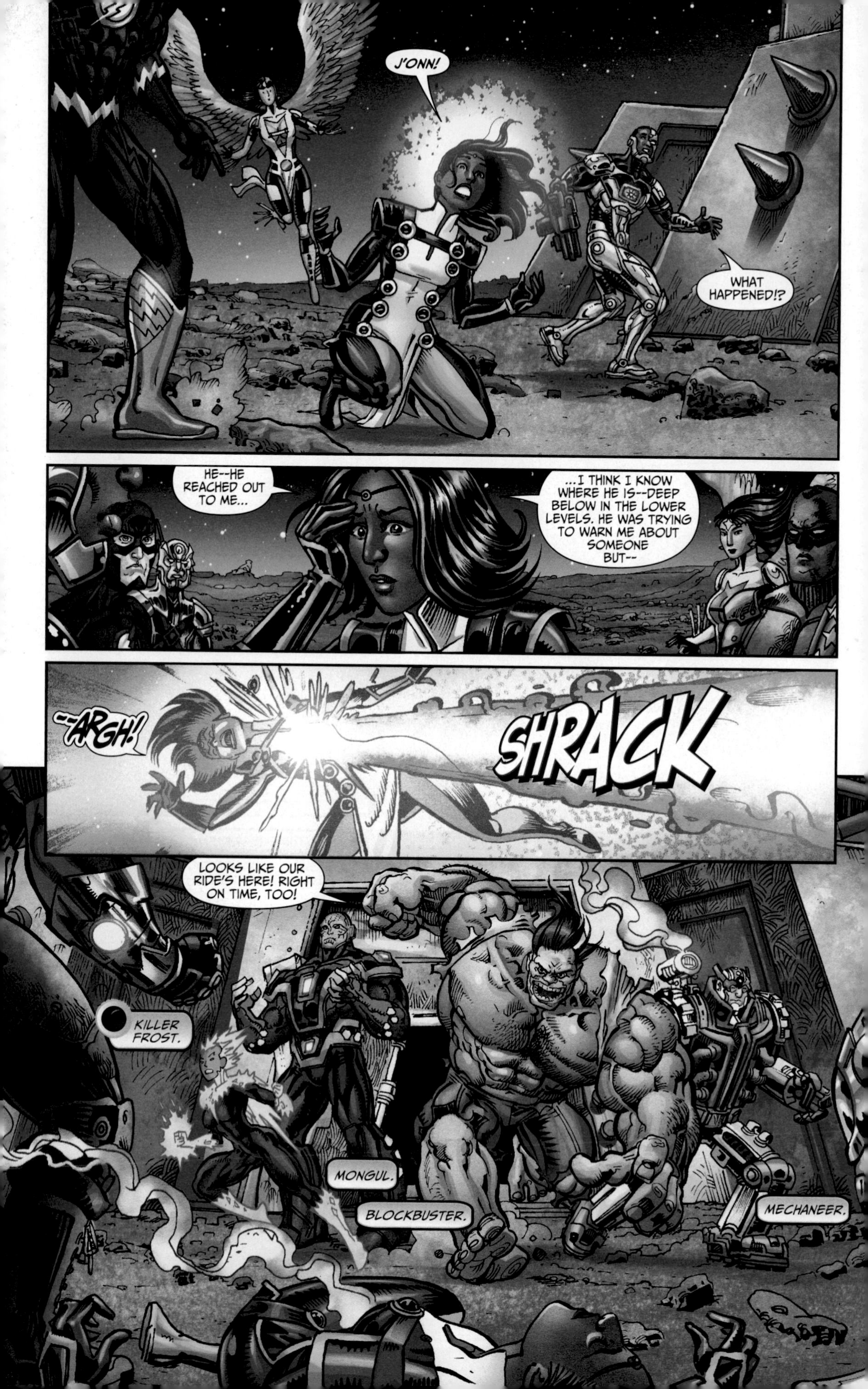

J'ONN!
WHAT HAPPENED!?
HE--HE REACHED OUT TO ME...
...I THINK I KNOW WHERE HE IS--DEEP BELOW IN THE LOWER LEVELS. HE WAS TRYING TO WARN ME ABOUT SOMEONE BUT--
--ARGH!
SHRACK
LOOKS LIKE OUR RIDE'S HERE! RIGHT ON TIME, TOO!
KILLER FROST.
MONGUL.
BLOCKBUSTER.
MECHANEER.

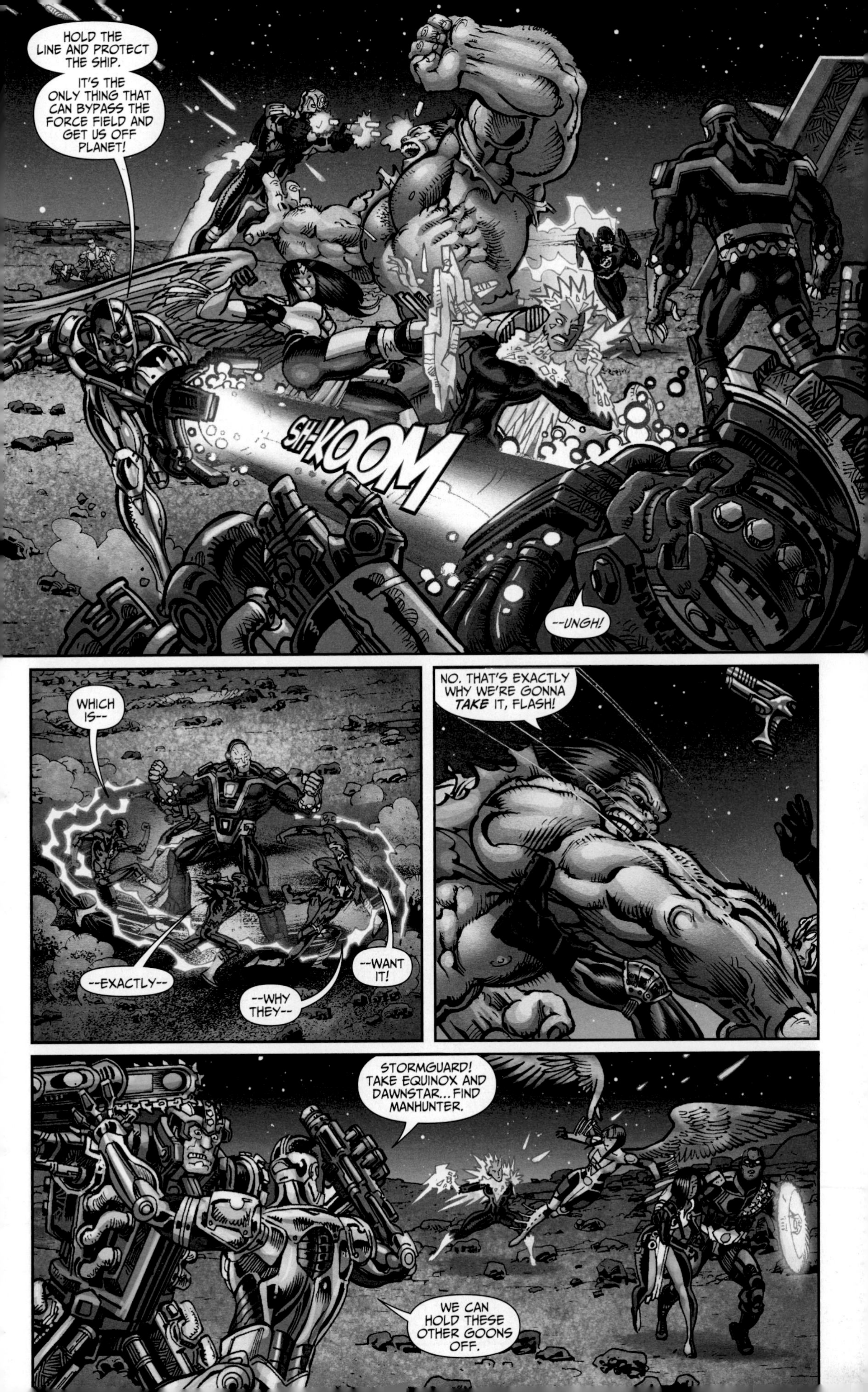
HOLD THE LINE AND PROTECT THE SHIP.
IT'S THE ONLY THING THAT CAN BYPASS THE FORCE FIELD AND GET US OFF PLANET!
SH-KOOM
--UNGH!
WHICH IS--
--EXACTLY--
--WHY THEY--
--WANT IT!
NO. THAT'S EXACTLY WHY WE'RE GONNA TAKE IT, FLASH!
STORMGUARD! TAKE EQUINOX AND DAWNSTAR...FIND MANHUNTER.
WE CAN HOLD THESE OTHER GOONS OFF.

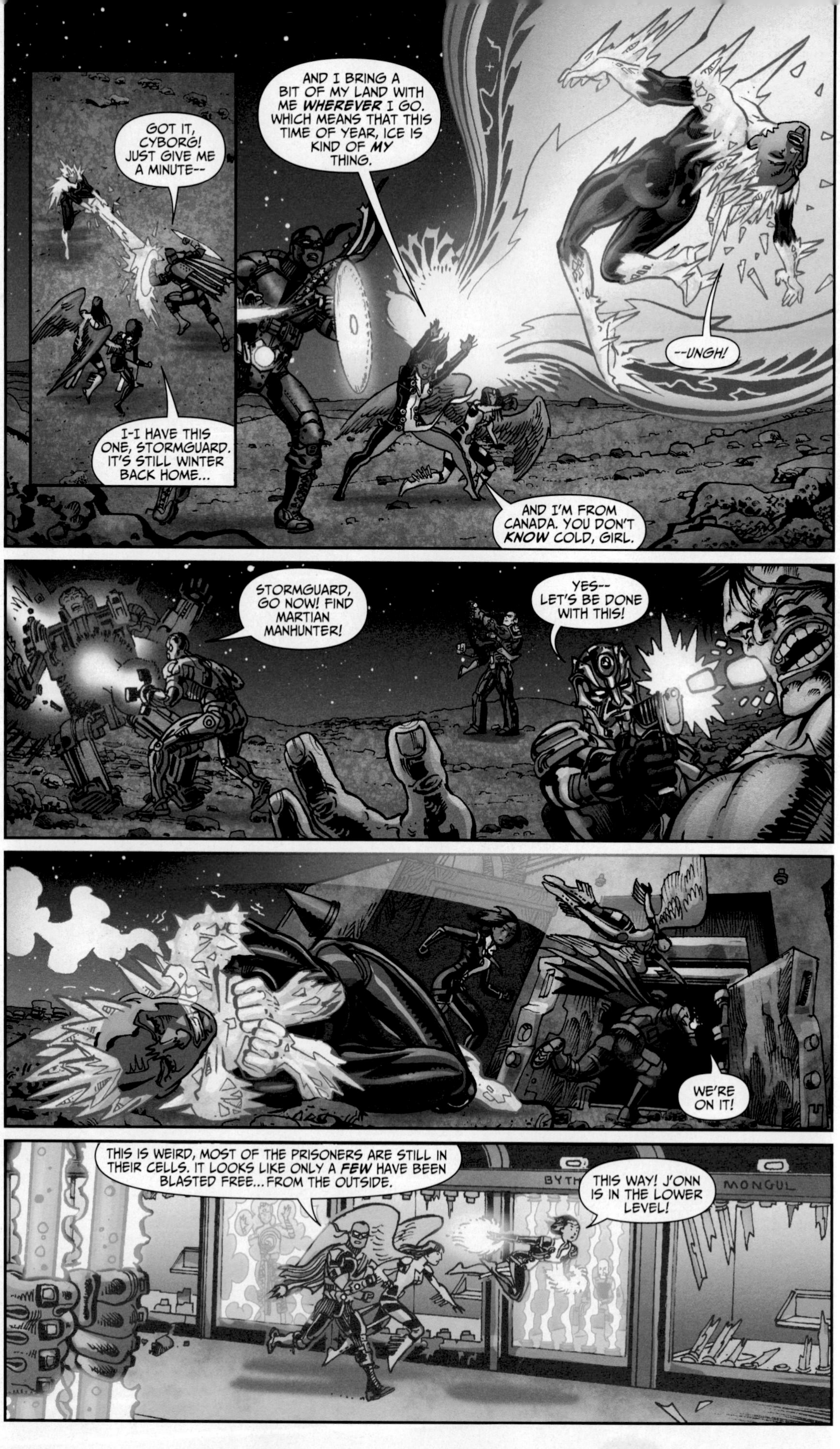
GOT IT, CYBORG! JUST GIVE ME A MINUTE--
I-I HAVE THIS ONE, STORMGUARD. IT'S STILL WINTER BACK HOME...
AND I BRING A BIT OF MY LAND WITH ME WHEREVER I GO. WHICH MEANS THAT THIS TIME OF YEAR, ICE IS KIND OF MY THING.
AND I'M FROM CANADA. YOU DON'T KNOW COLD, GIRL.
--UNGH!
STORMGUARD, GO NOW! FIND MARTIAN MANHUNTER!
YES-- LET'S BE DONE WITH THIS!
WE'RE ON IT!
THIS IS WEIRD, MOST OF THE PRISONERS ARE STILL IN THEIR CELLS. IT LOOKS LIKE ONLY A FEW HAVE BEEN BLASTED FREE...FROM THE OUTSIDE.
BYTH
MONGUL
THIS WAY! J'ONN IS IN THE LOWER LEVEL!

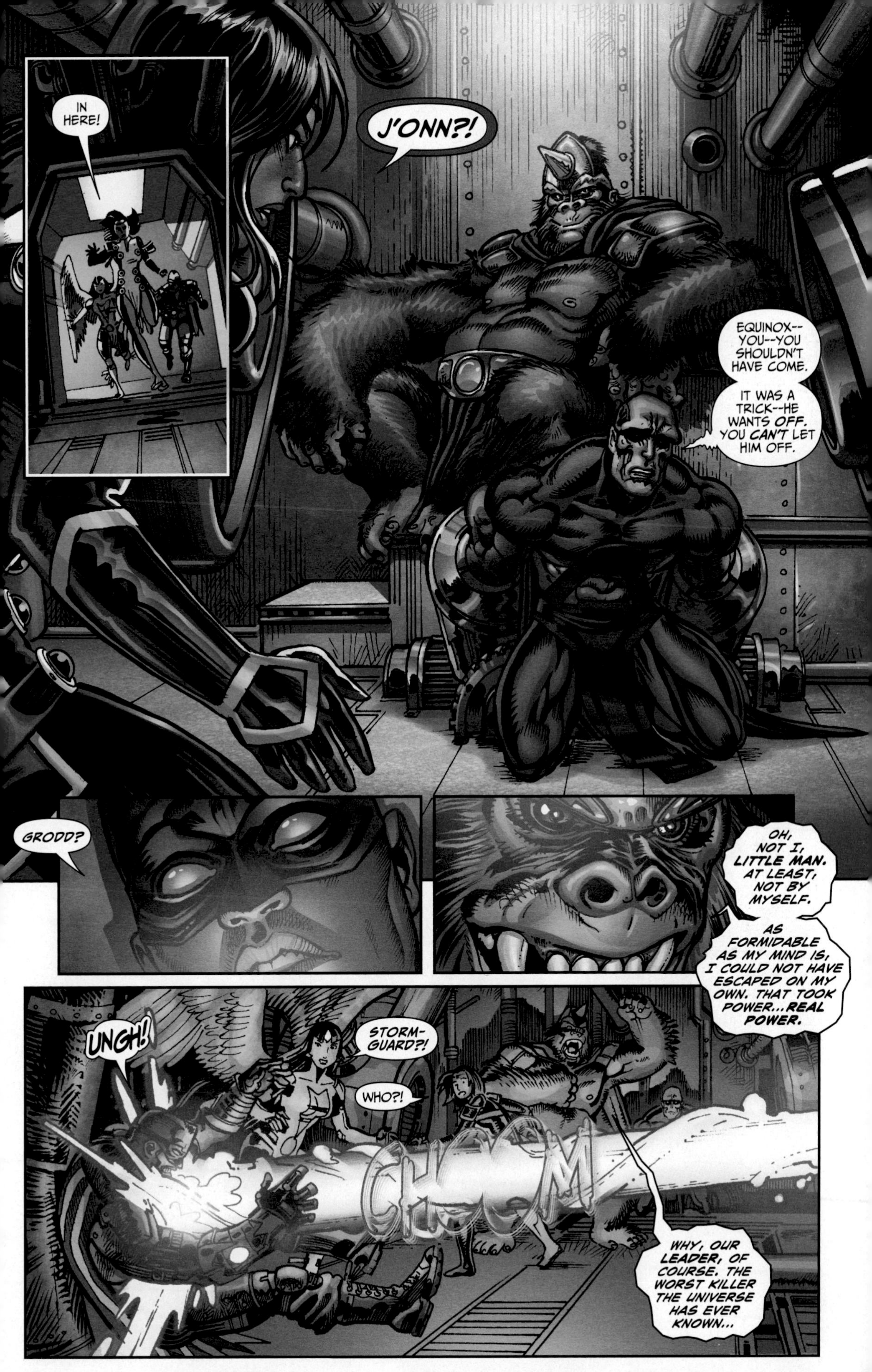
IN HERE!
J'ONN?!
EQUINOX-- YOU--YOU SHOULDN'T HAVE COME.
IT WAS A TRICK--HE WANTS OFF. YOU CAN'T LET HIM OFF.
GRODD?
OH, NOT I, LITTLE MAN. AT LEAST, NOT BY MYSELF.
AS FORMIDABLE AS MY MIND IS, I COULD NOT HAVE ESCAPED ON MY OWN. THAT TOOK POWER...REAL POWER.
UNGH!
STORM-GUARD?!
WHO?!
CHOOOM
WHY, OUR LEADER, OF COURSE. THE WORST KILLER THE UNIVERSE HAS EVER KNOWN...

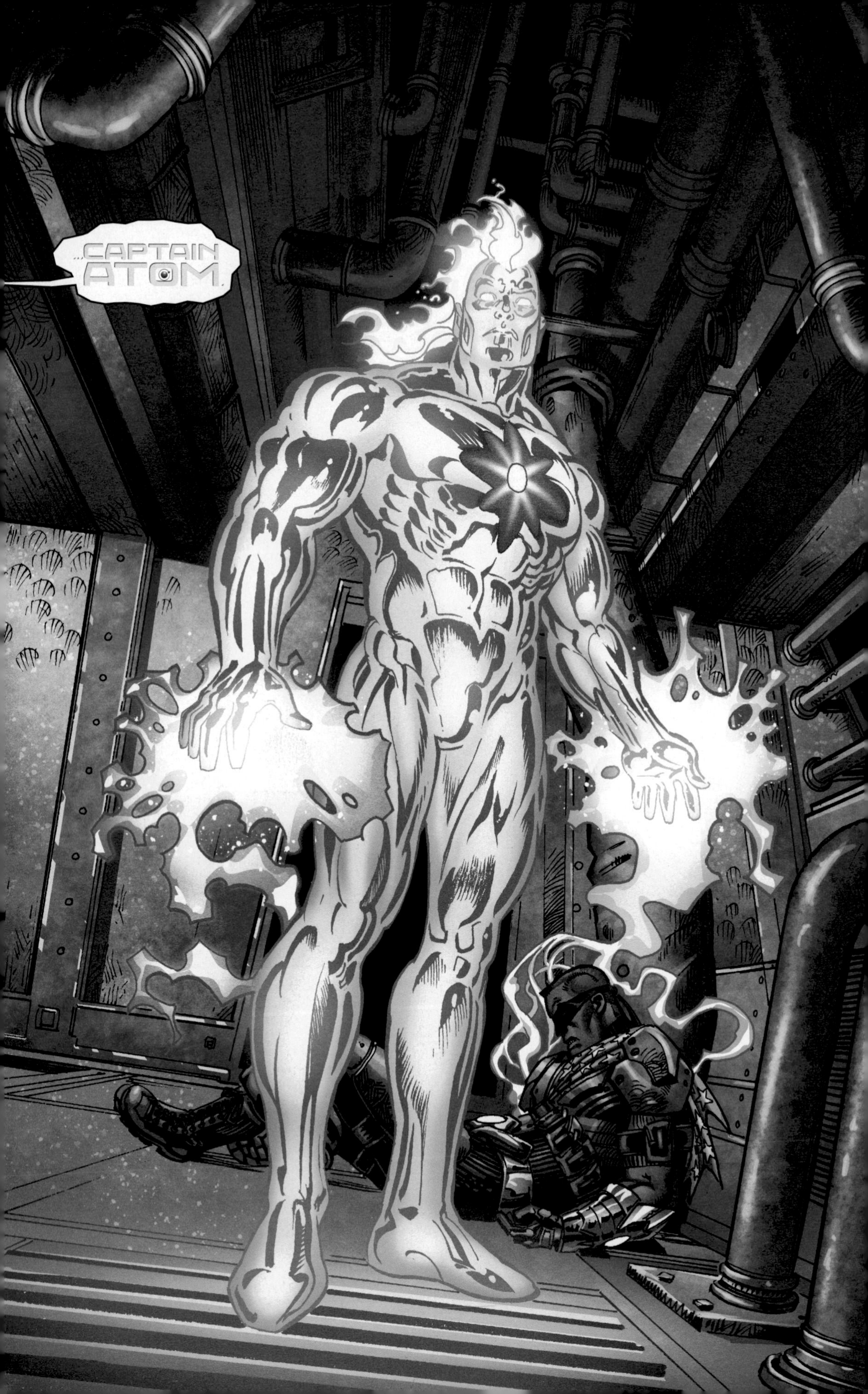
...CAPTAIN ATOM.

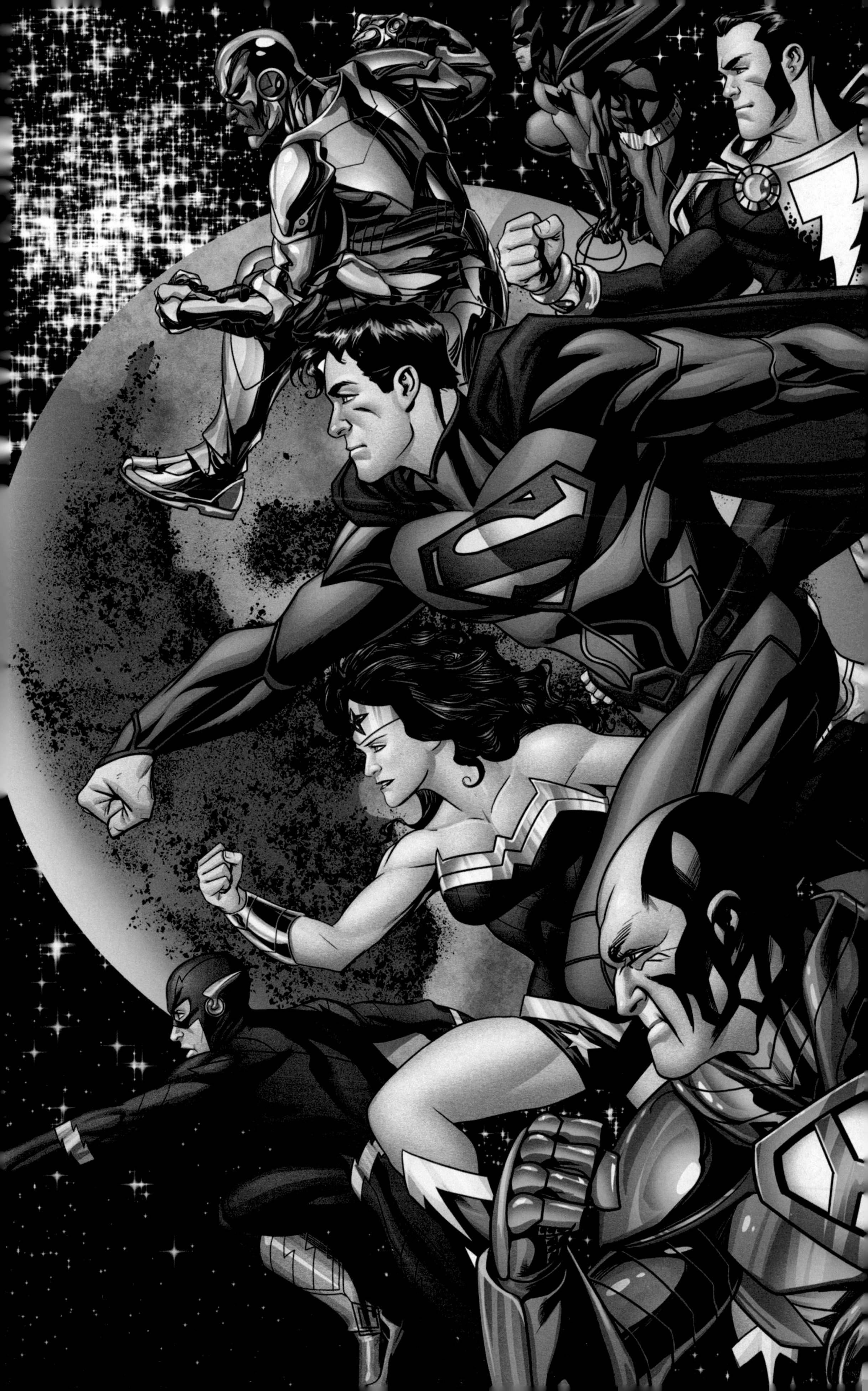

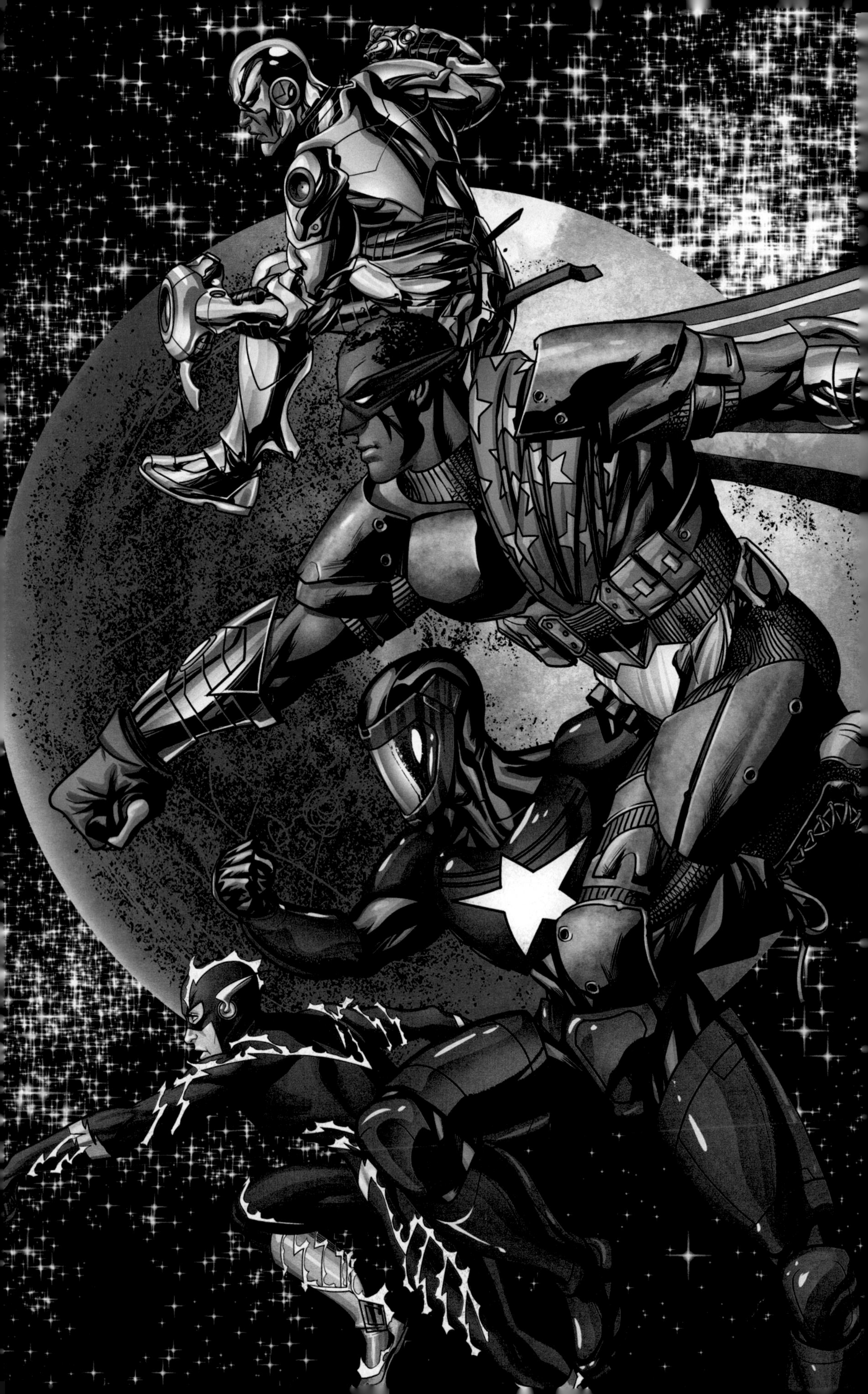

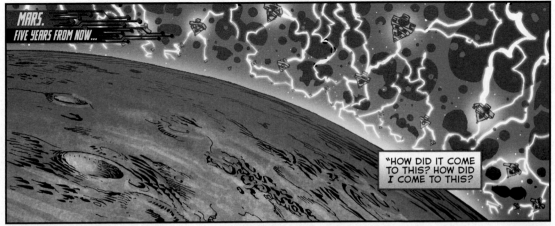

MARS.
FIVE YEARS FROM NOW...

"HOW DID IT COME TO THIS? HOW DID *I* COME TO THIS?"

"LOCKED AWAY IN A PRISON BUILT BY THE JUSTICE LEAGUE TO HOUSE THE WORST MURDERERS AND CRIMINALS IN THE UNIVERSE--

"--THOSE *TOO DANGEROUS* TO KEEP ON EARTH.

"HOW DID I BECOME ONE OF THESE MURDERERS? I USED TO BE SOME-THING ELSE. SOME-THING *BETTER*..."

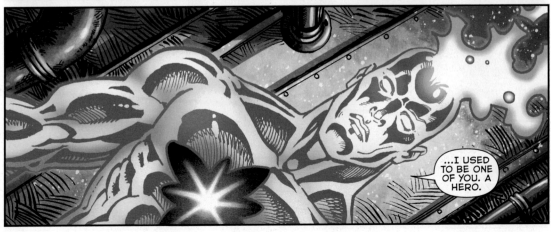

...I USED TO BE ONE OF YOU. A HERO.

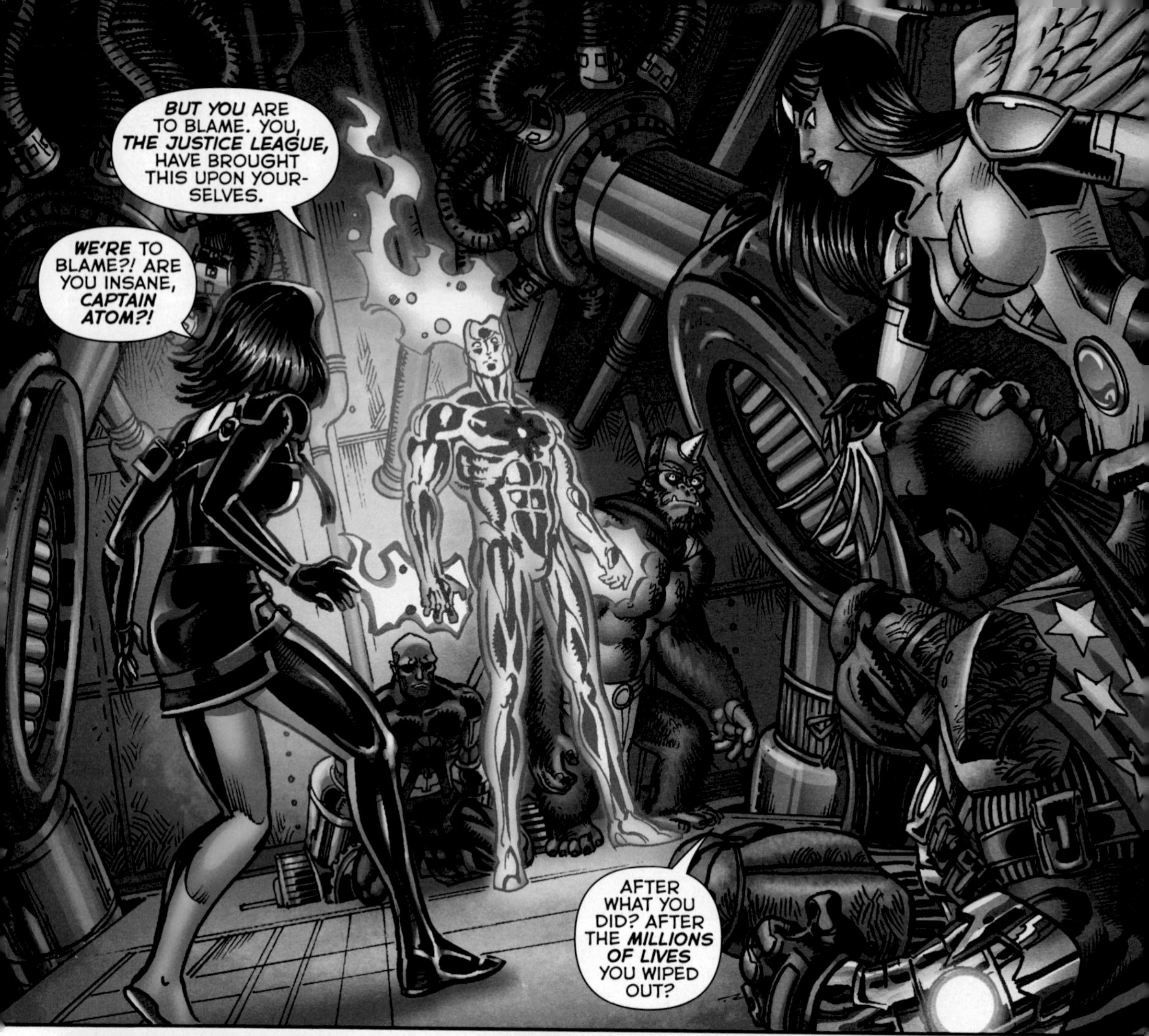
BUT YOU ARE TO BLAME. YOU, THE JUSTICE LEAGUE, HAVE BROUGHT THIS UPON YOUR-SELVES.
WE'RE TO BLAME?! ARE YOU INSANE, CAPTAIN ATOM?!
AFTER WHAT YOU DID? AFTER THE MILLIONS OF LIVES YOU WIPED OUT?

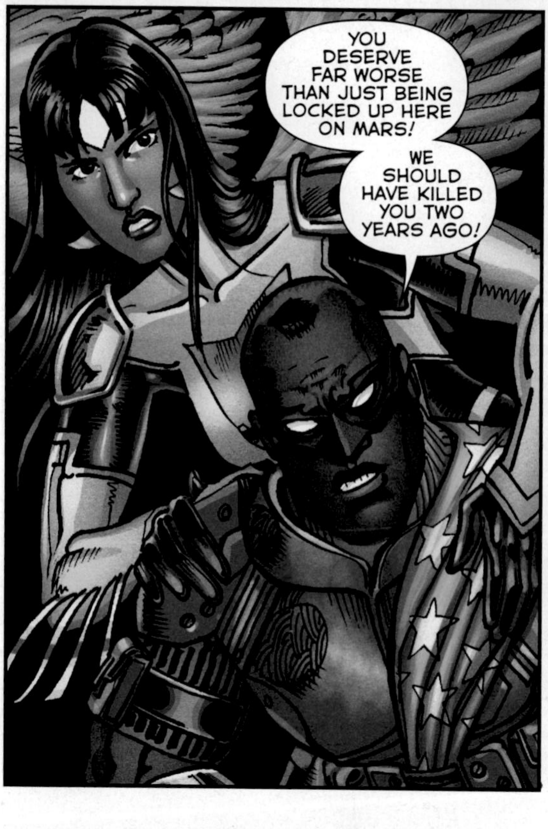
YOU DESERVE FAR WORSE THAN JUST BEING LOCKED UP HERE ON MARS!
WE SHOULD HAVE KILLED YOU TWO YEARS AGO!

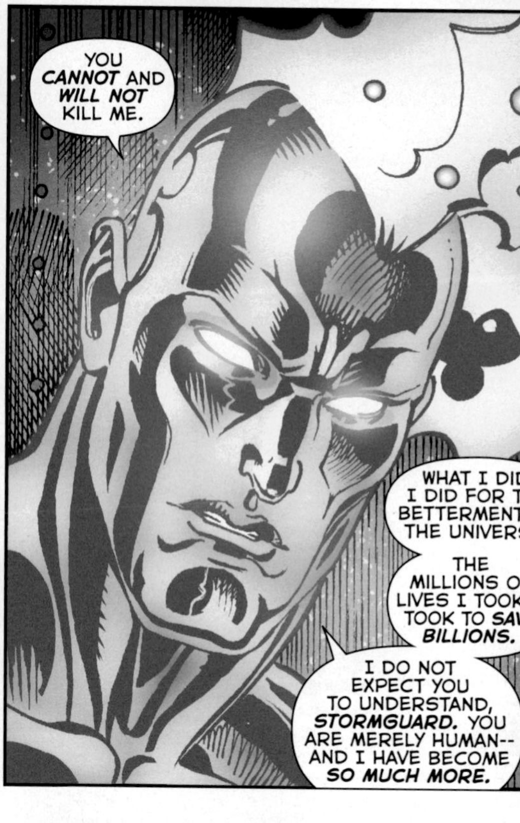
YOU CANNOT AND WILL NOT KILL ME.
WHAT I DID, I DID FOR THE BETTERMENT OF THE UNIVERSE.
THE MILLIONS OF LIVES I TOOK, I TOOK TO SAVE BILLIONS.
I DO NOT EXPECT YOU TO UNDERSTAND, STORMGUARD. YOU ARE MERELY HUMAN-- AND I HAVE BECOME SO MUCH MORE.

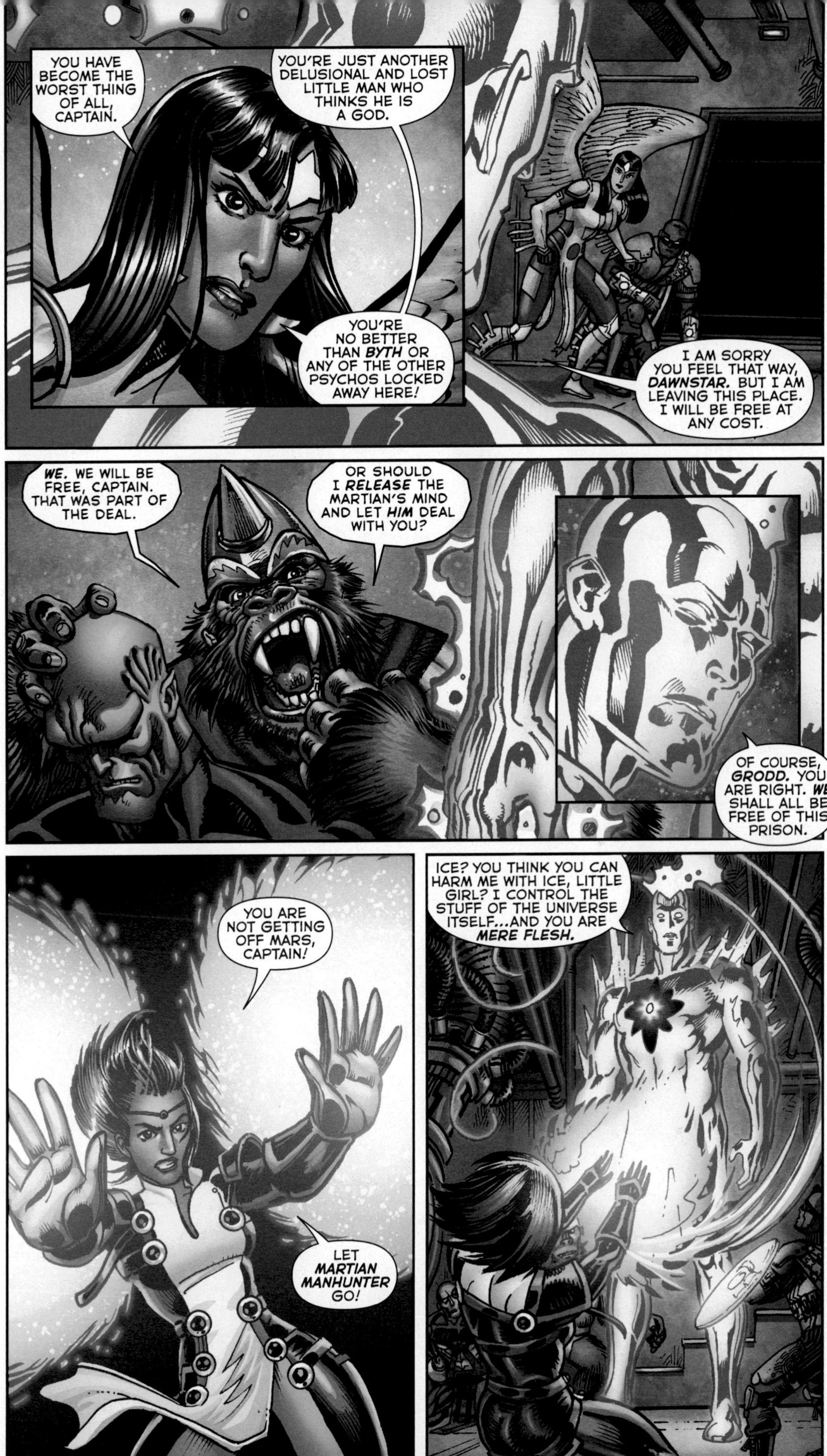
YOU HAVE BECOME THE WORST THING OF ALL, CAPTAIN.
YOU'RE JUST ANOTHER DELUSIONAL AND LOST LITTLE MAN WHO THINKS HE IS A GOD.
YOU'RE NO BETTER THAN BYTH OR ANY OF THE OTHER PSYCHOS LOCKED AWAY HERE!
I AM SORRY YOU FEEL THAT WAY, DAWNSTAR. BUT I AM LEAVING THIS PLACE. I WILL BE FREE AT ANY COST.
WE. WE WILL BE FREE, CAPTAIN. THAT WAS PART OF THE DEAL.
OR SHOULD I RELEASE THE MARTIAN'S MIND AND LET HIM DEAL WITH YOU?
OF COURSE, GRODD. YOU ARE RIGHT. WE SHALL ALL BE FREE OF THIS PRISON.
YOU ARE NOT GETTING OFF MARS, CAPTAIN!
LET MARTIAN MANHUNTER GO!
ICE? YOU THINK YOU CAN HARM ME WITH ICE, LITTLE GIRL? I CONTROL THE STUFF OF THE UNIVERSE ITSELF...AND YOU ARE MERE FLESH.

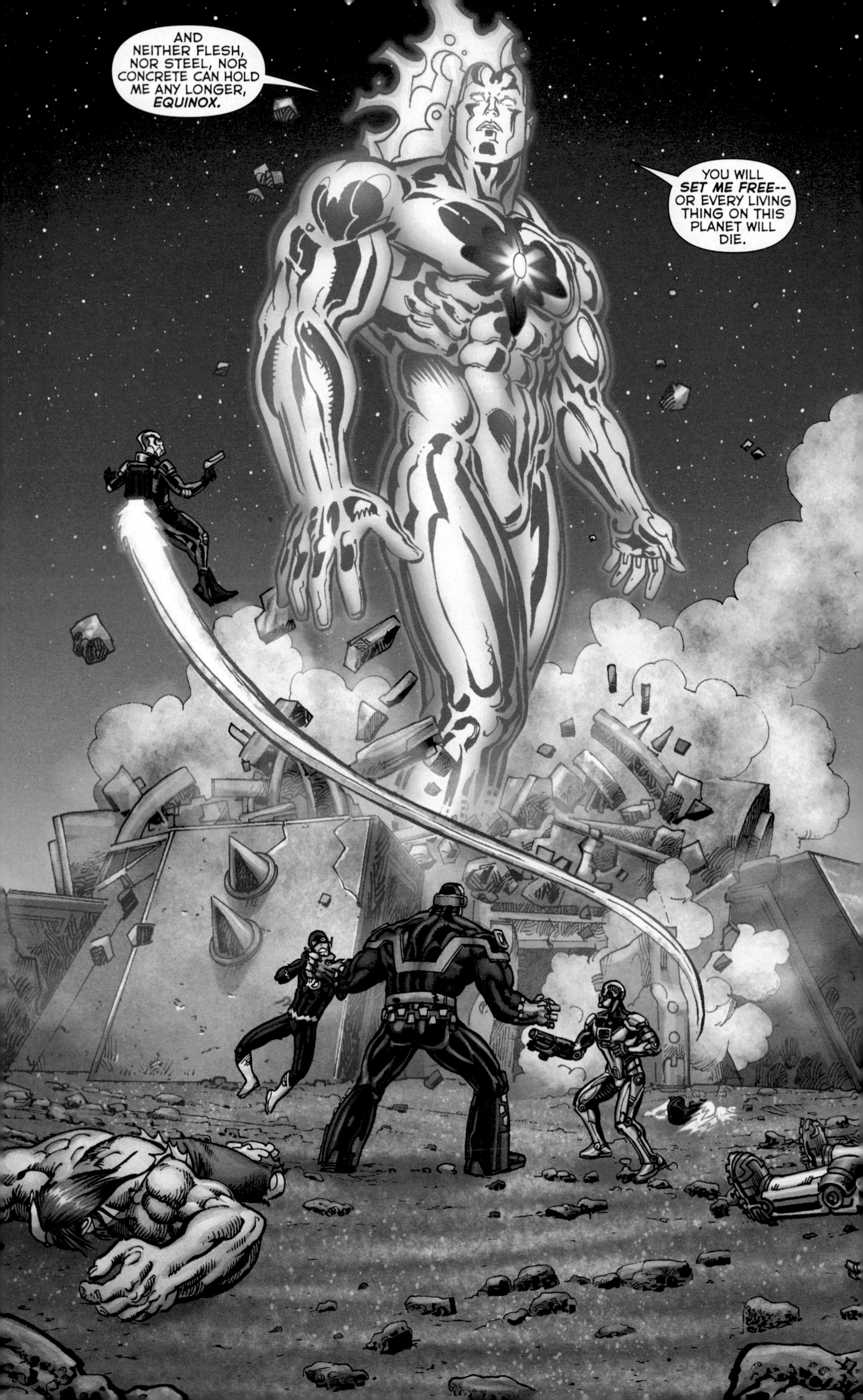
AND NEITHER FLESH, NOR STEEL, NOR CONCRETE CAN HOLD ME ANY LONGER, EQUINOX.
YOU WILL SET ME FREE-- OR EVERY LIVING THING ON THIS PLANET WILL DIE.

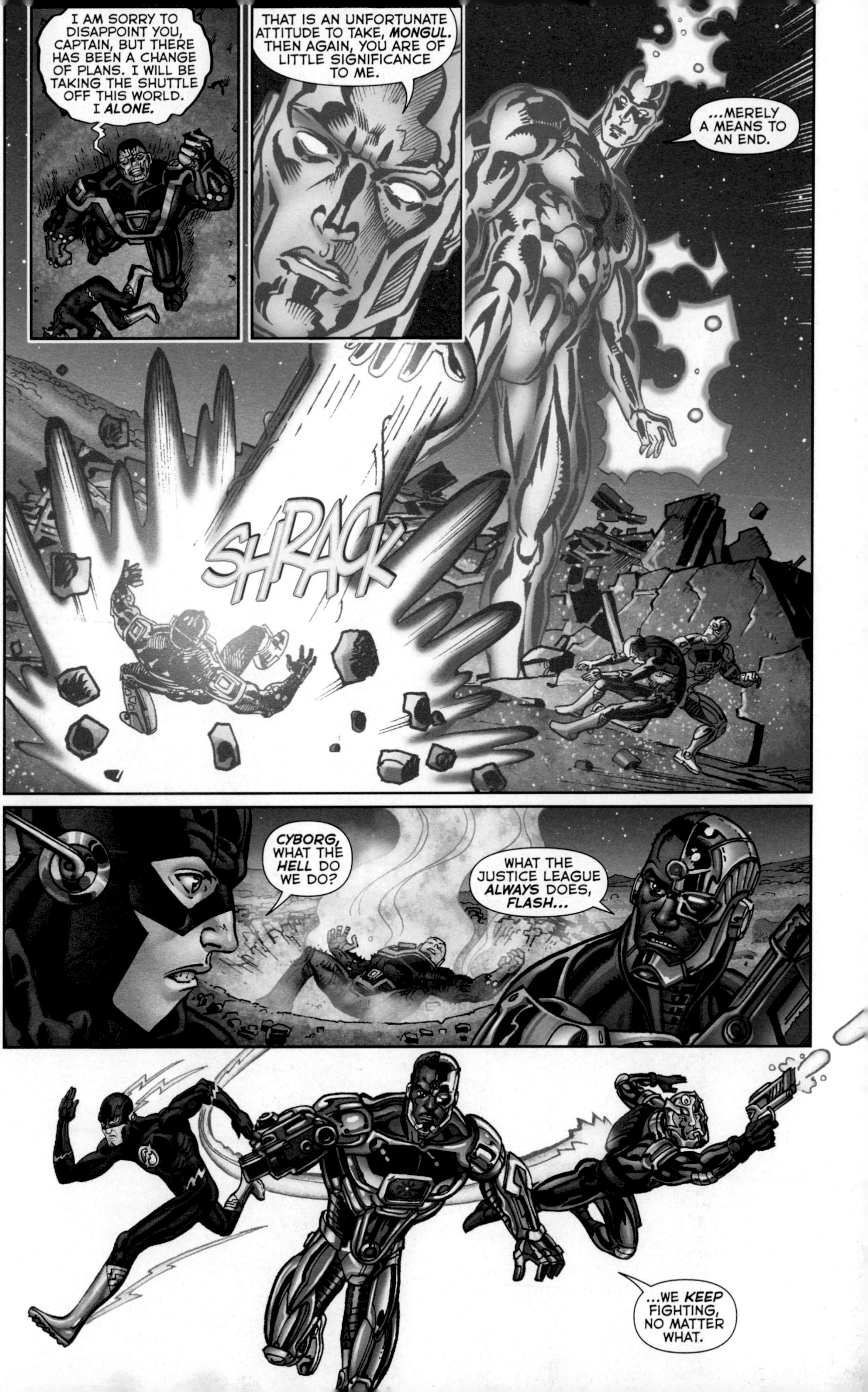
I AM SORRY TO DISAPPOINT YOU, CAPTAIN, BUT THERE HAS BEEN A CHANGE OF PLANS. I WILL BE TAKING THE SHUTTLE OFF THIS WORLD. I ALONE.
THAT IS AN UNFORTUNATE ATTITUDE TO TAKE, MONGUL. THEN AGAIN, YOU ARE OF LITTLE SIGNIFICANCE TO ME.
...MERELY A MEANS TO AN END.
SHRACK
CYBORG, WHAT THE HELL DO WE DO?
WHAT THE JUSTICE LEAGUE ALWAYS DOES, FLASH...
...WE KEEP FIGHTING, NO MATTER WHAT.

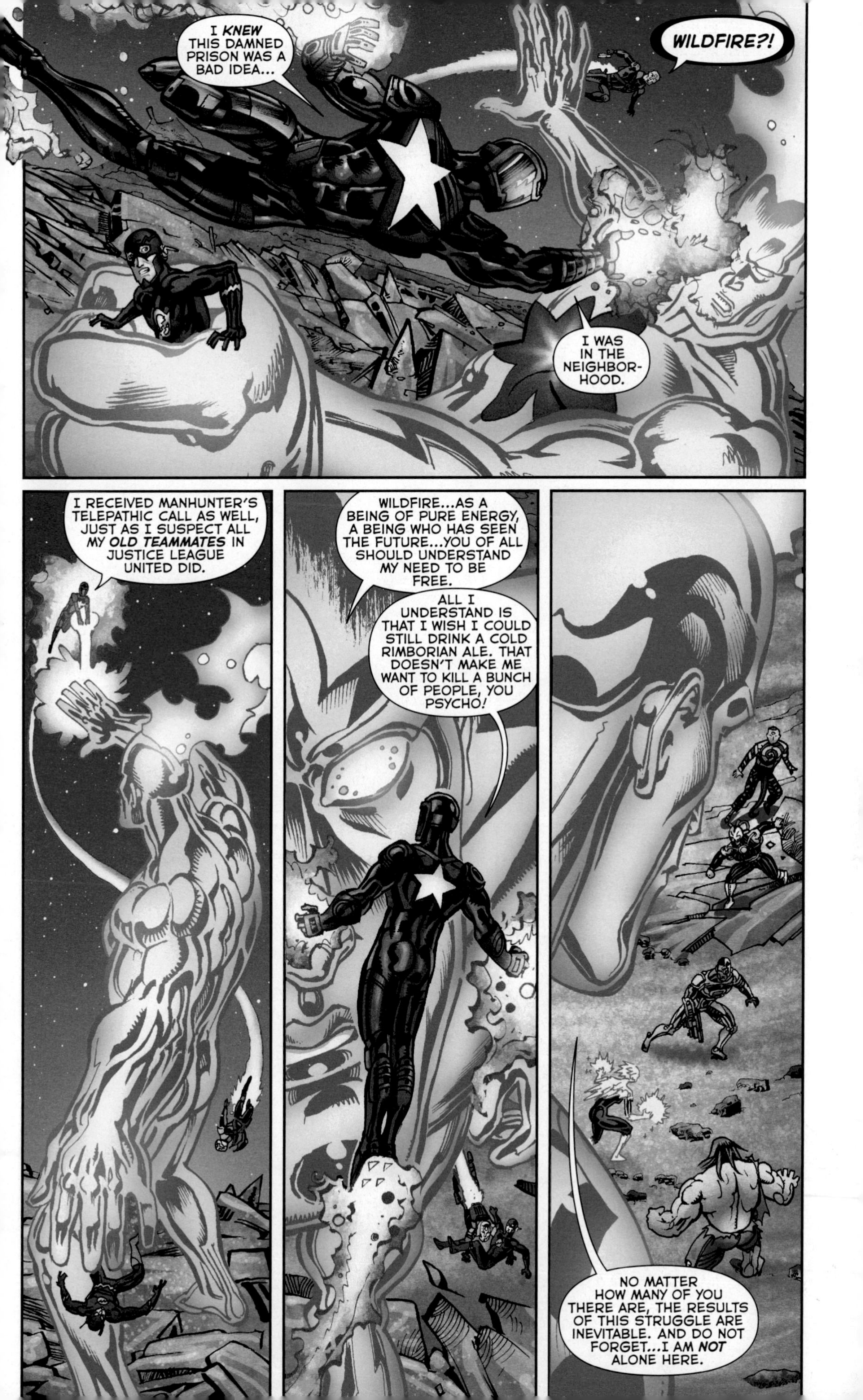
I KNEW THIS DAMNED PRISON WAS A BAD IDEA...
WILDFIRE?!
I WAS IN THE NEIGHBOR-HOOD.
I RECEIVED MANHUNTER'S TELEPATHIC CALL AS WELL, JUST AS I SUSPECT ALL MY OLD TEAMMATES IN JUSTICE LEAGUE UNITED DID.
WILDFIRE...AS A BEING OF PURE ENERGY, A BEING WHO HAS SEEN THE FUTURE...YOU OF ALL SHOULD UNDERSTAND MY NEED TO BE FREE.
ALL I UNDERSTAND IS THAT I WISH I COULD STILL DRINK A COLD RIMBORIAN ALE. THAT DOESN'T MAKE ME WANT TO KILL A BUNCH OF PEOPLE, YOU PSYCHO!
NO MATTER HOW MANY OF YOU THERE ARE, THE RESULTS OF THIS STRUGGLE ARE INEVITABLE. AND DO NOT FORGET...I AM NOT ALONE HERE.

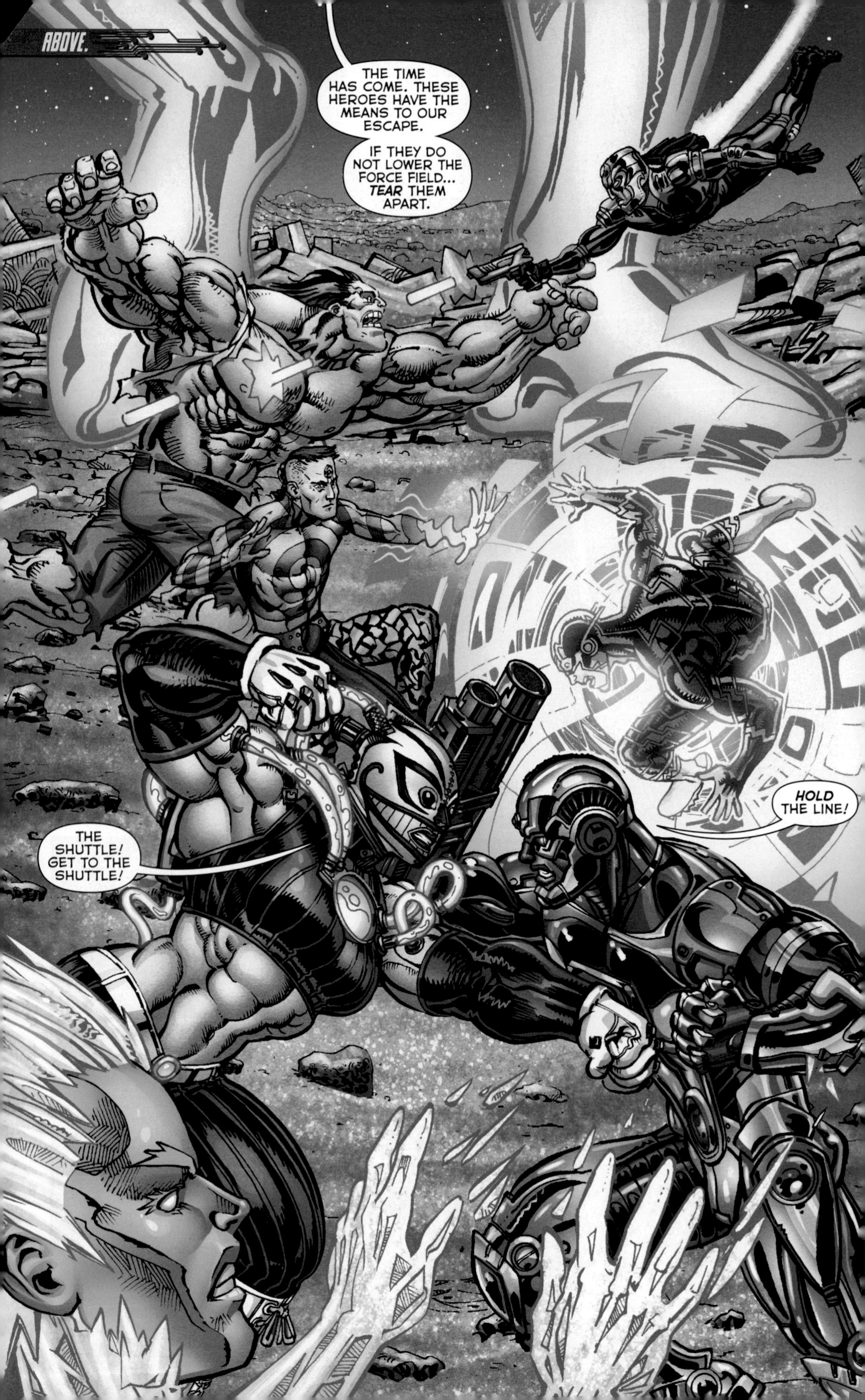
ABOVE.
THE TIME HAS COME. THESE HEROES HAVE THE MEANS TO OUR ESCAPE.
IF THEY DO NOT LOWER THE FORCE FIELD... *TEAR* THEM APART.
HOLD THE LINE!
THE SHUTTLE! GET TO THE SHUTTLE!

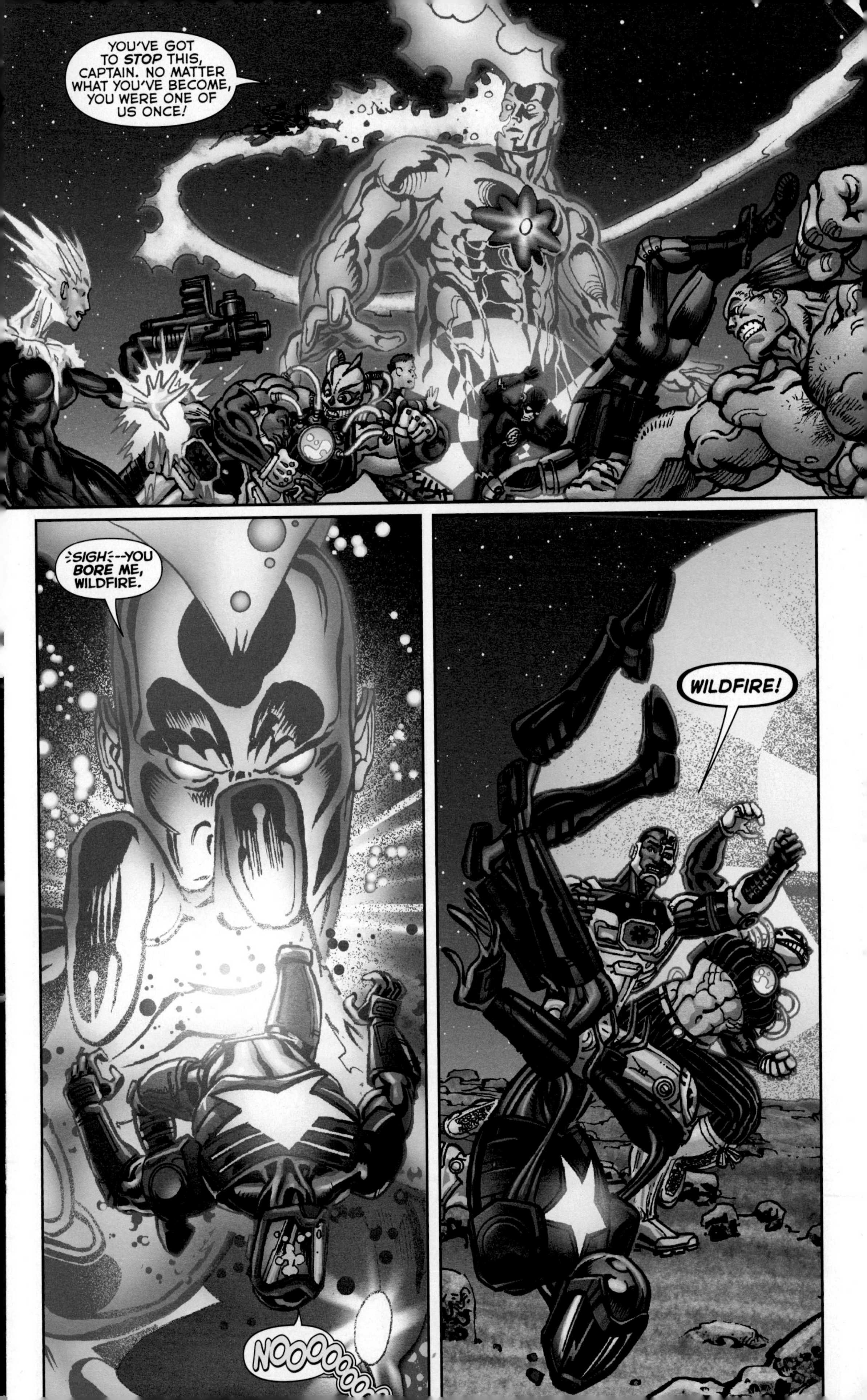
YOU'VE GOT TO STOP THIS, CAPTAIN. NO MATTER WHAT YOU'VE BECOME, YOU WERE ONE OF US ONCE!
SIGH--YOU BORE ME, WILDFIRE.
NOOOOOOO
WILDFIRE!

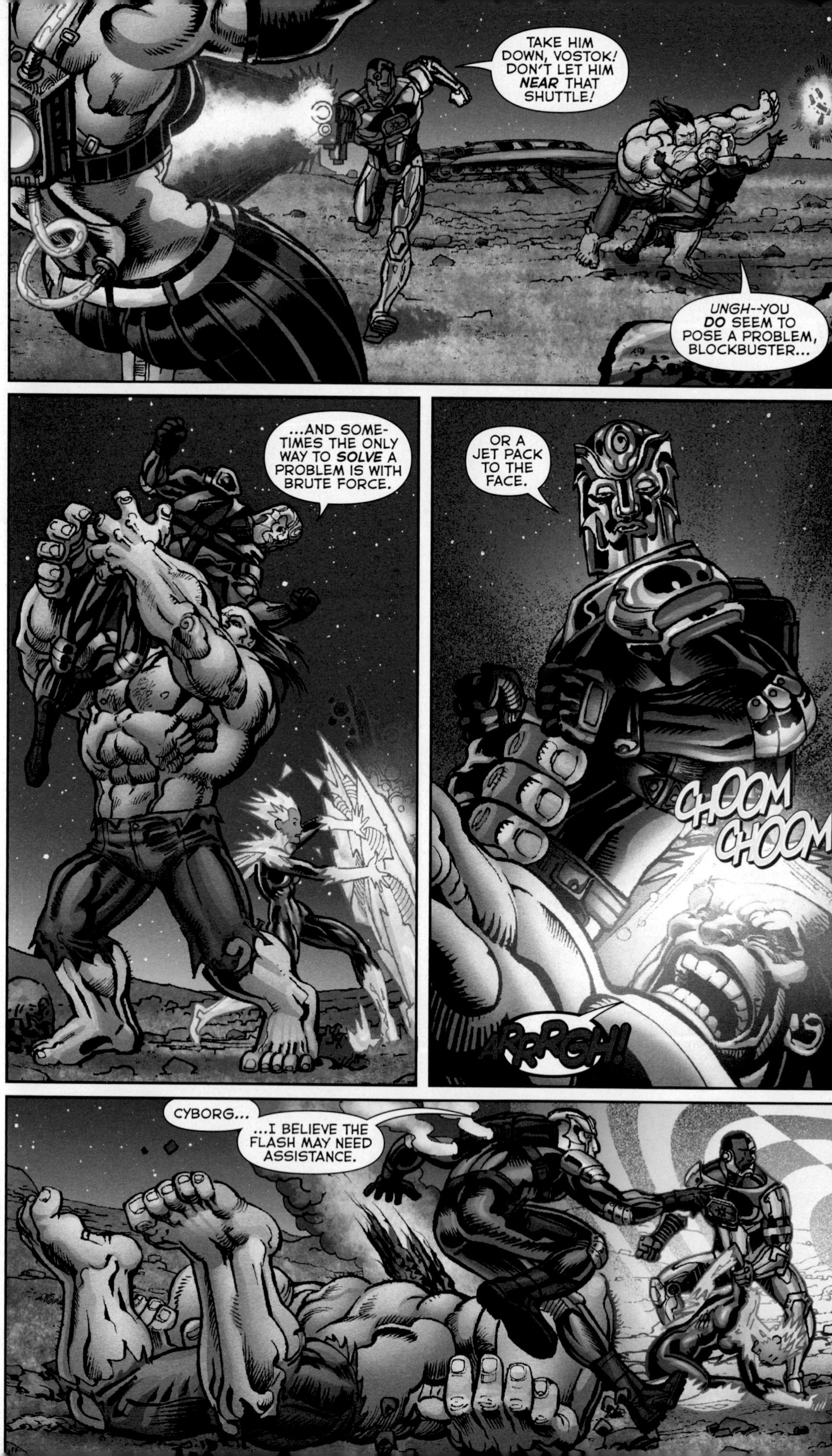
TAKE HIM DOWN, VOSTOK! DON'T LET HIM *NEAR* THAT SHUTTLE!
UNGH--YOU ***DO*** SEEM TO POSE A PROBLEM, BLOCKBUSTER...
...AND SOMETIMES THE ONLY WAY TO ***SOLVE*** A PROBLEM IS WITH BRUTE FORCE.
OR A JET PACK TO THE FACE.
CHOOM
CHOOM
ARRRGH!
CYBORG...
...I BELIEVE THE FLASH MAY NEED ASSISTANCE.

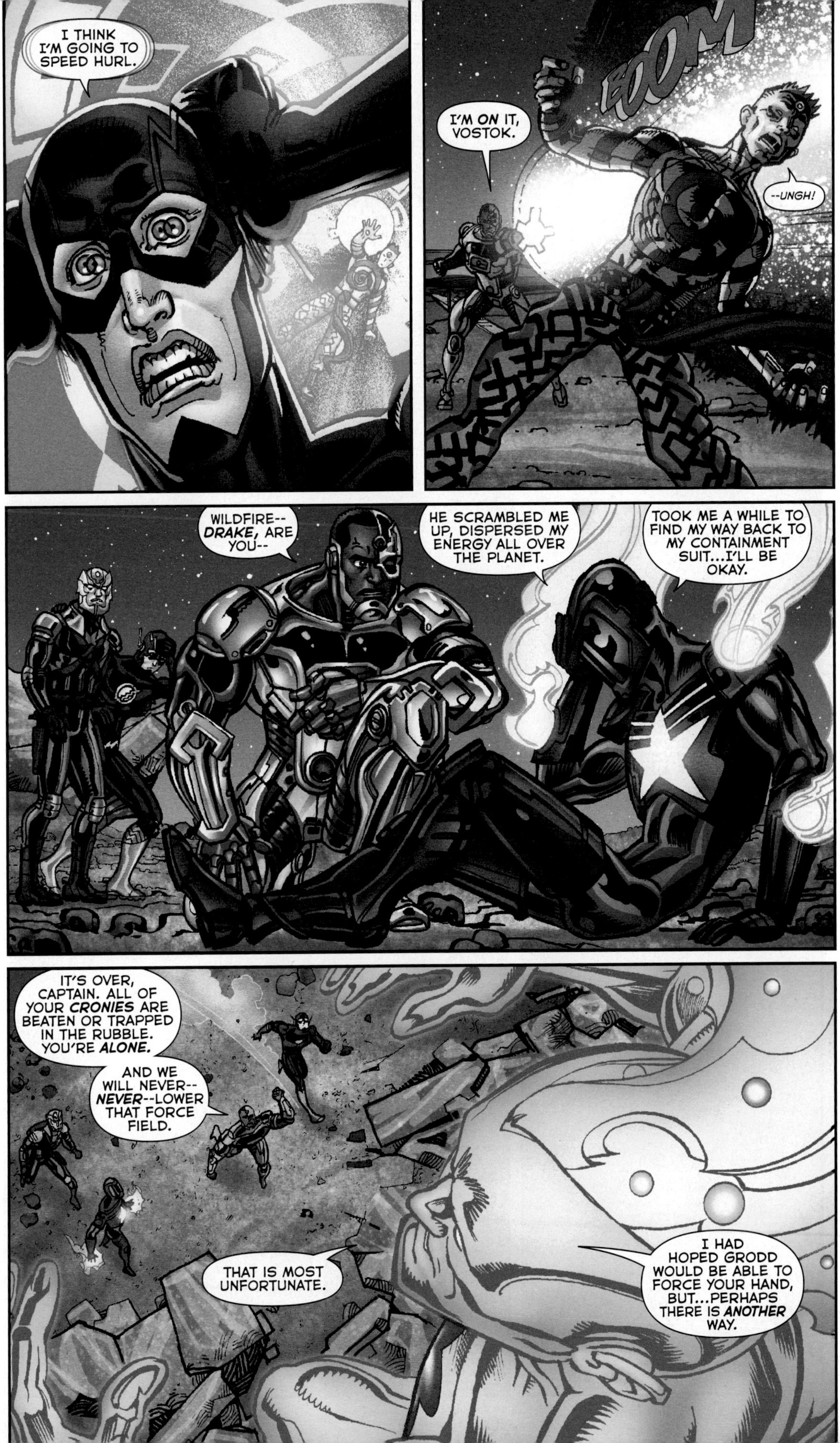
I THINK I'M GOING TO SPEED HURL.
BOOM
I'M ON IT, VOSTOK.
--UNGH!
WILDFIRE-- DRAKE, ARE YOU--
HE SCRAMBLED ME UP, DISPERSED MY ENERGY ALL OVER THE PLANET.
TOOK ME A WHILE TO FIND MY WAY BACK TO MY CONTAINMENT SUIT...I'LL BE OKAY.
IT'S OVER, CAPTAIN. ALL OF YOUR CRONIES ARE BEATEN OR TRAPPED IN THE RUBBLE. YOU'RE ALONE.
AND WE WILL NEVER-- NEVER--LOWER THAT FORCE FIELD.
THAT IS MOST UNFORTUNATE.
I HAD HOPED GRODD WOULD BE ABLE TO FORCE YOUR HAND, BUT...PERHAPS THERE IS ANOTHER WAY.

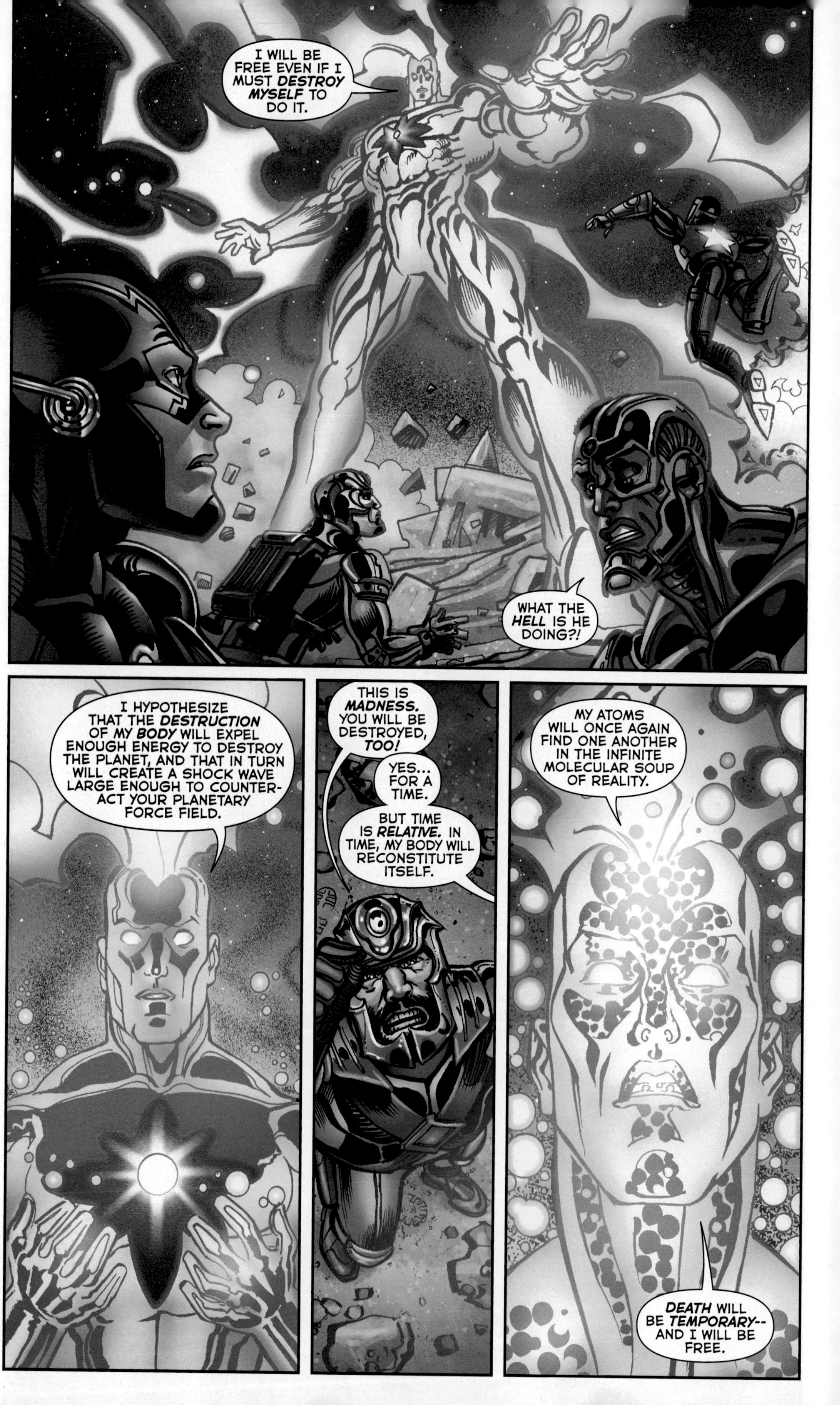
I WILL BE FREE EVEN IF I MUST *DESTROY MYSELF* TO DO IT.
WHAT THE *HELL* IS HE DOING?!
I HYPOTHESIZE THAT THE *DESTRUCTION* OF *MY BODY* WILL EXPEL ENOUGH ENERGY TO DESTROY THE PLANET, AND THAT IN TURN WILL CREATE A SHOCK WAVE LARGE ENOUGH TO COUNTER-ACT YOUR PLANETARY FORCE FIELD.
THIS IS *MADNESS.* YOU WILL BE DESTROYED, *TOO!*
YES... FOR A TIME.
BUT TIME IS *RELATIVE.* IN TIME, MY BODY WILL RECONSTITUTE ITSELF.
MY ATOMS WILL ONCE AGAIN FIND ONE ANOTHER IN THE INFINITE MOLECULAR SOUP OF REALITY.
DEATH WILL BE *TEMPORARY*-- AND I WILL BE FREE.

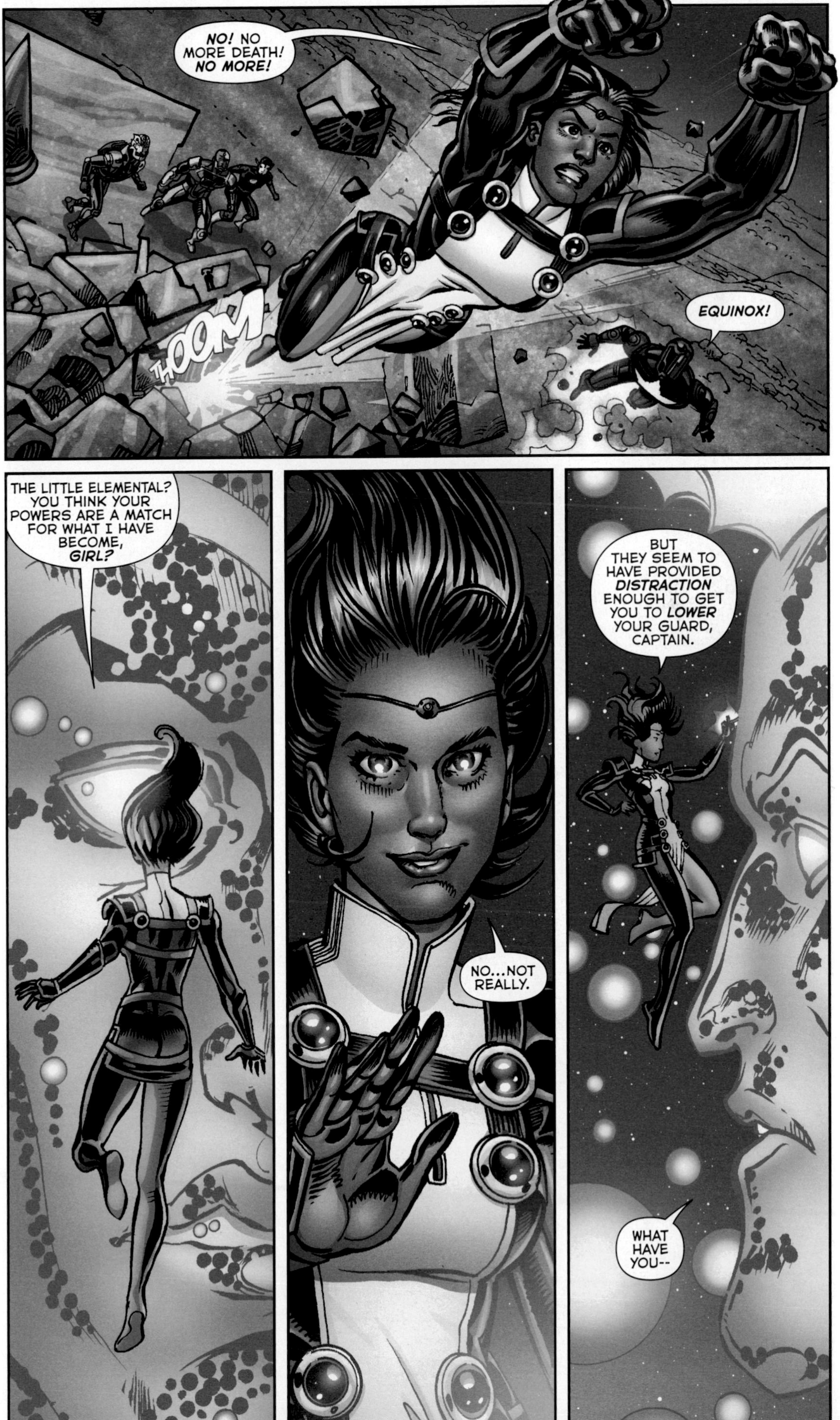

NO! NO MORE DEATH! NO MORE!
THOOM
EQUINOX!
THE LITTLE ELEMENTAL? YOU THINK YOUR POWERS ARE A MATCH FOR WHAT I HAVE BECOME, GIRL?
NO...NOT REALLY.
BUT THEY SEEM TO HAVE PROVIDED DISTRACTION ENOUGH TO GET YOU TO LOWER YOUR GUARD, CAPTAIN.
WHAT HAVE YOU--

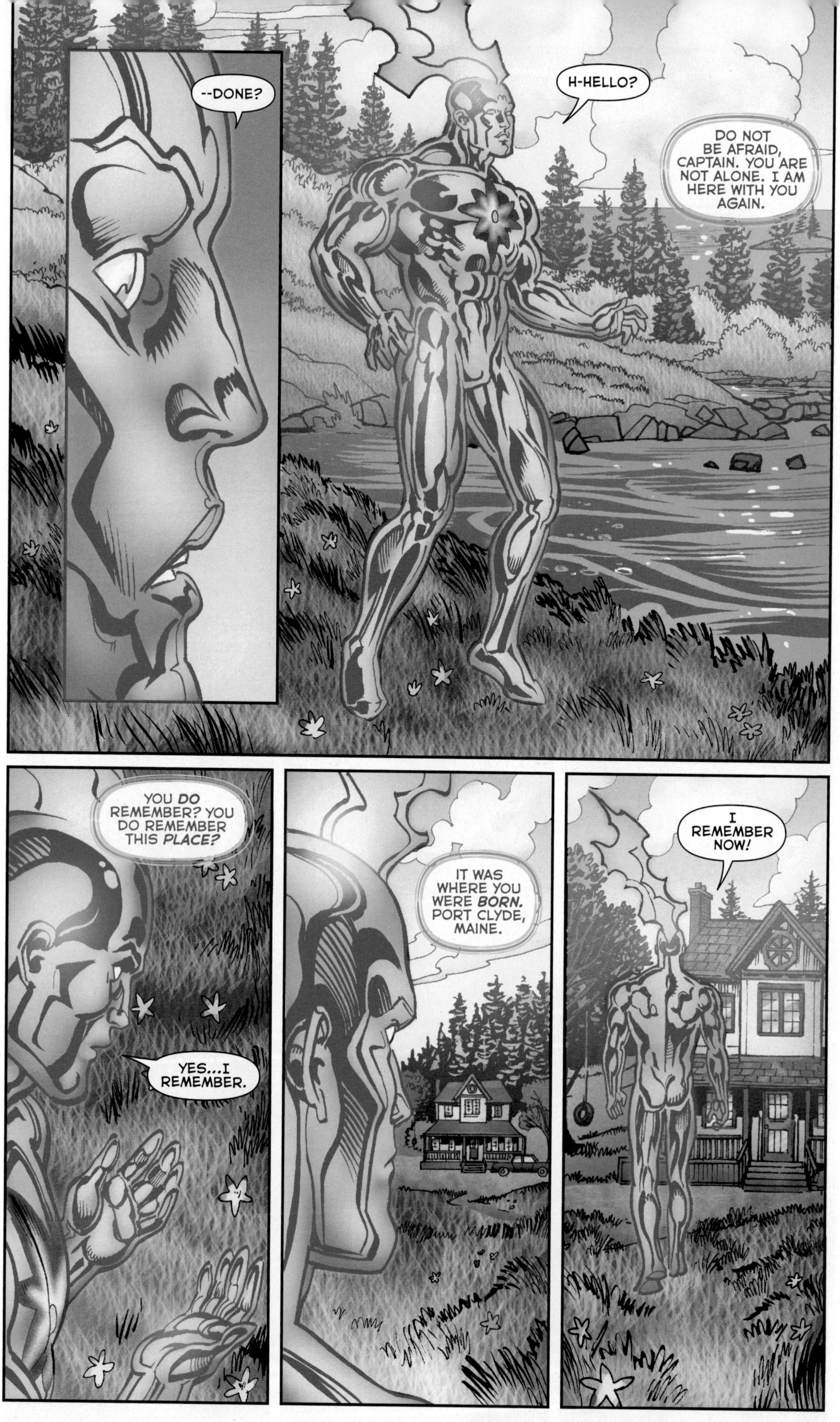
--DONE?
H-HELLO?
DO NOT BE AFRAID, CAPTAIN. YOU ARE NOT ALONE. I AM HERE WITH YOU AGAIN.
YOU DO REMEMBER? YOU DO REMEMBER THIS PLACE?
YES...I REMEMBER.
IT WAS WHERE YOU WERE BORN. PORT CLYDE, MAINE.
I REMEMBER NOW!

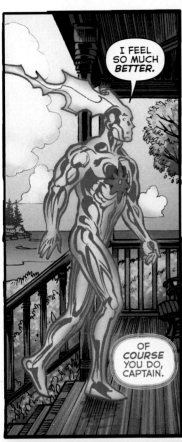

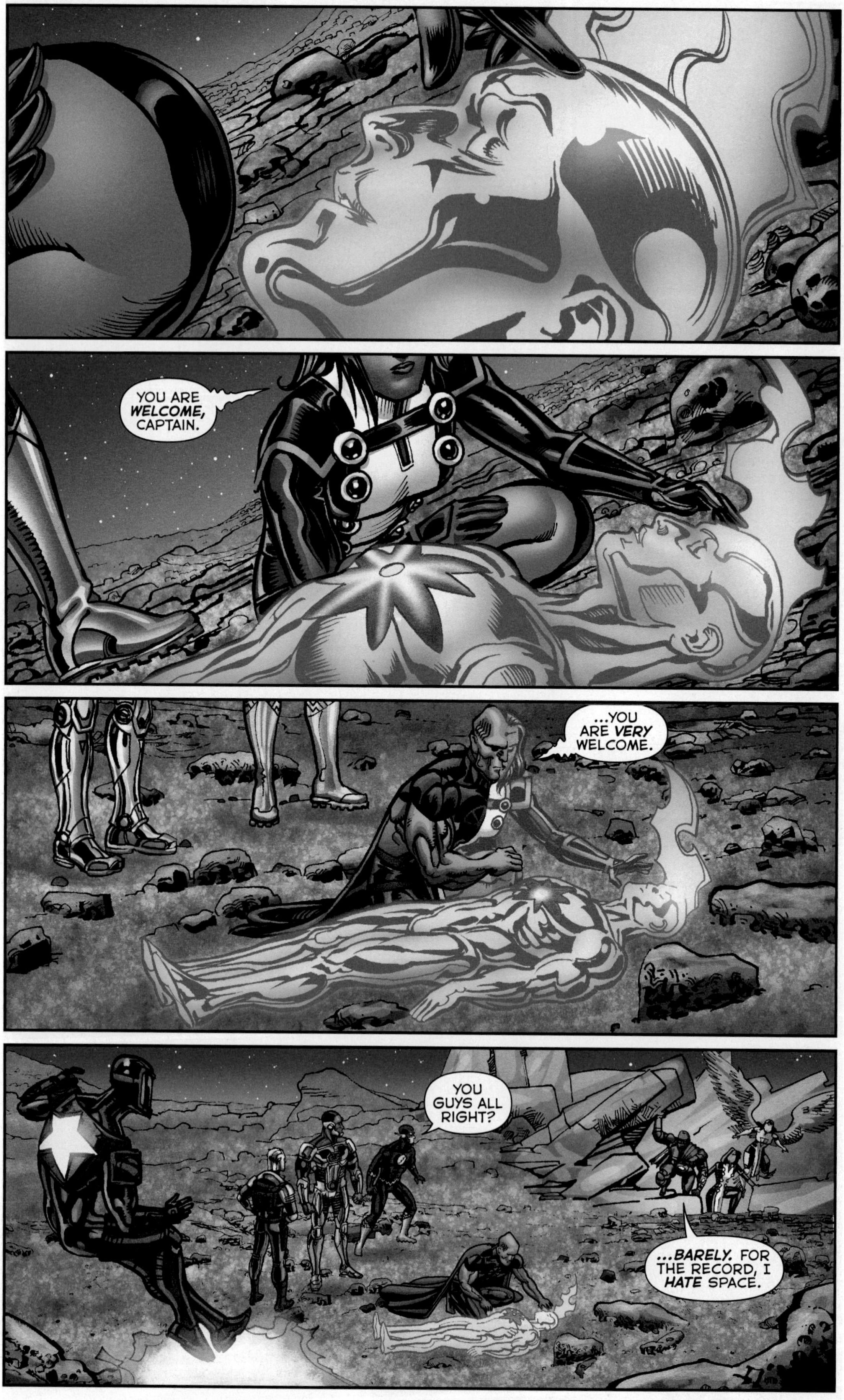
YOU ARE WELCOME, CAPTAIN.
...YOU ARE VERY WELCOME.
YOU GUYS ALL RIGHT?
...BARELY. FOR THE RECORD, I HATE SPACE.

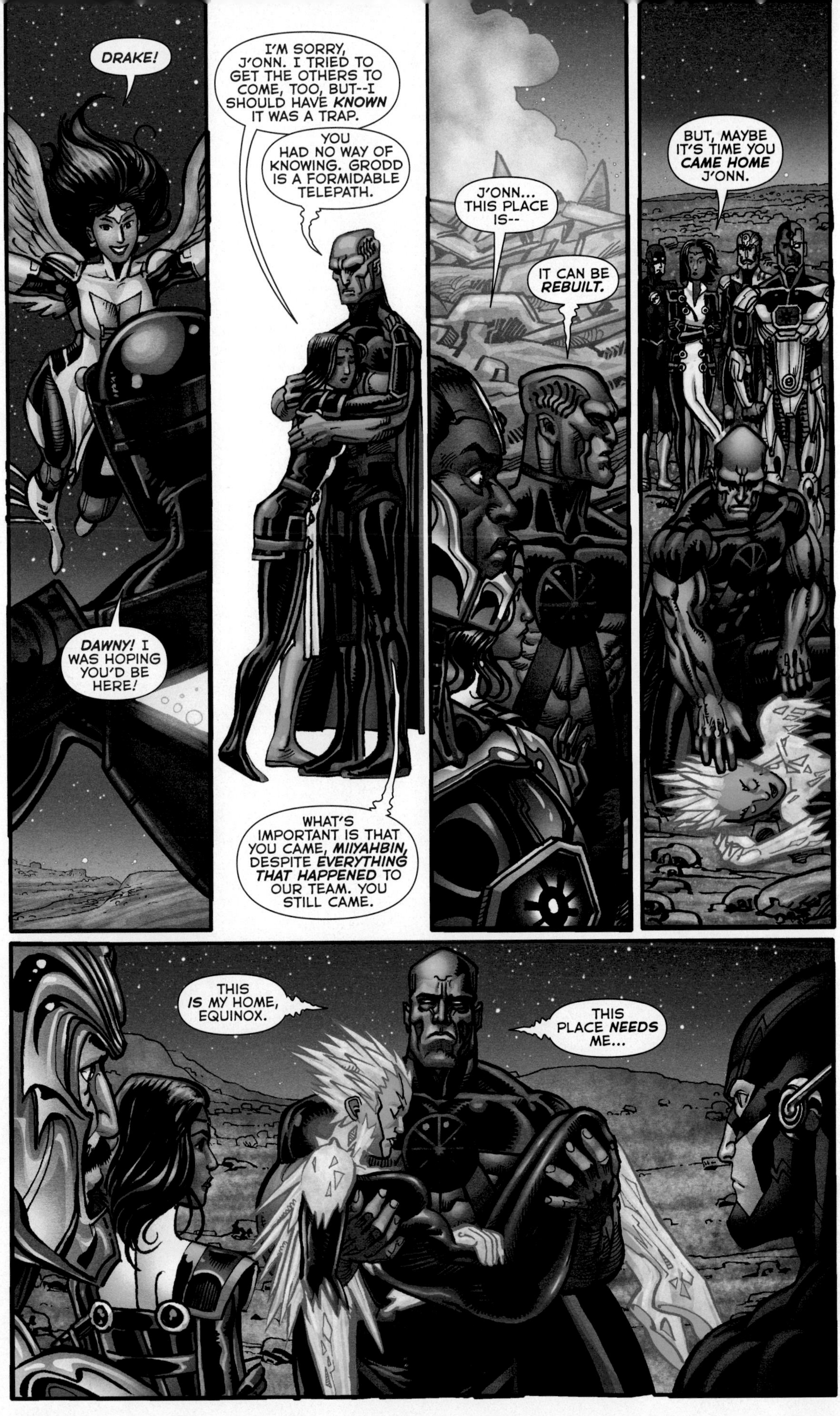
DRAKE!
DAWNY! I WAS HOPING YOU'D BE HERE!
I'M SORRY, J'ONN. I TRIED TO GET THE OTHERS TO COME, TOO, BUT--I SHOULD HAVE KNOWN IT WAS A TRAP.
YOU HAD NO WAY OF KNOWING. GRODD IS A FORMIDABLE TELEPATH.
WHAT'S IMPORTANT IS THAT YOU CAME, MIIYAHBIN, DESPITE EVERYTHING THAT HAPPENED TO OUR TEAM. YOU STILL CAME.
J'ONN... THIS PLACE IS--
IT CAN BE REBUILT.
BUT, MAYBE IT'S TIME YOU CAME HOME J'ONN.
THIS IS MY HOME, EQUINOX.
THIS PLACE NEEDS ME...

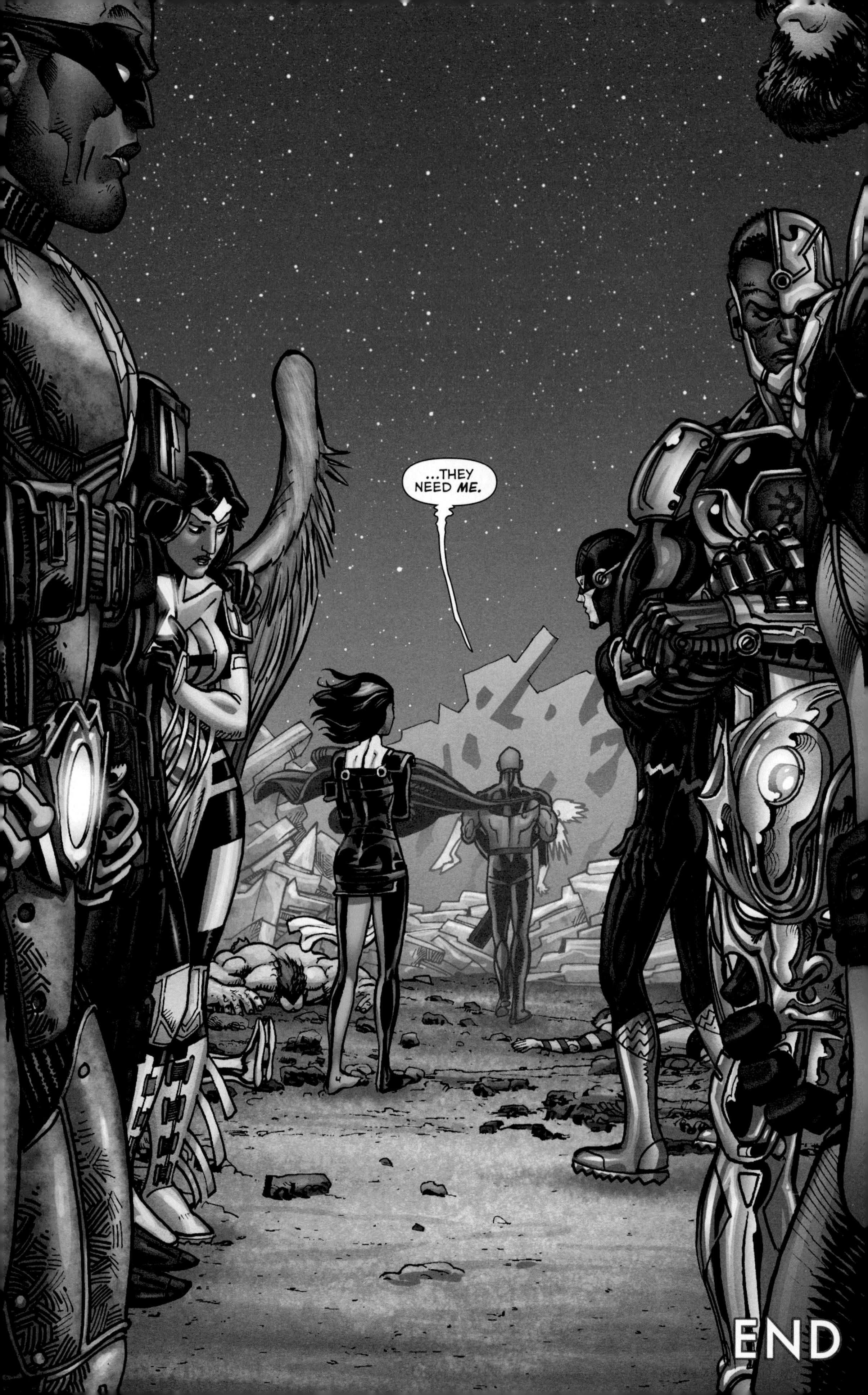
...THEY NEED *ME.*
END

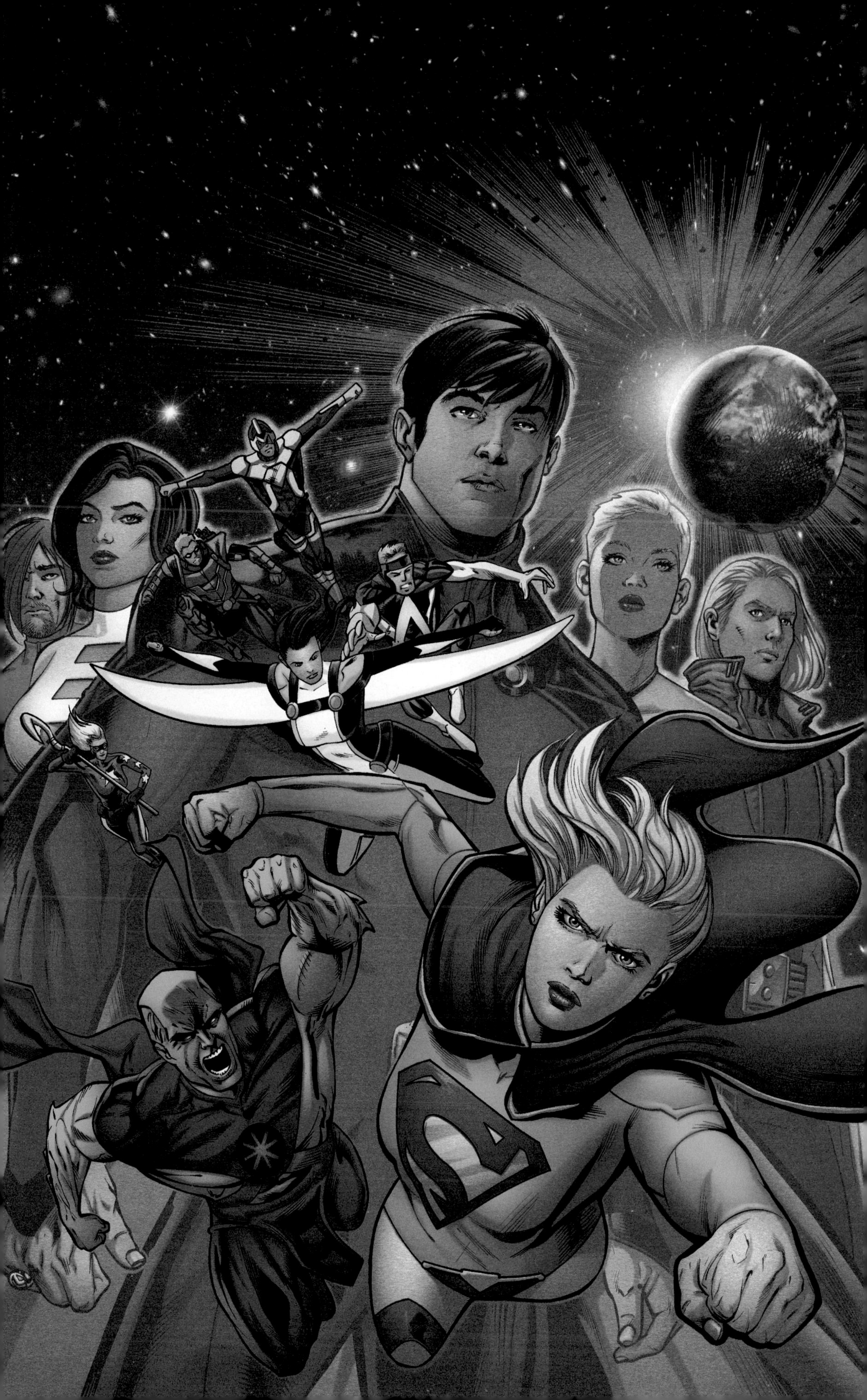

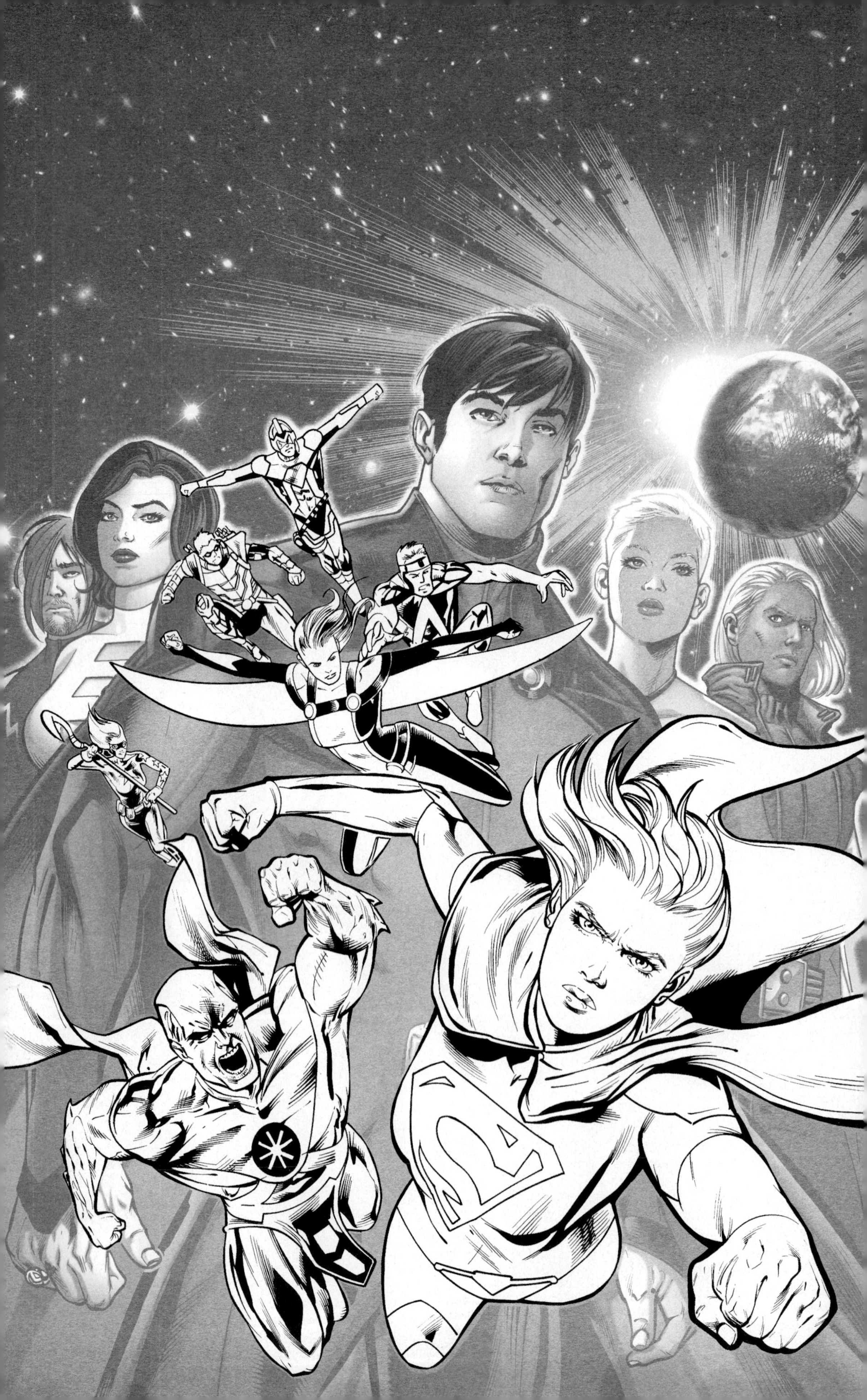

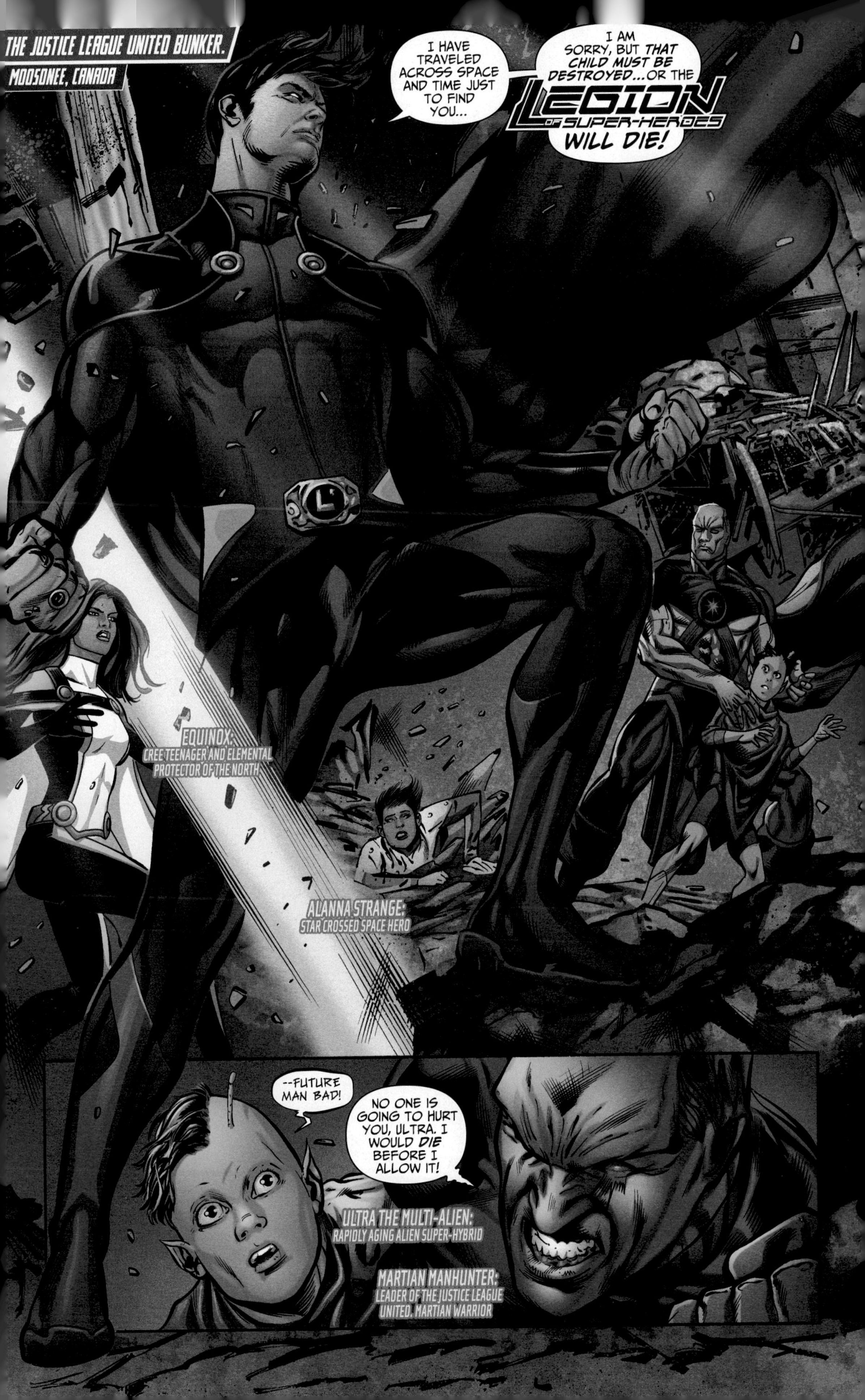
THE JUSTICE LEAGUE UNITED BUNKER.
MOOSONEE, CANADA
I HAVE TRAVELED ACROSS SPACE AND TIME JUST TO FIND YOU...
I AM SORRY, BUT THAT CHILD MUST BE DESTROYED...OR THE LEGION OF SUPER-HEROES WILL DIE!
EQUINOX: CREE TEENAGER AND ELEMENTAL PROTECTOR OF THE NORTH
ALANNA STRANGE: STAR CROSSED SPACE HERO
--FUTURE MAN BAD!
NO ONE IS GOING TO HURT YOU, ULTRA. I WOULD DIE BEFORE I ALLOW IT!
ULTRA THE MULTI-ALIEN: RAPIDLY AGING ALIEN SUPER-HYBRID
MARTIAN MANHUNTER: LEADER OF THE JUSTICE LEAGUE UNITED. MARTIAN WARRIOR

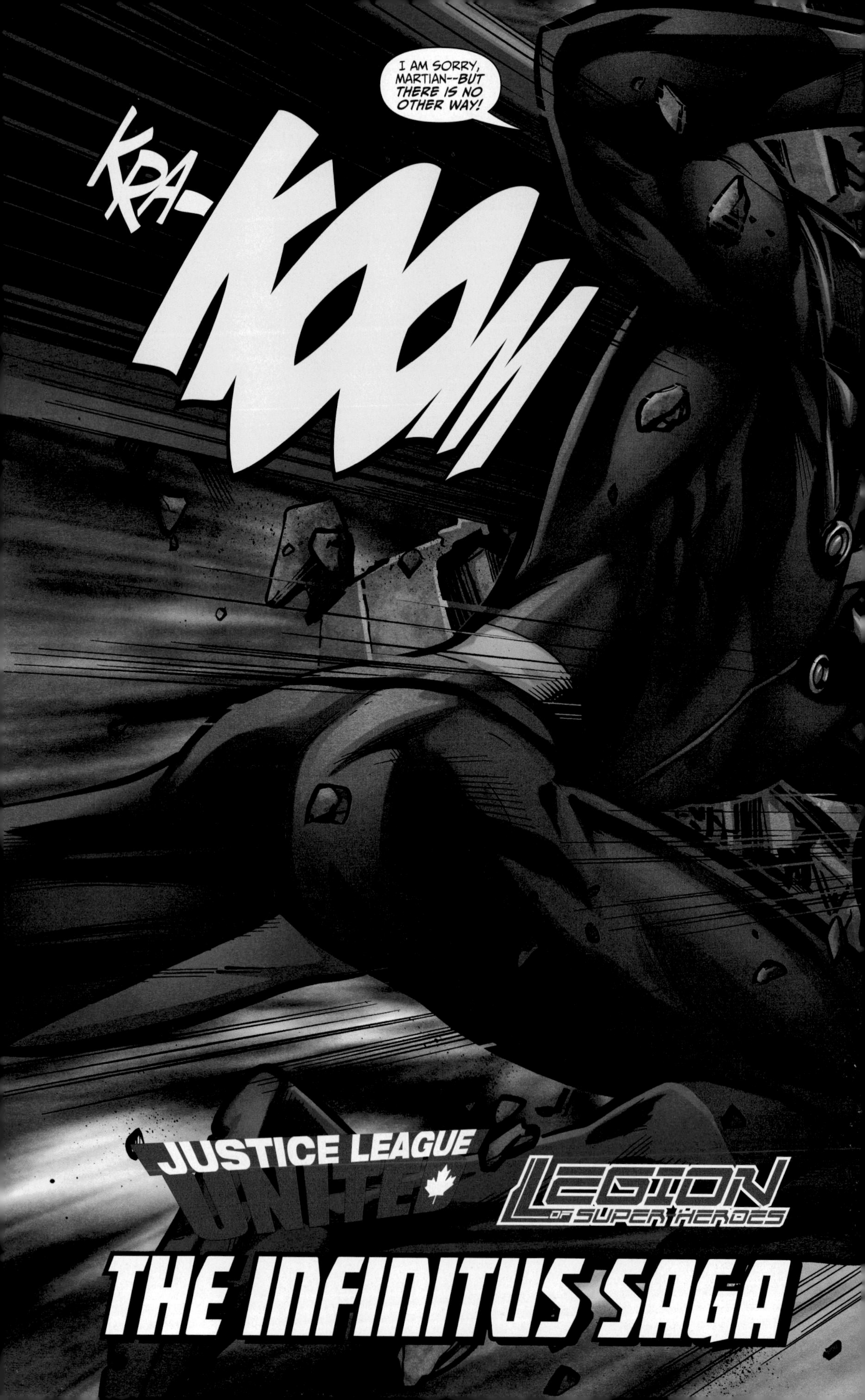
I AM SORRY, MARTIAN--BUT THERE IS NO OTHER WAY!
KRA-KOOM
JUSTICE LEAGUE UNITED
LEGION OF SUPER-HEROES
THE INFINITUS SAGA

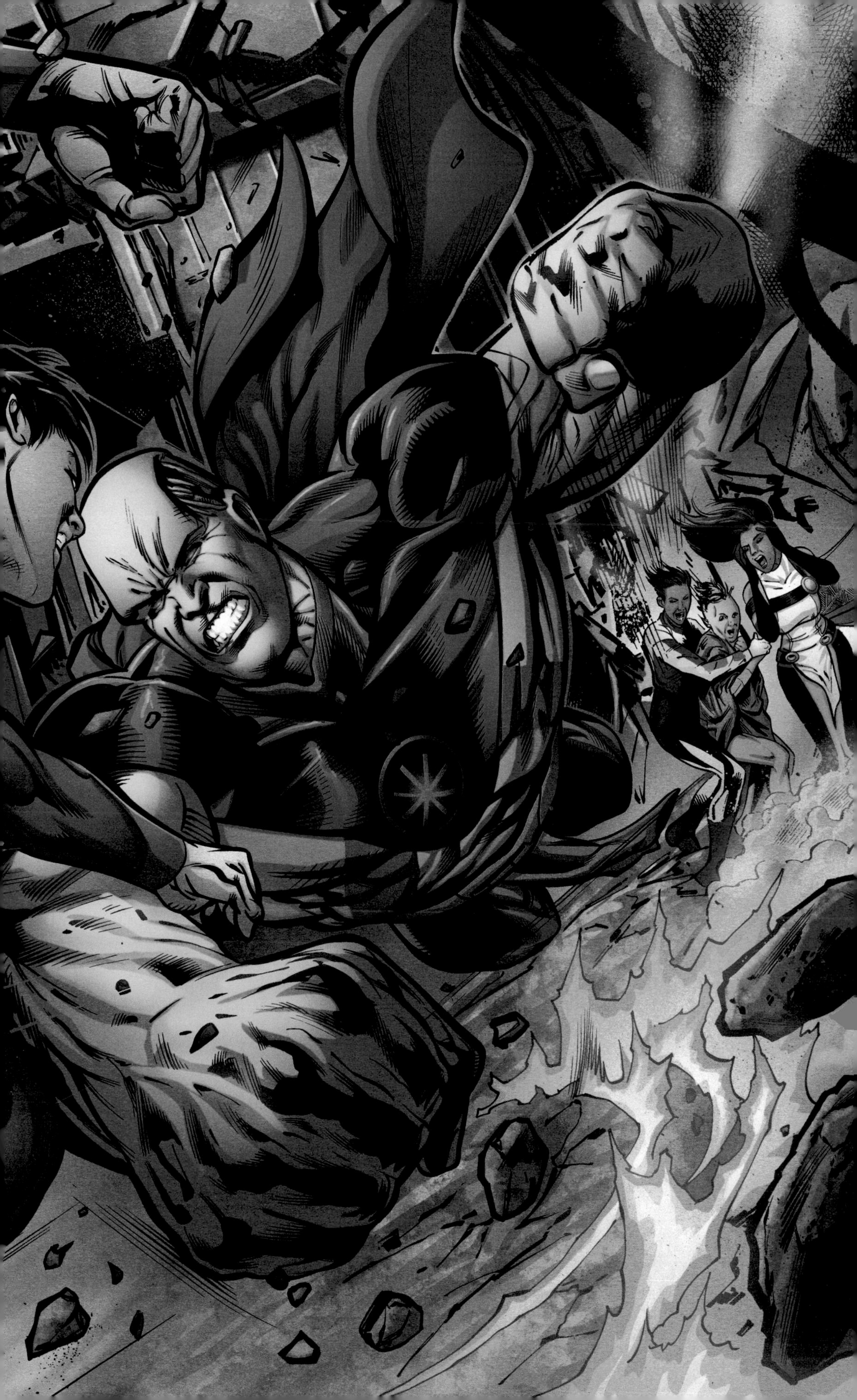

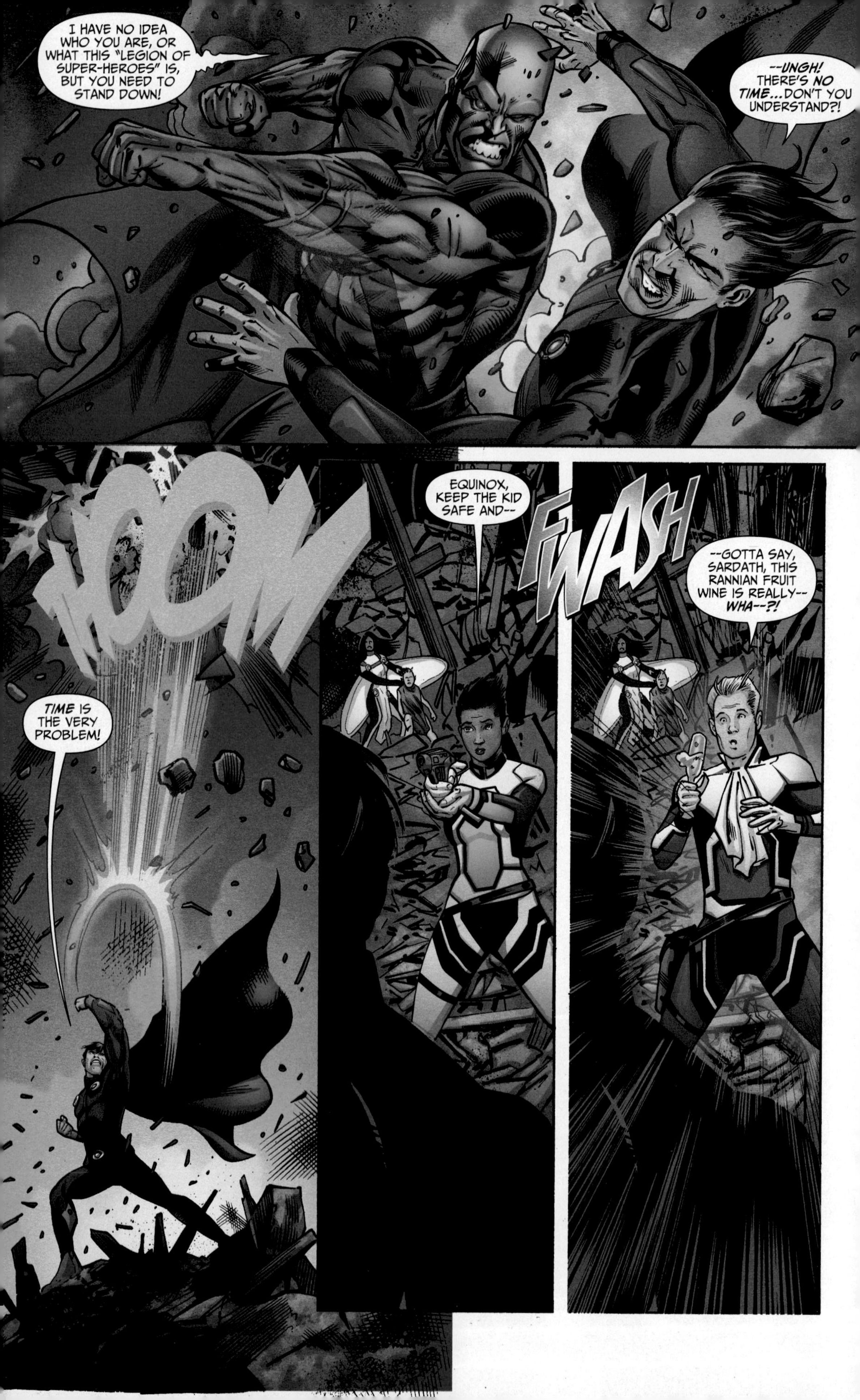
I HAVE NO IDEA WHO YOU ARE, OR WHAT THIS "LEGION OF SUPER-HEROES" IS, BUT YOU NEED TO STAND DOWN!
--UNGH! THERE'S NO TIME...DON'T YOU UNDERSTAND?!
FOOOM
TIME IS THE VERY PROBLEM!
EQUINOX, KEEP THE KID SAFE AND--
FWASH
--GOTTA SAY, SARDATH, THIS RANNIAN FRUIT WINE IS REALLY-- WHA--?!

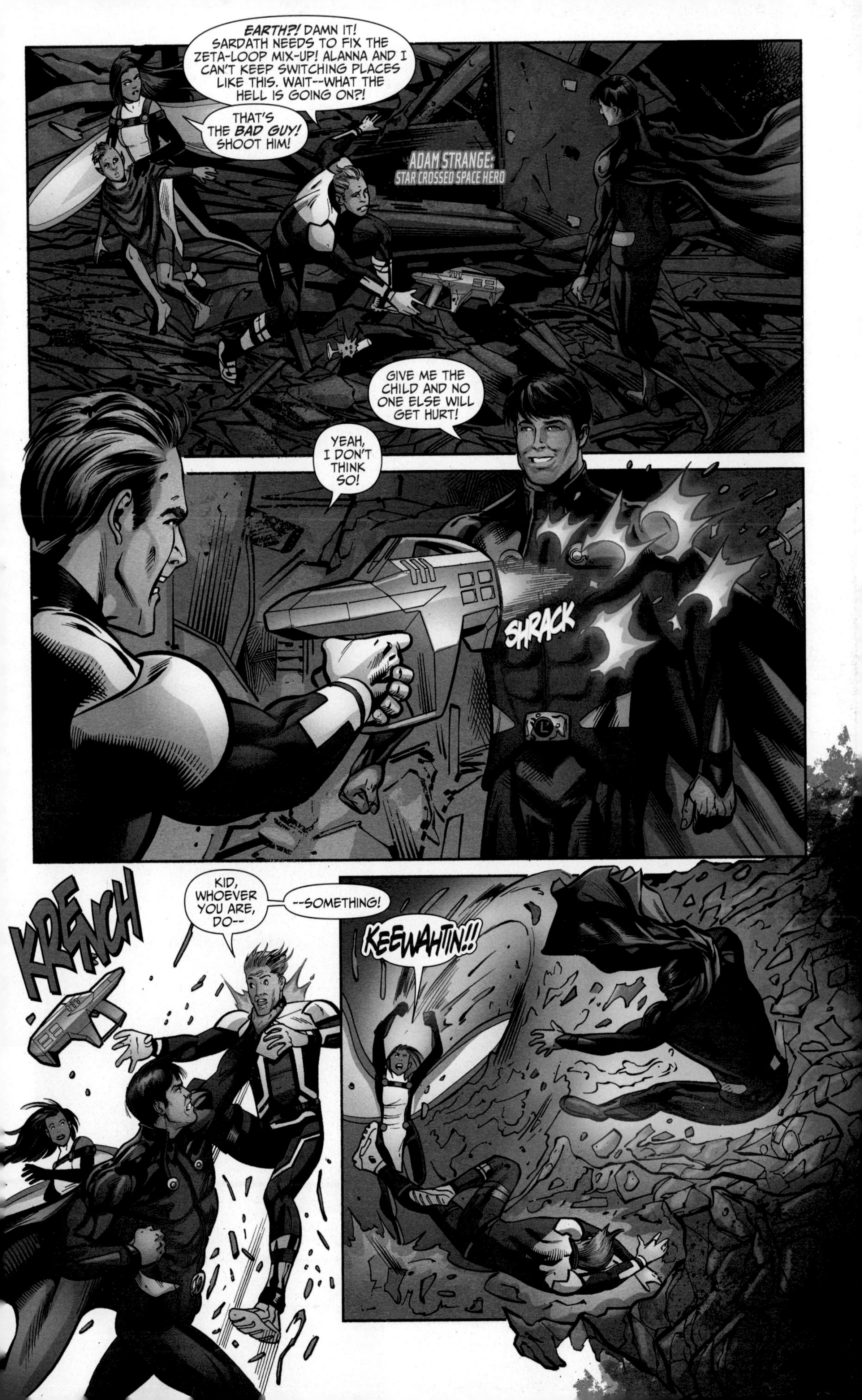
EARTH?! DAMN IT! SARDATH NEEDS TO FIX THE ZETA-LOOP MIX-UP! ALANNA AND I CAN'T KEEP SWITCHING PLACES LIKE THIS. WAIT--WHAT THE HELL IS GOING ON?!
THAT'S THE BAD GUY! SHOOT HIM!
ADAM STRANGE: STAR CROSSED SPACE HERO
GIVE ME THE CHILD AND NO ONE ELSE WILL GET HURT!
YEAH, I DON'T THINK SO!
SHRACK
KRENCH
KID, WHOEVER YOU ARE, DO--
--SOMETHING!
KEEWAHTIN!!

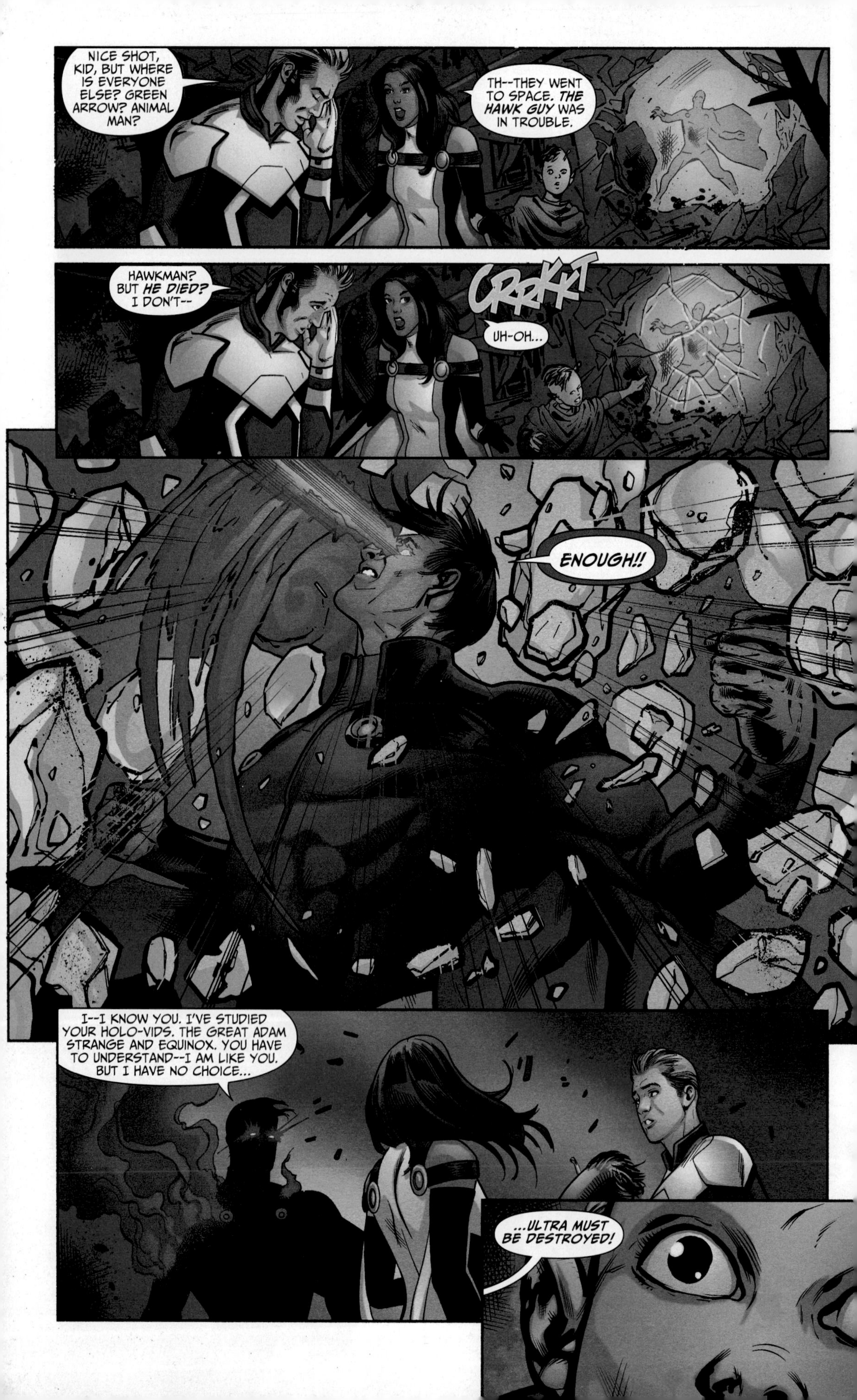
NICE SHOT, KID, BUT WHERE IS EVERYONE ELSE? GREEN ARROW? ANIMAL MAN?
TH--THEY WENT TO SPACE. *THE HAWK GUY* WAS IN TROUBLE.
HAWKMAN? BUT *HE DIED?* I DON'T--
CRRKKT
UH-OH...
ENOUGH!!
I--I KNOW YOU. I'VE STUDIED YOUR HOLO-VIDS. THE GREAT ADAM STRANGE AND EQUINOX. YOU HAVE TO UNDERSTAND--I AM LIKE YOU. BUT I HAVE NO CHOICE...
...ULTRA MUST BE DESTROYED!

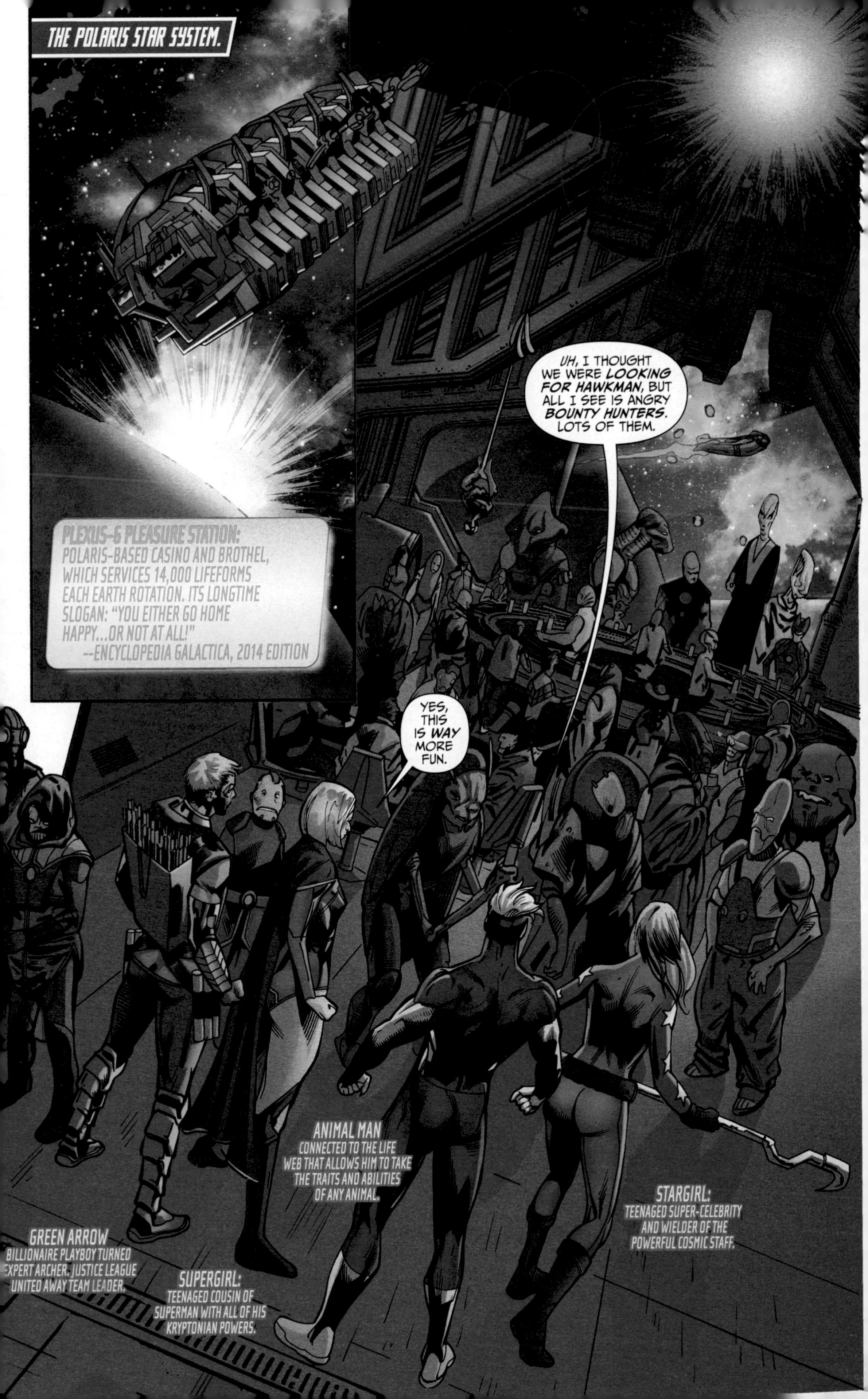
THE POLARIS STAR SYSTEM.
PLEXUS-6 PLEASURE STATION: POLARIS-BASED CASINO AND BROTHEL, WHICH SERVICES 14,000 LIFEFORMS EACH EARTH ROTATION. ITS LONGTIME SLOGAN: "YOU EITHER GO HOME HAPPY...OR NOT AT ALL!" --ENCYCLOPEDIA GALACTICA, 2014 EDITION
UH, I THOUGHT WE WERE LOOKING FOR HAWKMAN, BUT ALL I SEE IS ANGRY BOUNTY HUNTERS. LOTS OF THEM.
YES, THIS IS WAY MORE FUN.
GREEN ARROW BILLIONAIRE PLAYBOY TURNED EXPERT ARCHER. JUSTICE LEAGUE UNITED AWAY TEAM LEADER.
SUPERGIRL: TEENAGED COUSIN OF SUPERMAN WITH ALL OF HIS KRYPTONIAN POWERS.
ANIMAL MAN CONNECTED TO THE LIFE WEB THAT ALLOWS HIM TO TAKE THE TRAITS AND ABILITIES OF ANY ANIMAL.
STARGIRL: TEENAGED SUPER-CELEBRITY AND WIELDER OF THE POWERFUL COSMIC STAFF.

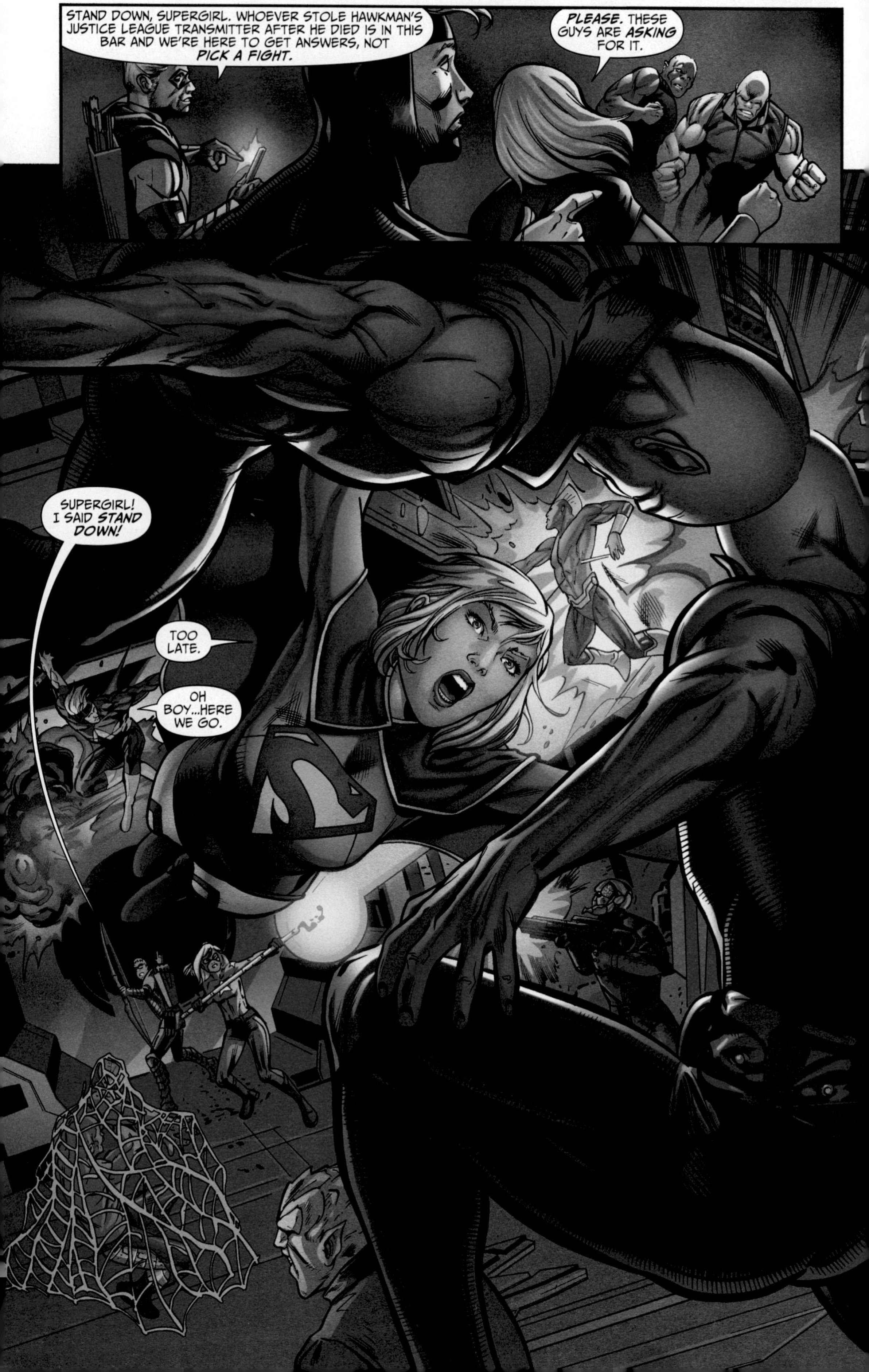
STAND DOWN, SUPERGIRL. WHOEVER STOLE HAWKMAN'S JUSTICE LEAGUE TRANSMITTER AFTER HE DIED IS IN THIS BAR AND WE'RE HERE TO GET ANSWERS, NOT PICK A FIGHT.
PLEASE. THESE GUYS ARE ASKING FOR IT.
SUPERGIRL! I SAID STAND DOWN!
TOO LATE.
OH BOY...HERE WE GO.

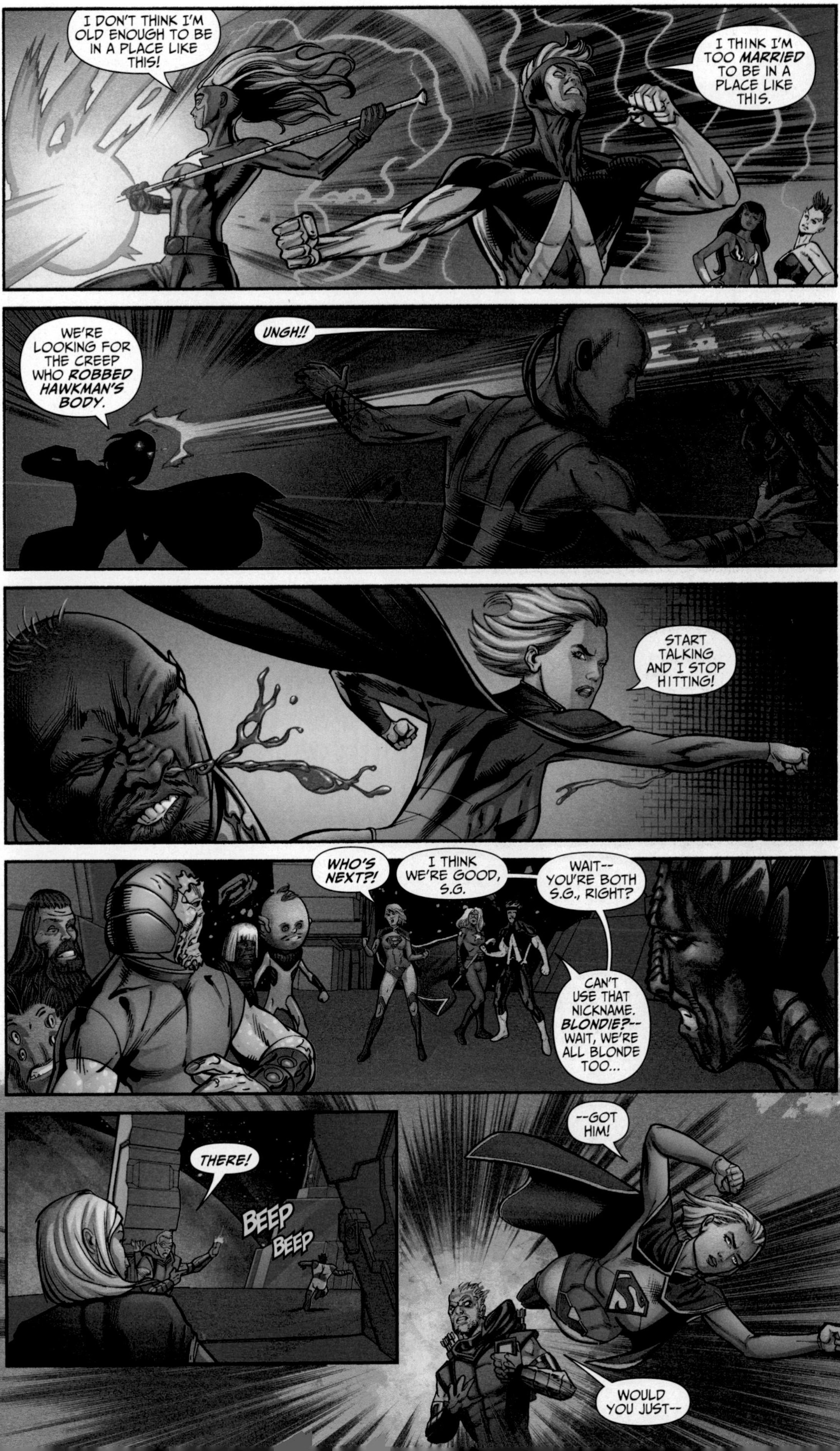
I DON'T THINK I'M OLD ENOUGH TO BE IN A PLACE LIKE THIS!
I THINK I'M TOO MARRIED TO BE IN A PLACE LIKE THIS.
WE'RE LOOKING FOR THE CREEP WHO ROBBED HAWKMAN'S BODY.
UNGH!!
START TALKING AND I STOP HITTING!
WHO'S NEXT?!
I THINK WE'RE GOOD, S.G.
WAIT-- YOU'RE BOTH S.G., RIGHT?
CAN'T USE THAT NICKNAME. BLONDIE?-- WAIT, WE'RE ALL BLONDE TOO...
THERE!
BEEP
BEEP
--GOT HIM!
WOULD YOU JUST--

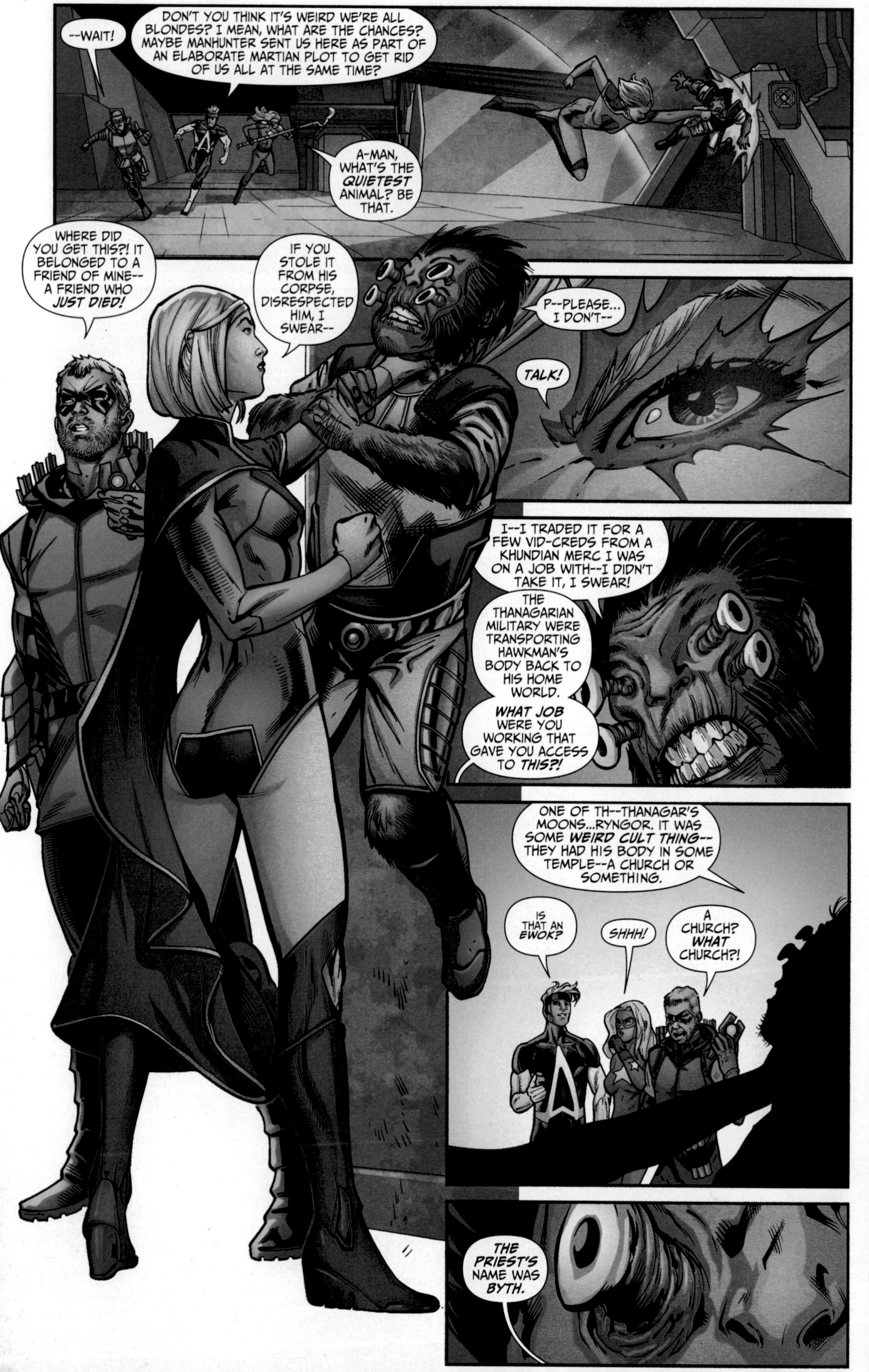
--WAIT!
DON'T YOU THINK IT'S WEIRD WE'RE ALL BLONDES? I MEAN, WHAT ARE THE CHANCES? MAYBE MANHUNTER SENT US HERE AS PART OF AN ELABORATE MARTIAN PLOT TO GET RID OF US ALL AT THE SAME TIME?
A-MAN, WHAT'S THE QUIETEST ANIMAL? BE THAT.
WHERE DID YOU GET THIS?! IT BELONGED TO A FRIEND OF MINE-- A FRIEND WHO JUST DIED!
IF YOU STOLE IT FROM HIS CORPSE, DISRESPECTED HIM, I SWEAR--
P--PLEASE... I DON'T--
TALK!
I--I TRADED IT FOR A FEW VID-CREDS FROM A KHUNDIAN MERC I WAS ON A JOB WITH--I DIDN'T TAKE IT, I SWEAR!
THE THANAGARIAN MILITARY WERE TRANSPORTING HAWKMAN'S BODY BACK TO HIS HOME WORLD.
WHAT JOB WERE YOU WORKING THAT GAVE YOU ACCESS TO THIS?!
ONE OF TH--THANAGAR'S MOONS...RYNGOR. IT WAS SOME WEIRD CULT THING-- THEY HAD HIS BODY IN SOME TEMPLE--A CHURCH OR SOMETHING.
IS THAT AN EWOK?
SHHH!
A CHURCH? WHAT CHURCH?!
THE PRIEST'S NAME WAS BYTH.

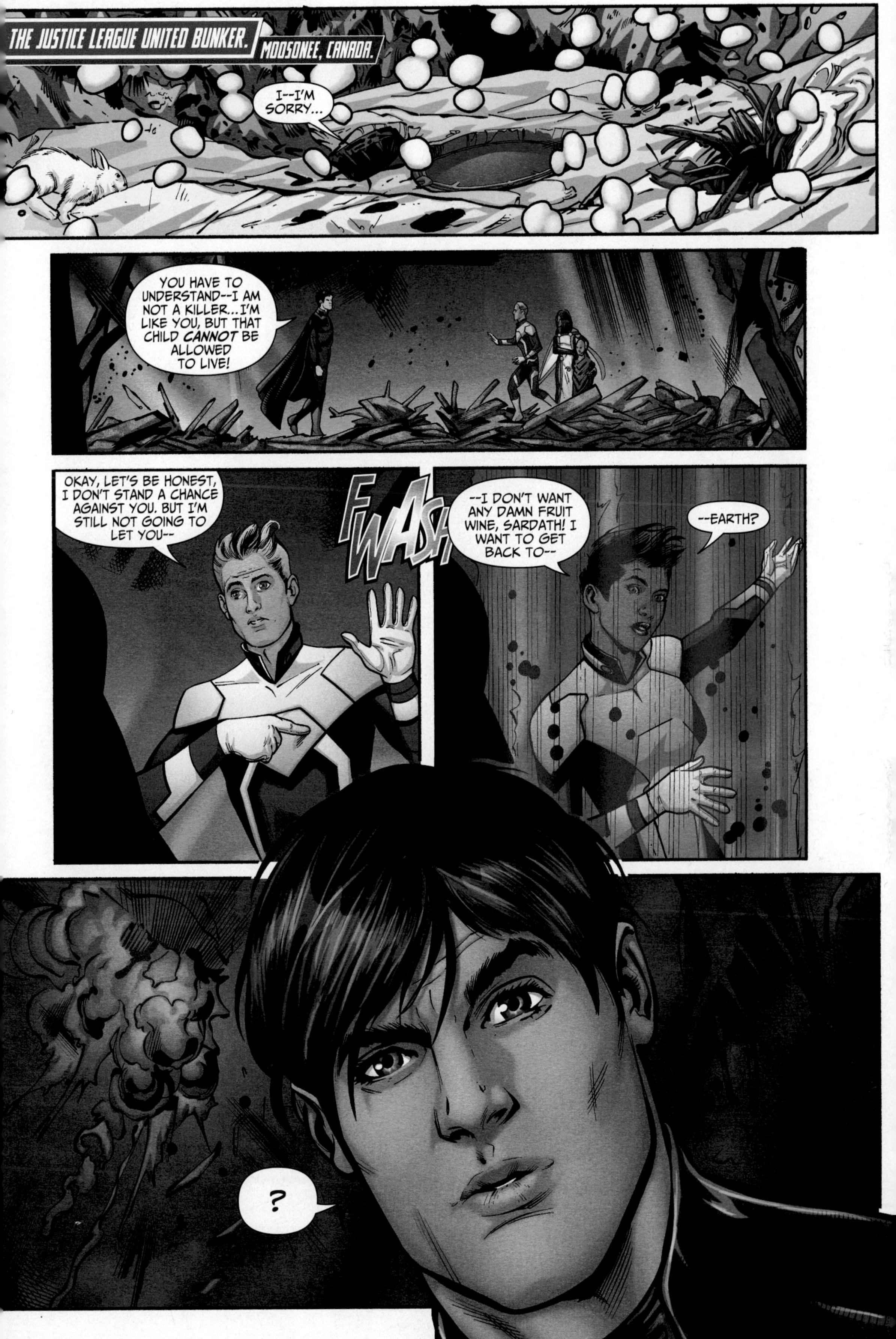
THE JUSTICE LEAGUE UNITED BUNKER.
MOOSONEE, CANADA.
I--I'M SORRY...
YOU HAVE TO UNDERSTAND--I AM NOT A KILLER...I'M LIKE YOU, BUT THAT CHILD CANNOT BE ALLOWED TO LIVE!
OKAY, LET'S BE HONEST, I DON'T STAND A CHANCE AGAINST YOU. BUT I'M STILL NOT GOING TO LET YOU--
FWASH
--I DON'T WANT ANY DAMN FRUIT WINE, SARDATH! I WANT TO GET BACK TO--
--EARTH?
?

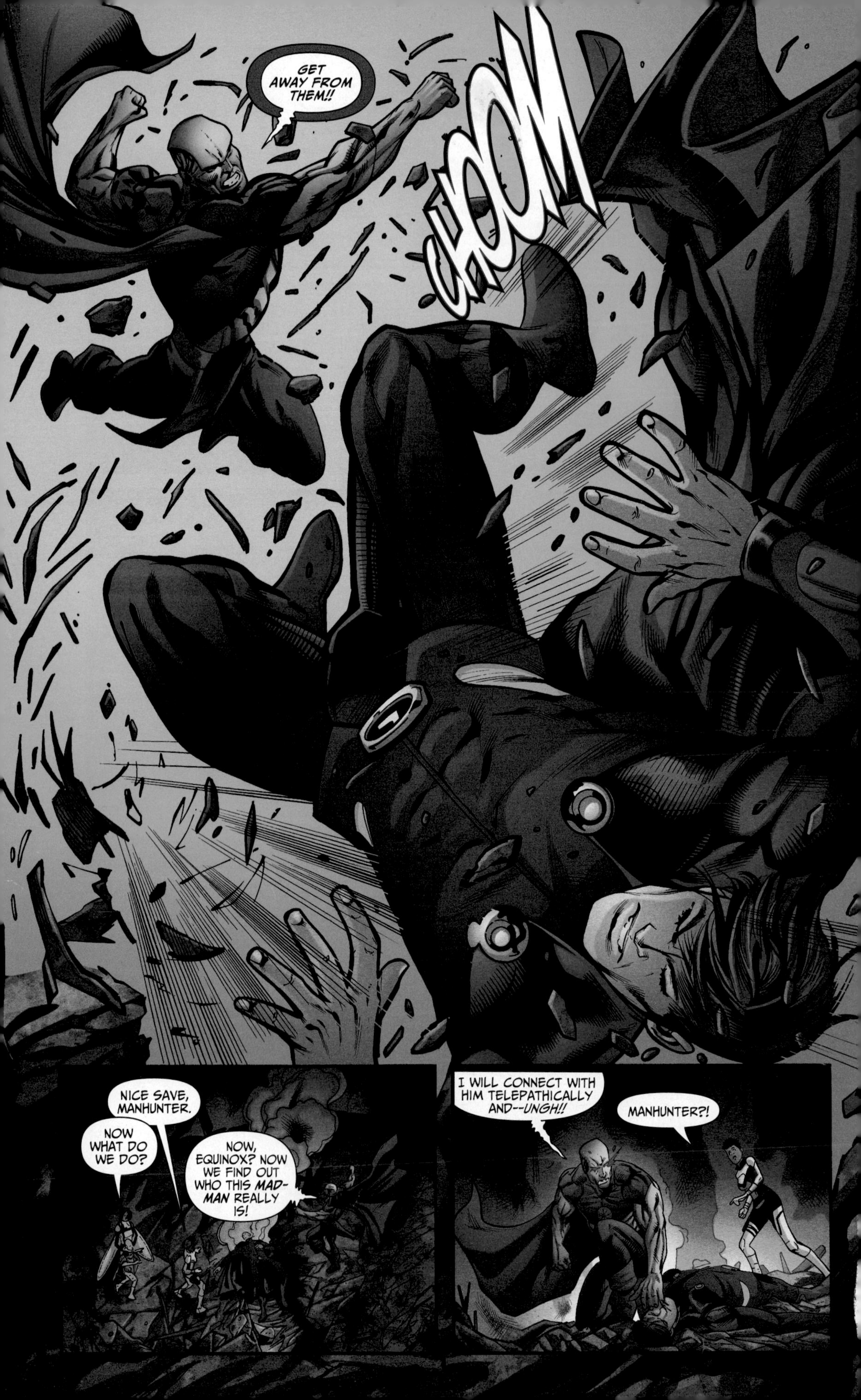
GET AWAY FROM THEM!!
CHOOOM
NICE SAVE, MANHUNTER.
NOW WHAT DO WE DO?
NOW, EQUINOX? NOW WE FIND OUT WHO THIS MAD-MAN REALLY IS!
I WILL CONNECT WITH HIM TELEPATHICALLY AND--UNGH!!
MANHUNTER?!

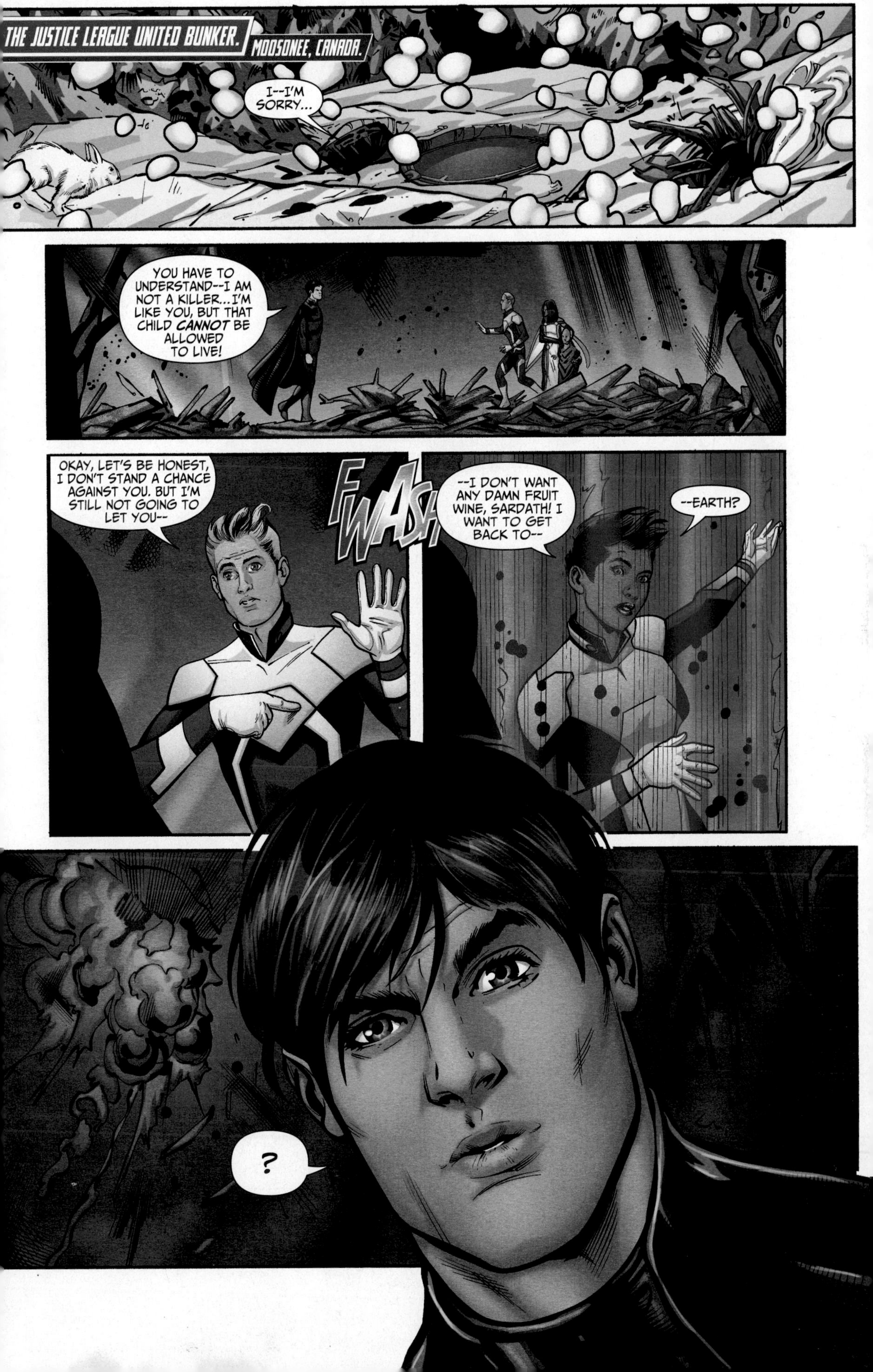
THE JUSTICE LEAGUE UNITED BUNKER.
MOOSONEE, CANADA.
I--I'M SORRY...
YOU HAVE TO UNDERSTAND--I AM NOT A KILLER...I'M LIKE YOU, BUT THAT CHILD CANNOT BE ALLOWED TO LIVE!
OKAY, LET'S BE HONEST, I DON'T STAND A CHANCE AGAINST YOU. BUT I'M STILL NOT GOING TO LET YOU--
FWASH
--I DON'T WANT ANY DAMN FRUIT WINE, SARDATH! I WANT TO GET BACK TO--
--EARTH?
?

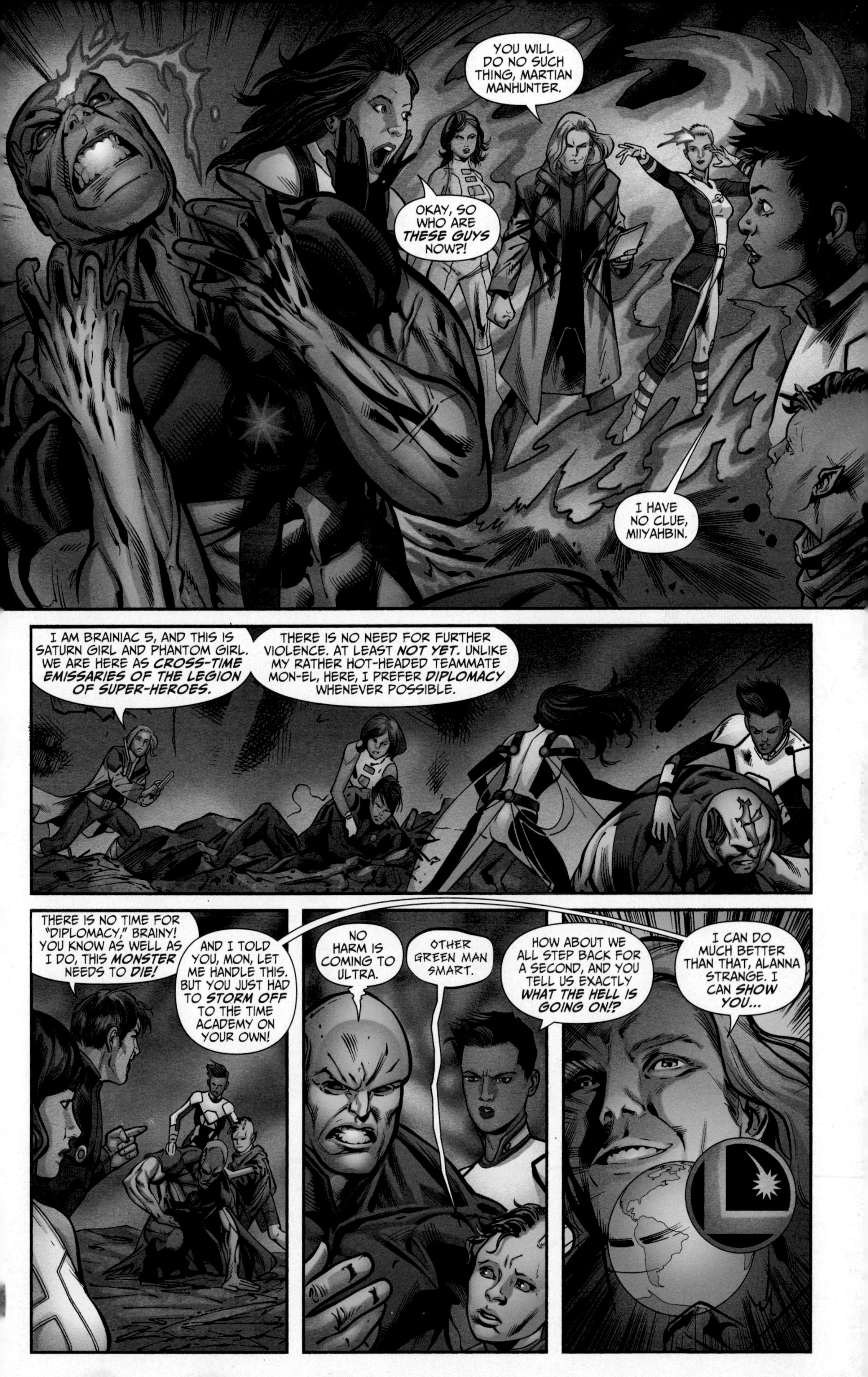

YOU WILL DO NO SUCH THING, MARTIAN MANHUNTER.
OKAY, SO WHO ARE THESE GUYS NOW?!
I HAVE NO CLUE, MIIYAHBIN.
I AM BRAINIAC 5, AND THIS IS SATURN GIRL AND PHANTOM GIRL. WE ARE HERE AS CROSS-TIME EMISSARIES OF THE LEGION OF SUPER-HEROES.
THERE IS NO NEED FOR FURTHER VIOLENCE. AT LEAST NOT YET. UNLIKE MY RATHER HOT-HEADED TEAMMATE MON-EL, HERE, I PREFER DIPLOMACY WHENEVER POSSIBLE.
THERE IS NO TIME FOR "DIPLOMACY," BRAINY! YOU KNOW AS WELL AS I DO, THIS MONSTER NEEDS TO DIE!
AND I TOLD YOU, MON, LET ME HANDLE THIS. BUT YOU JUST HAD TO STORM OFF TO THE TIME ACADEMY ON YOUR OWN!
NO HARM IS COMING TO ULTRA.
OTHER GREEN MAN SMART.
HOW ABOUT WE ALL STEP BACK FOR A SECOND, AND YOU TELL US EXACTLY WHAT THE HELL IS GOING ON!?
I CAN DO MUCH BETTER THAN THAT, ALANNA STRANGE. I CAN SHOW YOU...

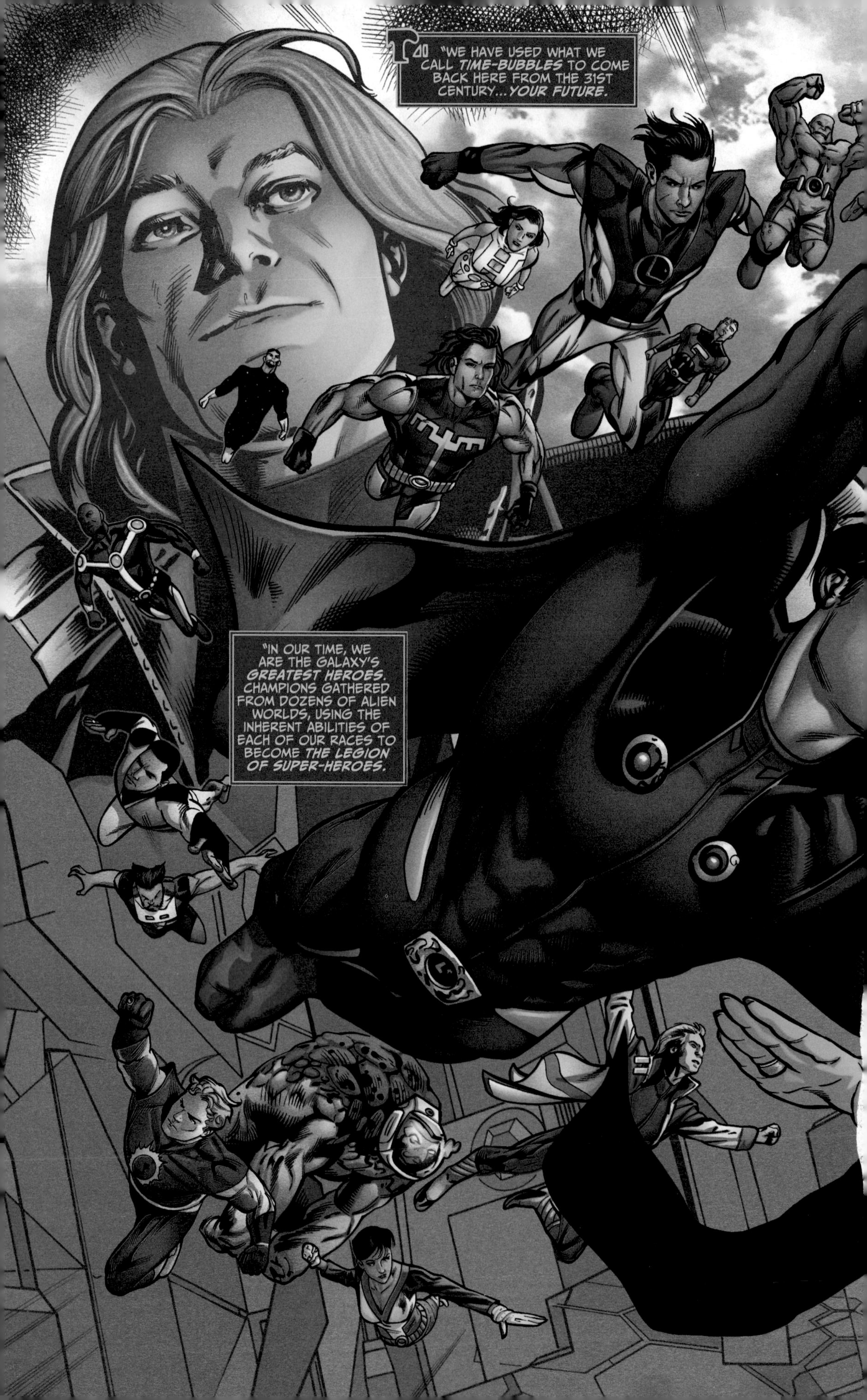
"WE HAVE USED WHAT WE CALL *TIME-BUBBLES* TO COME BACK HERE FROM THE 31ST CENTURY... *YOUR FUTURE.*
"IN OUR TIME, WE ARE THE GALAXY'S *GREATEST HEROES.* CHAMPIONS GATHERED FROM DOZENS OF ALIEN WORLDS, USING THE INHERENT ABILITIES OF EACH OF OUR RACES TO BECOME *THE LEGION OF SUPER-HEROES.*

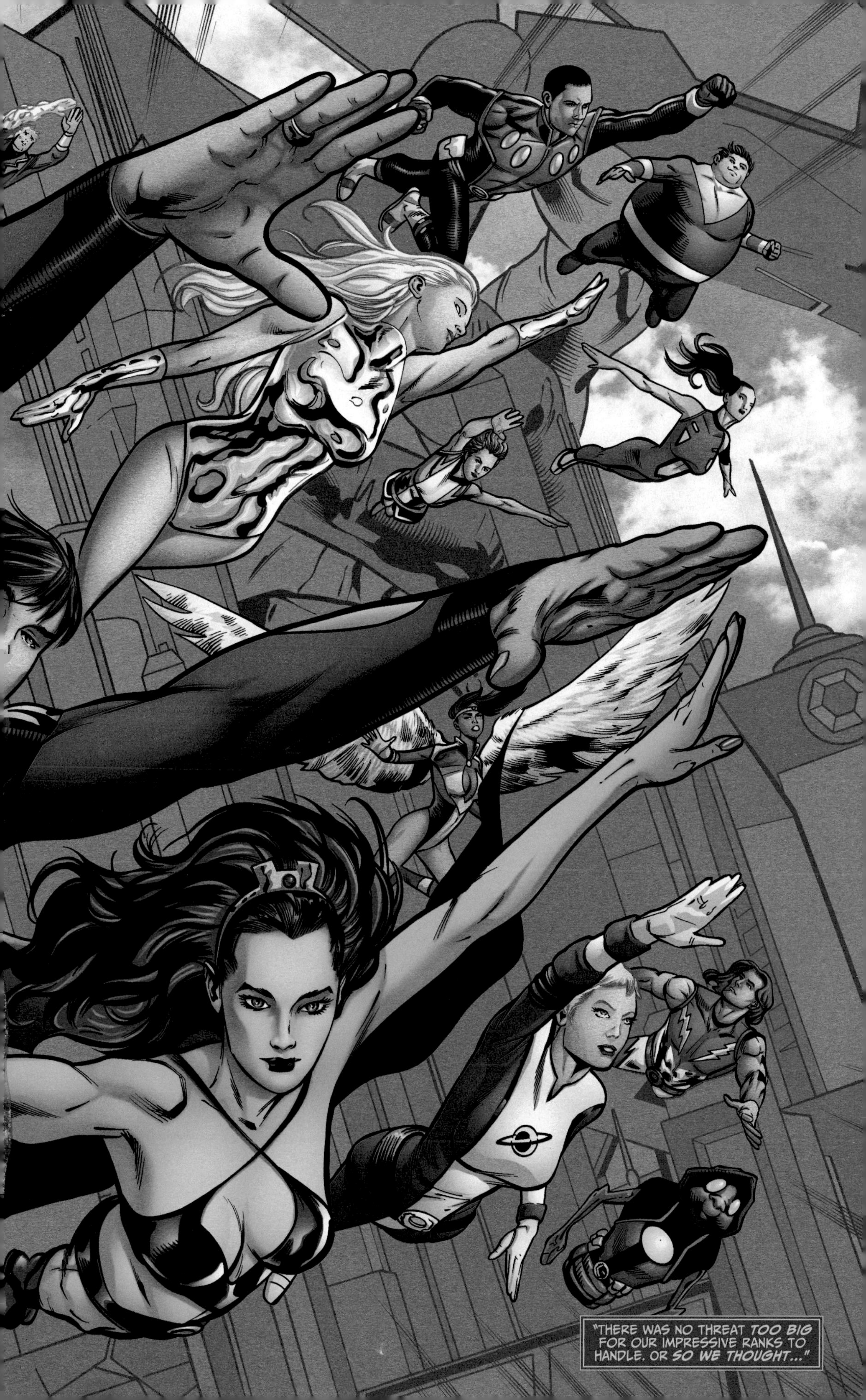
"THERE WAS NO THREAT TOO BIG FOR OUR IMPRESSIVE RANKS TO HANDLE. OR SO WE THOUGHT..."

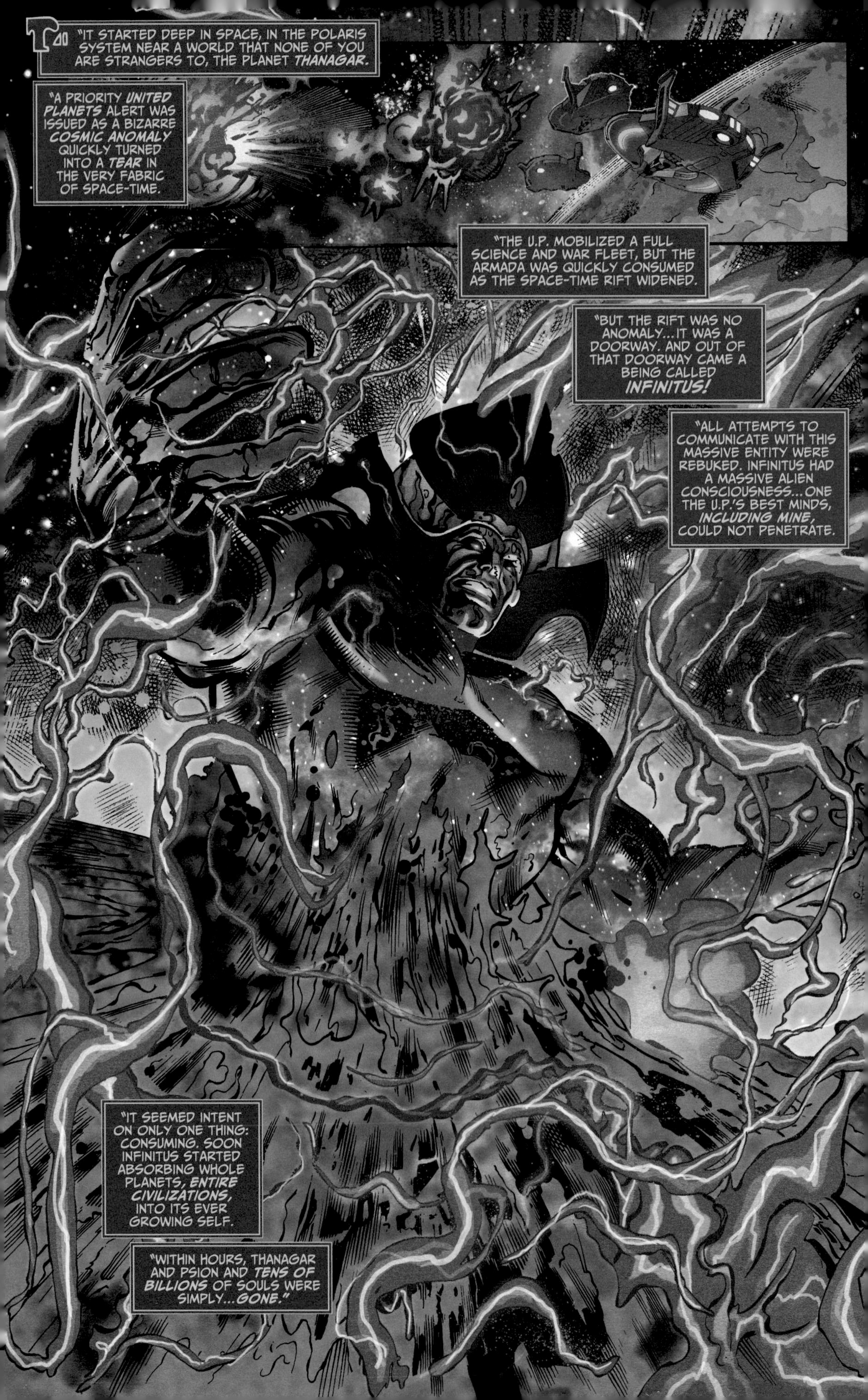
"IT STARTED DEEP IN SPACE, IN THE POLARIS SYSTEM NEAR A WORLD THAT NONE OF YOU ARE STRANGERS TO, THE PLANET THANAGAR.
"A PRIORITY UNITED PLANETS ALERT WAS ISSUED AS A BIZARRE COSMIC ANOMALY QUICKLY TURNED INTO A TEAR IN THE VERY FABRIC OF SPACE-TIME.
"THE U.P. MOBILIZED A FULL SCIENCE AND WAR FLEET, BUT THE ARMADA WAS QUICKLY CONSUMED AS THE SPACE-TIME RIFT WIDENED.
"BUT THE RIFT WAS NO ANOMALY...IT WAS A DOORWAY. AND OUT OF THAT DOORWAY CAME A BEING CALLED INFINITUS!
"ALL ATTEMPTS TO COMMUNICATE WITH THIS MASSIVE ENTITY WERE REBUKED. INFINITUS HAD A MASSIVE ALIEN CONSCIOUSNESS...ONE THE U.P.'S BEST MINDS, INCLUDING MINE, COULD NOT PENETRATE.
"IT SEEMED INTENT ON ONLY ONE THING: CONSUMING. SOON INFINITUS STARTED ABSORBING WHOLE PLANETS, ENTIRE CIVILIZATIONS, INTO ITS EVER GROWING SELF.
"WITHIN HOURS, THANAGAR AND PSION AND TENS OF BILLIONS OF SOULS WERE SIMPLY...GONE."

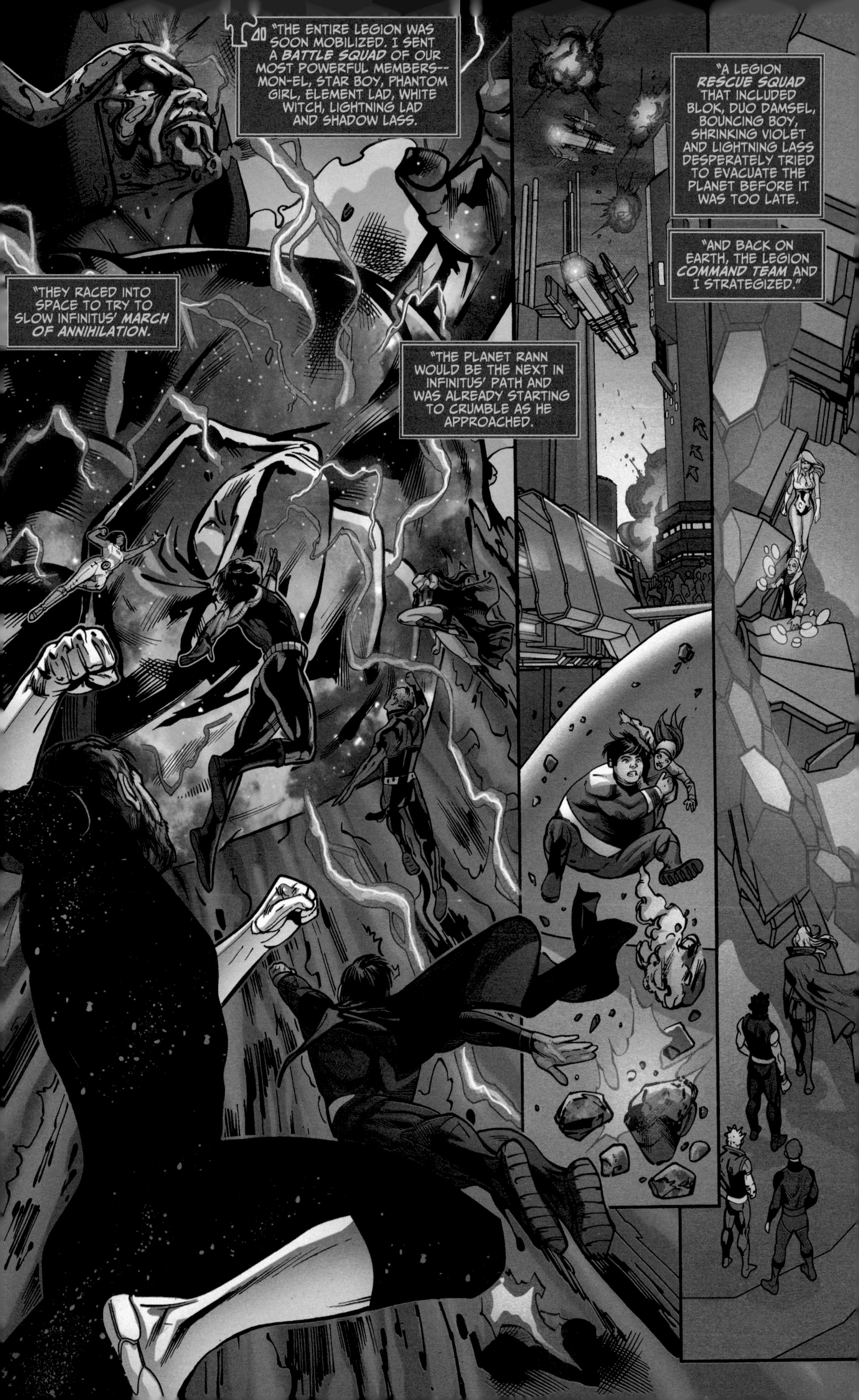
"THE ENTIRE LEGION WAS SOON MOBILIZED. I SENT A *BATTLE SQUAD* OF OUR MOST POWERFUL MEMBERS-- MON-EL, STAR BOY, PHANTOM GIRL, ELEMENT LAD, WHITE WITCH, LIGHTNING LAD AND SHADOW LASS.
"THEY RACED INTO SPACE TO TRY TO SLOW INFINITUS' *MARCH OF ANNIHILATION*.
"THE PLANET RANN WOULD BE THE NEXT IN INFINITUS' PATH AND WAS ALREADY STARTING TO CRUMBLE AS HE APPROACHED.
"A LEGION *RESCUE SQUAD* THAT INCLUDED BLOK, DUO DAMSEL, BOUNCING BOY, SHRINKING VIOLET AND LIGHTNING LASS DESPERATELY TRIED TO EVACUATE THE PLANET BEFORE IT WAS TOO LATE.
"AND BACK ON EARTH, THE LEGION *COMMAND TEAM* AND I STRATEGIZED."

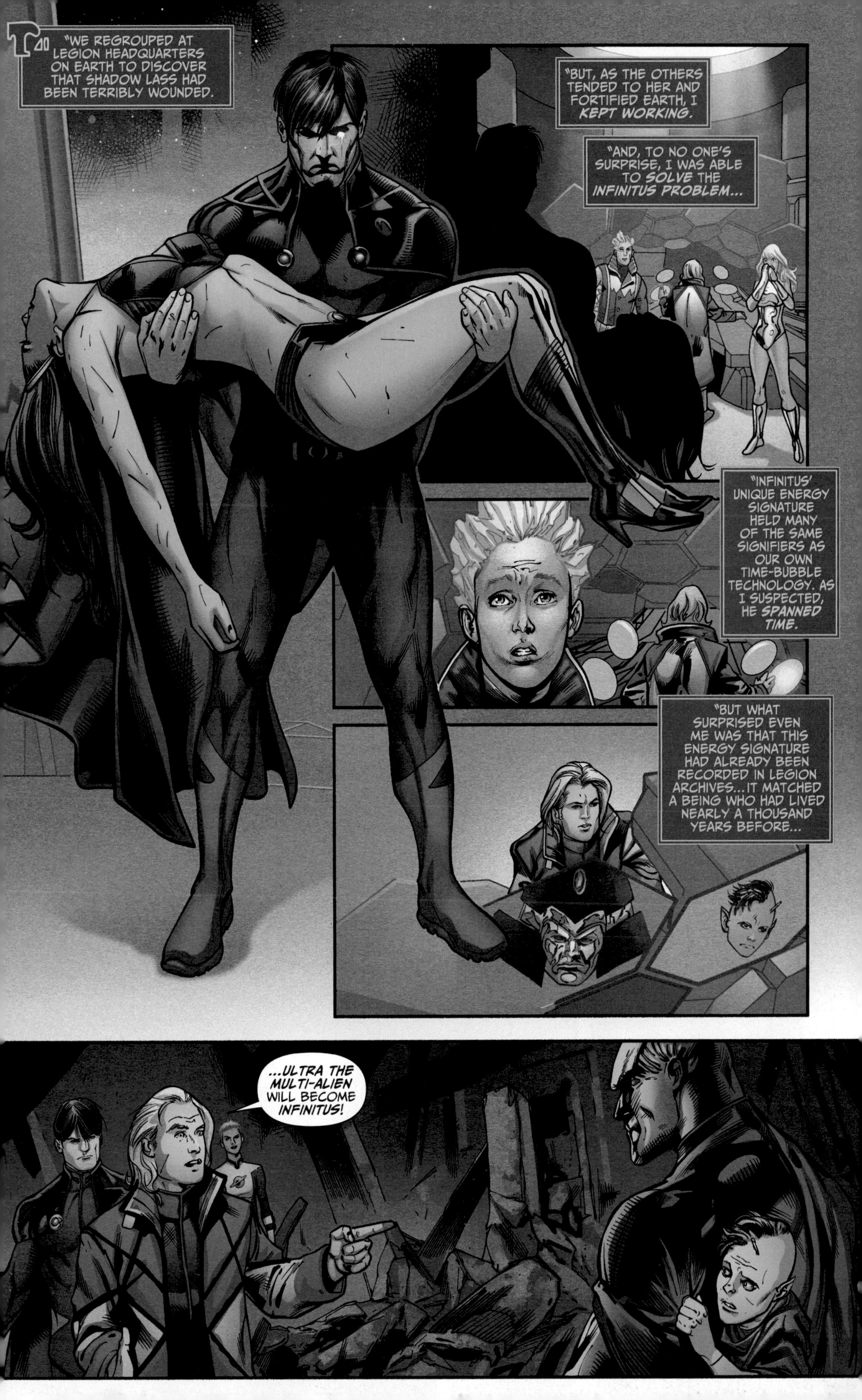

"WE REGROUPED AT LEGION HEADQUARTERS ON EARTH TO DISCOVER THAT SHADOW LASS HAD BEEN TERRIBLY WOUNDED.
"BUT, AS THE OTHERS TENDED TO HER AND FORTIFIED EARTH, I KEPT WORKING.
"AND, TO NO ONE'S SURPRISE, I WAS ABLE TO SOLVE THE INFINITUS PROBLEM...
"INFINITUS' UNIQUE ENERGY SIGNATURE HELD MANY OF THE SAME SIGNIFIERS AS OUR OWN TIME-BUBBLE TECHNOLOGY. AS I SUSPECTED, HE SPANNED TIME.
"BUT WHAT SURPRISED EVEN ME WAS THAT THIS ENERGY SIGNATURE HAD ALREADY BEEN RECORDED IN LEGION ARCHIVES...IT MATCHED A BEING WHO HAD LIVED NEARLY A THOUSAND YEARS BEFORE...
...ULTRA THE MULTI-ALIEN WILL BECOME INFINITUS!

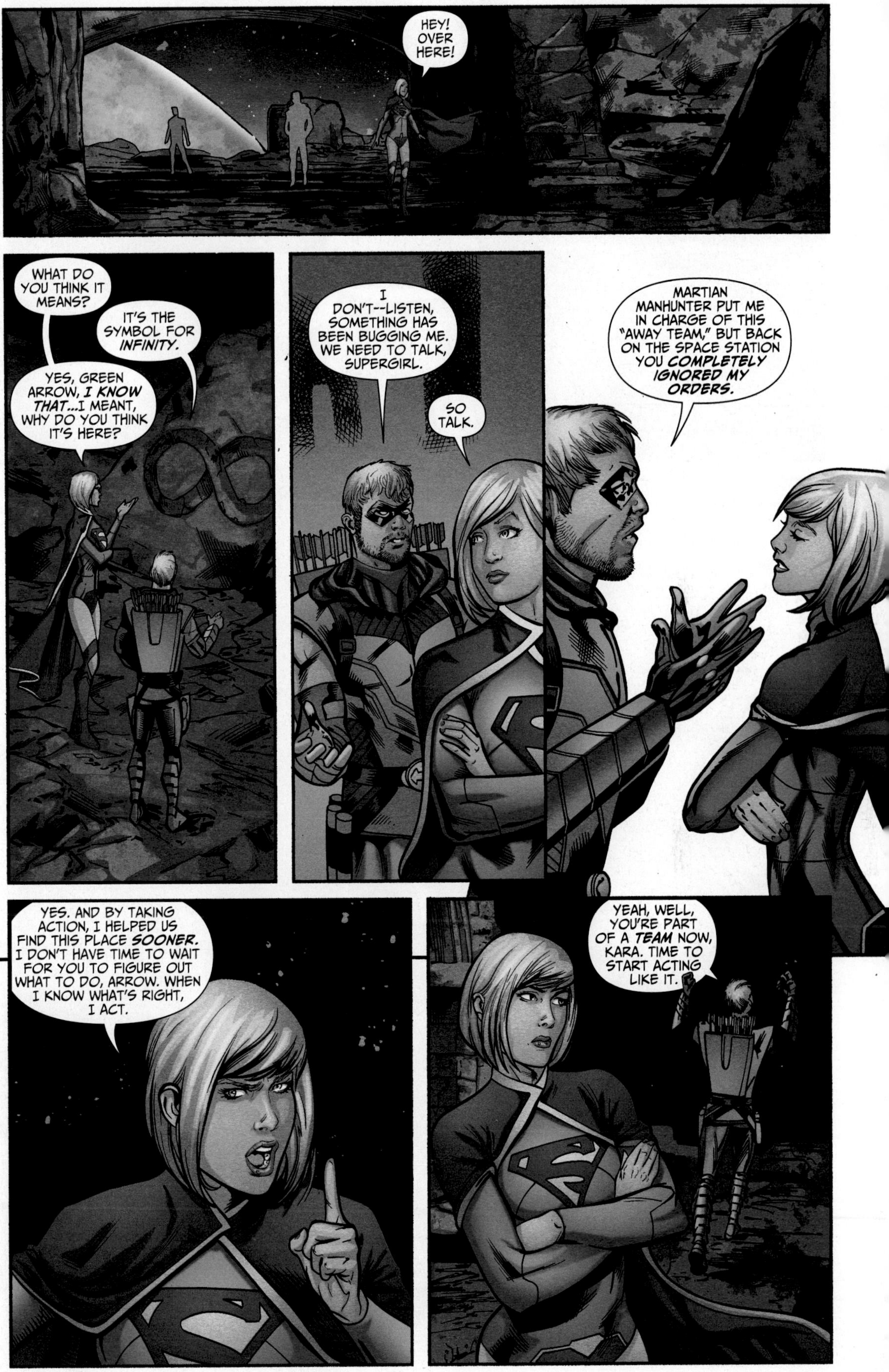
HEY! OVER HERE!
WHAT DO YOU THINK IT MEANS?
IT'S THE SYMBOL FOR *INFINITY.*
YES, GREEN ARROW, ***I KNOW THAT...*** I MEANT, WHY DO YOU THINK IT'S HERE?
I DON'T--LISTEN, SOMETHING HAS BEEN BUGGING ME. WE NEED TO TALK, SUPERGIRL.
SO TALK.
MARTIAN MANHUNTER PUT ME IN CHARGE OF THIS "AWAY TEAM," BUT BACK ON THE SPACE STATION YOU ***COMPLETELY IGNORED MY ORDERS.***
YES. AND BY TAKING ACTION, I HELPED US FIND THIS PLACE ***SOONER.*** I DON'T HAVE TIME TO WAIT FOR YOU TO FIGURE OUT WHAT TO DO, ARROW. WHEN I KNOW WHAT'S RIGHT, I ACT.
YEAH, WELL, YOU'RE PART OF A ***TEAM*** NOW, KARA. TIME TO START ACTING LIKE IT.

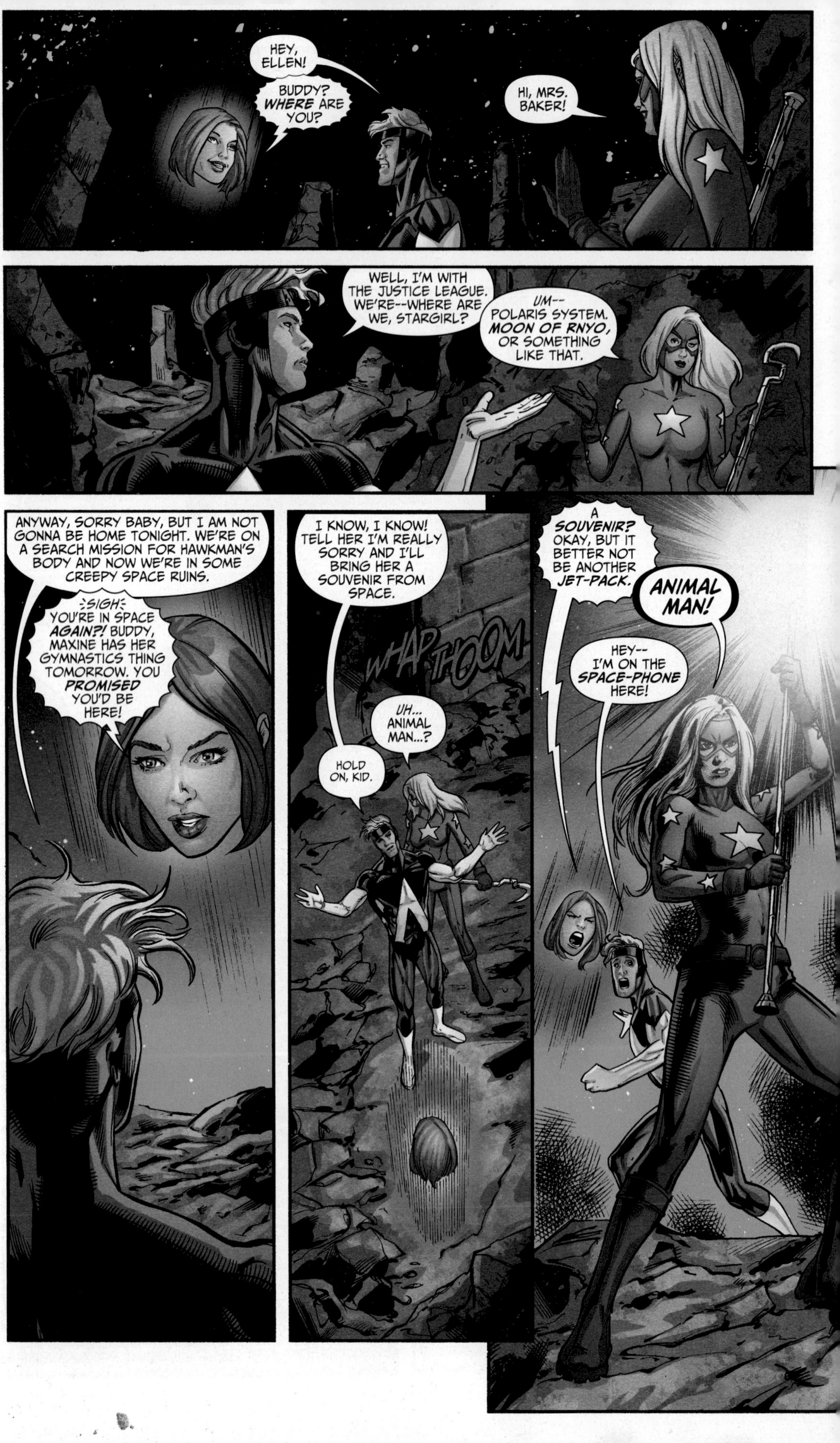
HEY, ELLEN!
BUDDY? WHERE ARE YOU?
HI, MRS. BAKER!
WELL, I'M WITH THE JUSTICE LEAGUE. WE'RE--WHERE ARE WE, STARGIRL?
UM-- POLARIS SYSTEM. MOON OF RNYO, OR SOMETHING LIKE THAT.
ANYWAY, SORRY BABY, BUT I AM NOT GONNA BE HOME TONIGHT. WE'RE ON A SEARCH MISSION FOR HAWKMAN'S BODY AND NOW WE'RE IN SOME CREEPY SPACE RUINS.
SIGH
YOU'RE IN SPACE AGAIN?! BUDDY, MAXINE HAS HER GYMNASTICS THING TOMORROW. YOU PROMISED YOU'D BE HERE!
I KNOW, I KNOW! TELL HER I'M REALLY SORRY AND I'LL BRING HER A SOUVENIR FROM SPACE.
WHAP THOOM
UH... ANIMAL MAN...?
HOLD ON, KID.
A SOUVENIR? OKAY, BUT IT BETTER NOT BE ANOTHER JET-PACK.
ANIMAL MAN!
HEY-- I'M ON THE SPACE-PHONE HERE!

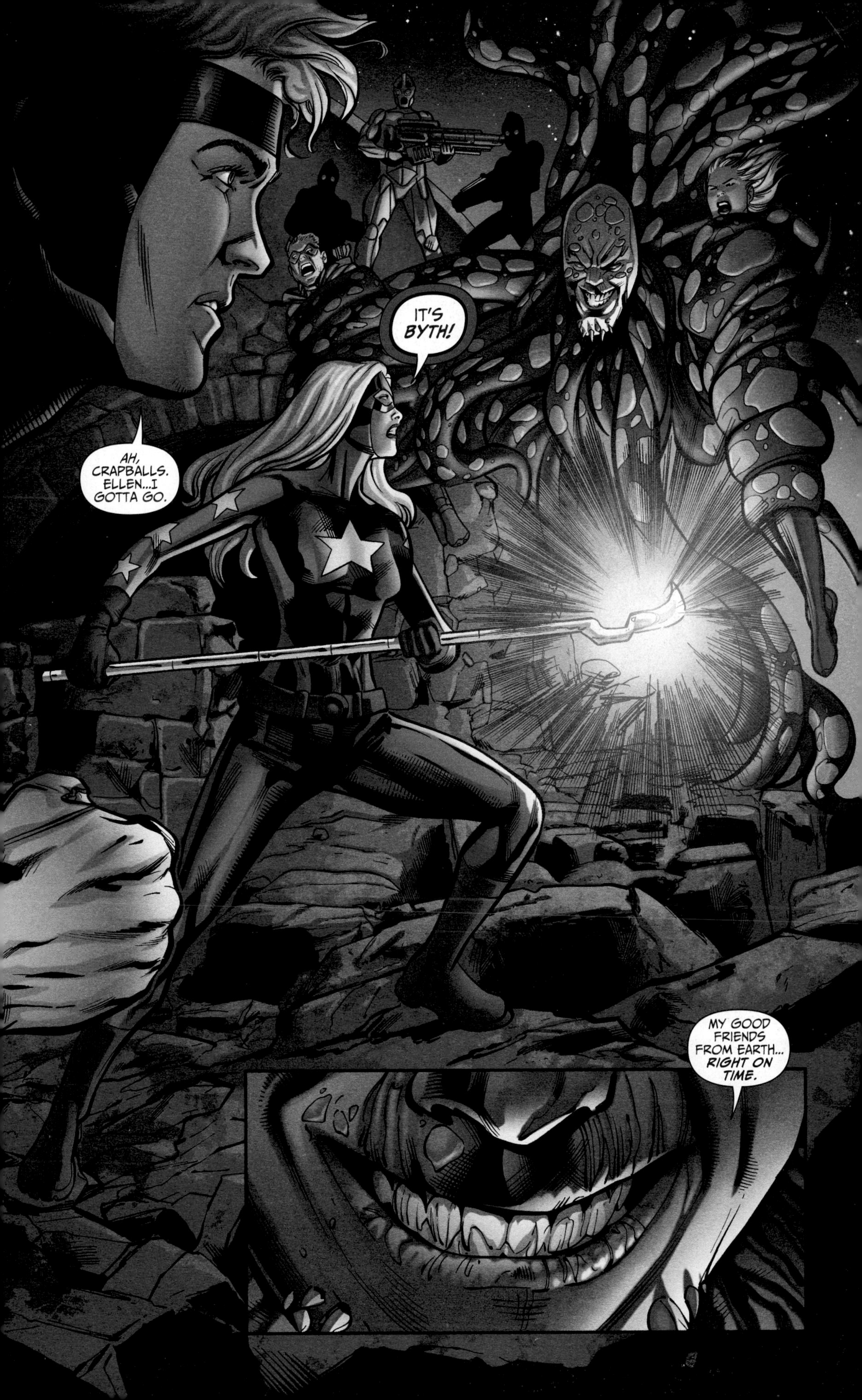
IT'S BYTH!
AH, CRAPBALLS. ELLEN...I GOTTA GO.
MY GOOD FRIENDS FROM EARTH... RIGHT ON TIME.

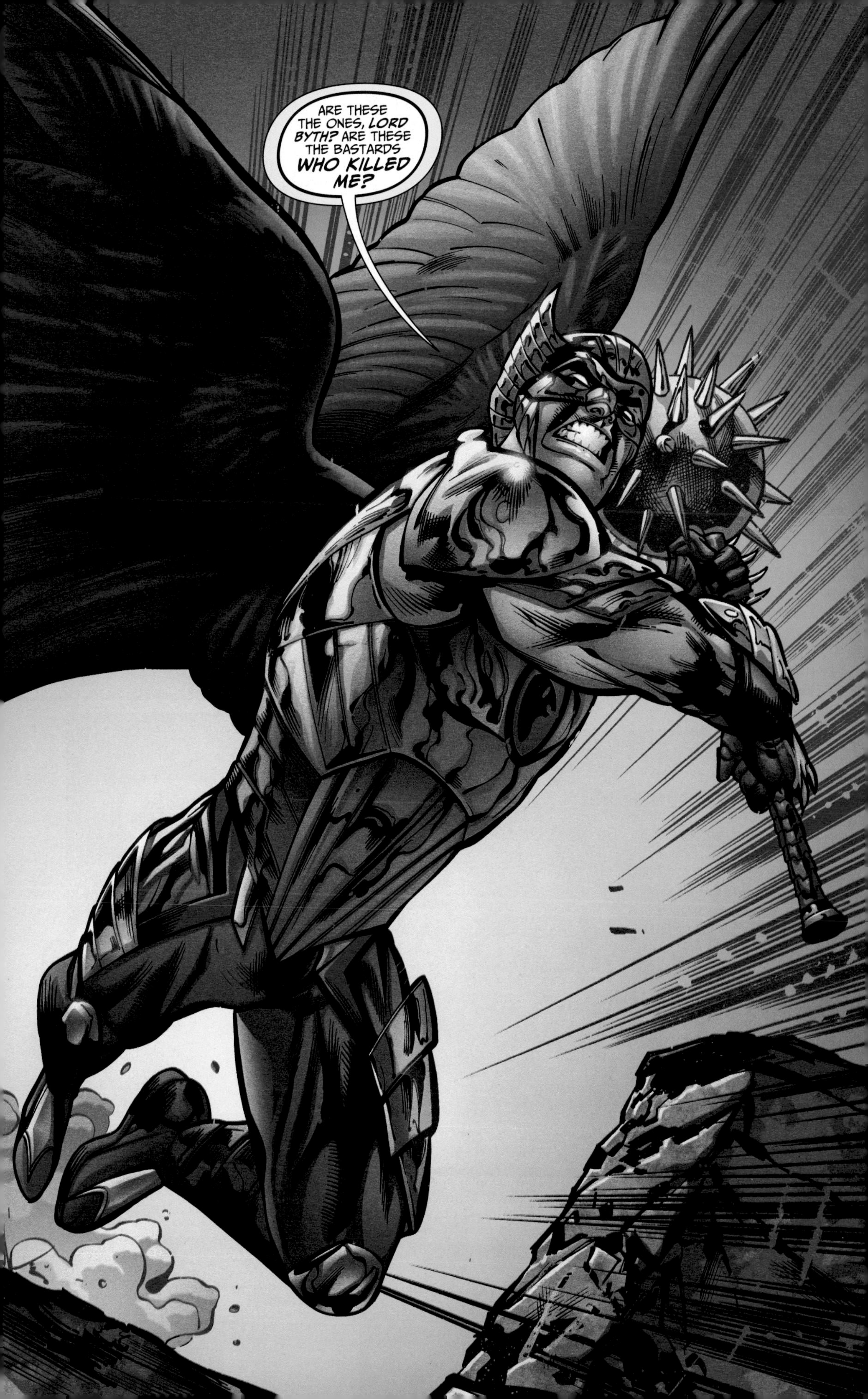
ARE THESE THE ONES, LORD BYTH? ARE THESE THE BASTARDS WHO KILLED ME?

WAIT--HOW IS THIS *CHILD* GOING TO BECOME THIS *INFINTUS* THING? I'M TOTALLY LOST.

YOU'RE LOST?!

THE *HOW* ISN'T *IMPORTANT!* THAT THING IS GOING TO *KILL SHADOW LASS!* I WILL *NOT* ALLOW THAT TO HAPPEN!

MON-EL, STOP! SHADOW LASS IS *NOT DEAD!*

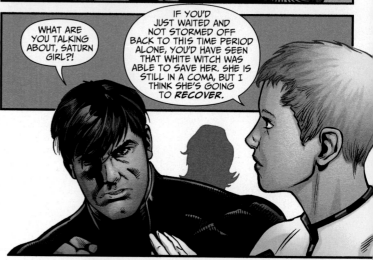

WHAT ARE YOU TALKING ABOUT, SATURN GIRL?!

IF YOU'D JUST WAITED AND NOT STORMED OFF BACK TO THIS TIME PERIOD *ALONE,* YOU'D HAVE SEEN THAT WHITE WITCH WAS ABLE TO SAVE HER. SHE IS STILL IN A COMA, BUT I THINK SHE'S GOING TO *RECOVER.*

IT'S TRUE, MON. SHE'S GOING TO BE OKAY.

THIS SHADOW LASS...IS SHE YOUR...?

YES. I--I THOUGHT I'D LOST HER.

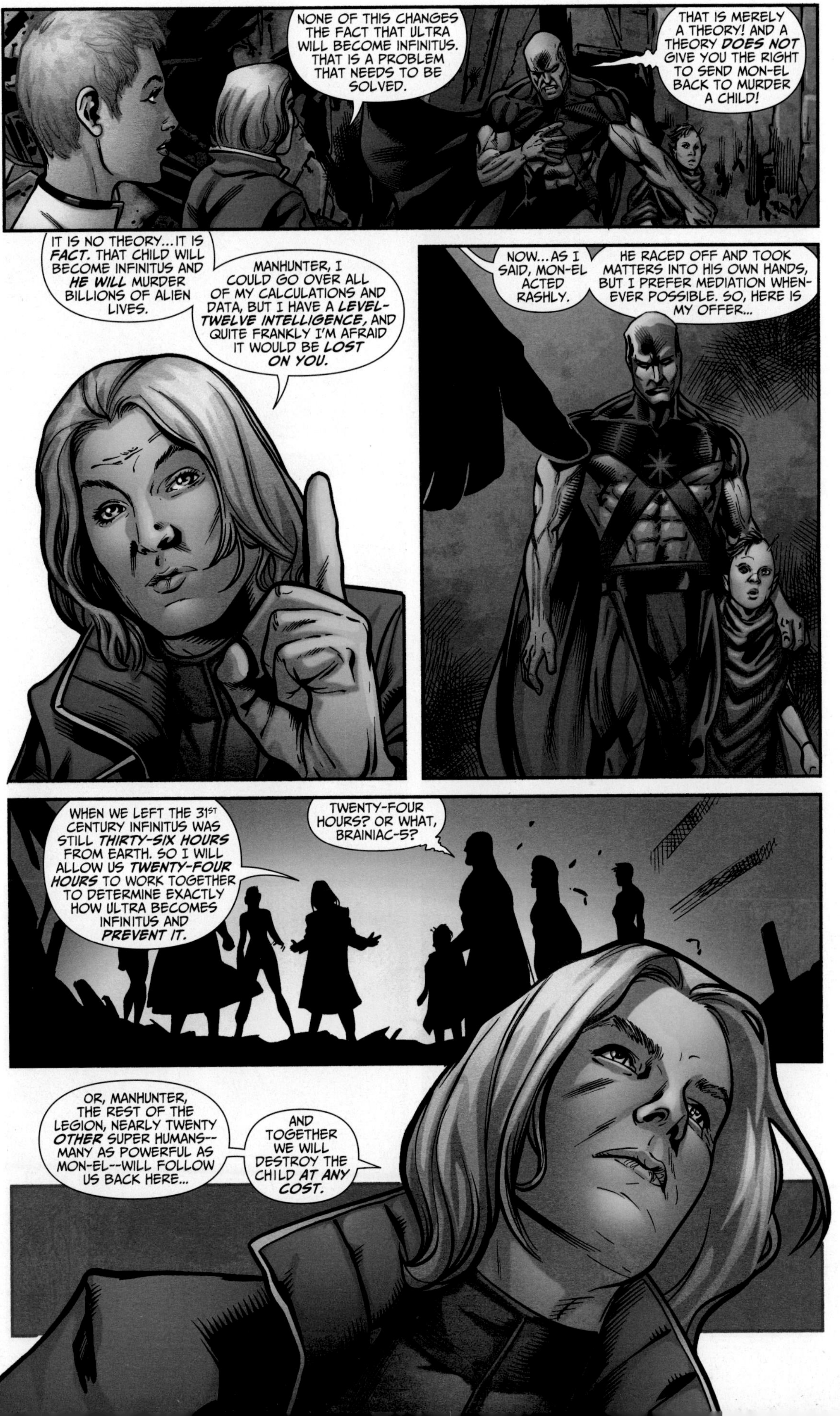

NONE OF THIS CHANGES THE FACT THAT ULTRA WILL BECOME INFINITUS. THAT IS A PROBLEM THAT NEEDS TO BE SOLVED.
THAT IS MERELY A THEORY! AND A THEORY DOES NOT GIVE YOU THE RIGHT TO SEND MON-EL BACK TO MURDER A CHILD!
IT IS NO THEORY...IT IS FACT. THAT CHILD WILL BECOME INFINITUS AND HE WILL MURDER BILLIONS OF ALIEN LIVES.
MANHUNTER, I COULD GO OVER ALL OF MY CALCULATIONS AND DATA, BUT I HAVE A LEVEL-TWELVE INTELLIGENCE, AND QUITE FRANKLY I'M AFRAID IT WOULD BE LOST ON YOU.
NOW...AS I SAID, MON-EL ACTED RASHLY.
HE RACED OFF AND TOOK MATTERS INTO HIS OWN HANDS, BUT I PREFER MEDIATION WHENEVER POSSIBLE. SO, HERE IS MY OFFER...
WHEN WE LEFT THE 31ST CENTURY INFINITUS WAS STILL THIRTY-SIX HOURS FROM EARTH. SO I WILL ALLOW US TWENTY-FOUR HOURS TO WORK TOGETHER TO DETERMINE EXACTLY HOW ULTRA BECOMES INFINITUS AND PREVENT IT.
TWENTY-FOUR HOURS? OR WHAT, BRAINIAC-5?
OR, MANHUNTER, THE REST OF THE LEGION, NEARLY TWENTY OTHER SUPER HUMANS--MANY AS POWERFUL AS MON-EL--WILL FOLLOW US BACK HERE...
AND TOGETHER WE WILL DESTROY THE CHILD AT ANY COST.

--ANHUNTER, COME IN!

GREEN ARROW?! THIS IS *NOT* A GOOD TIME.

YEAH, WELL, *MAKE IT A GOOD TIME*--WE GOT TROUBLE! WE FOUND HAWKMAN *AND* BYTH--

AH, THE *FIRST* GREEN ARROW... FASCINATING.

BYTH? HOW IS HE INVOLVED IN THIS?!

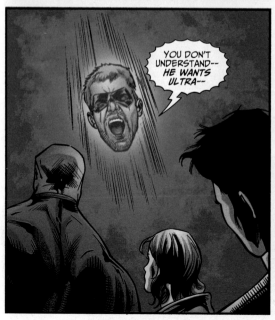

YOU DON'T UNDERSTAND-- *HE WANTS ULTRA*--

AND THAT'S NOT ALL. HAWKMAN IS ALI--

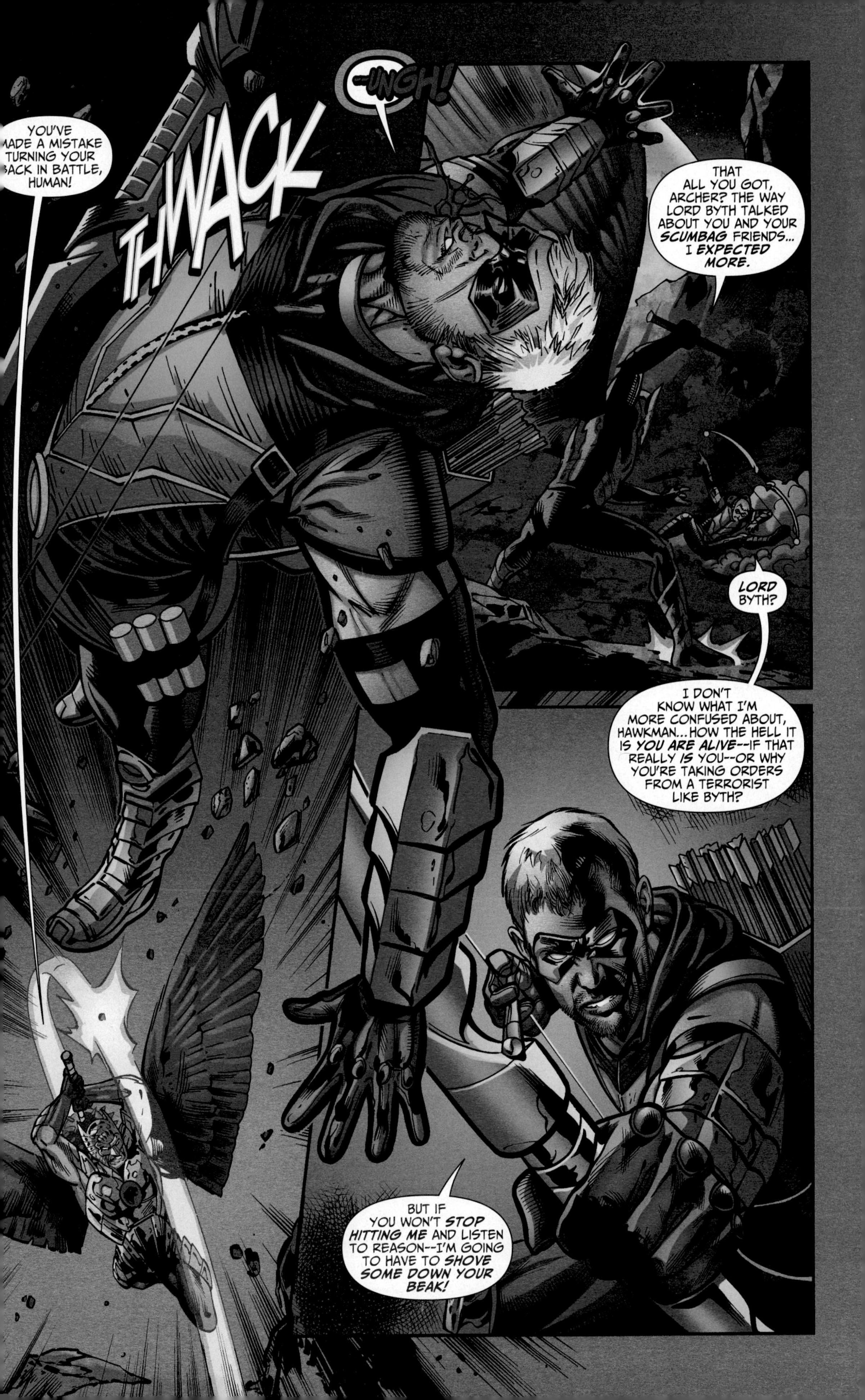
YOU'VE MADE A MISTAKE TURNING YOUR BACK IN BATTLE, HUMAN!
THWACK
-UNGH!
THAT ALL YOU GOT, ARCHER? THE WAY LORD BYTH TALKED ABOUT YOU AND YOUR SCUMBAG FRIENDS... I EXPECTED MORE.
LORD BYTH?
I DON'T KNOW WHAT I'M MORE CONFUSED ABOUT, HAWKMAN...HOW THE HELL IT IS YOU ARE ALIVE--IF THAT REALLY IS YOU--OR WHY YOU'RE TAKING ORDERS FROM A TERRORIST LIKE BYTH?
BUT IF YOU WON'T STOP HITTING ME AND LISTEN TO REASON--I'M GOING TO HAVE TO SHOVE SOME DOWN YOUR BEAK!

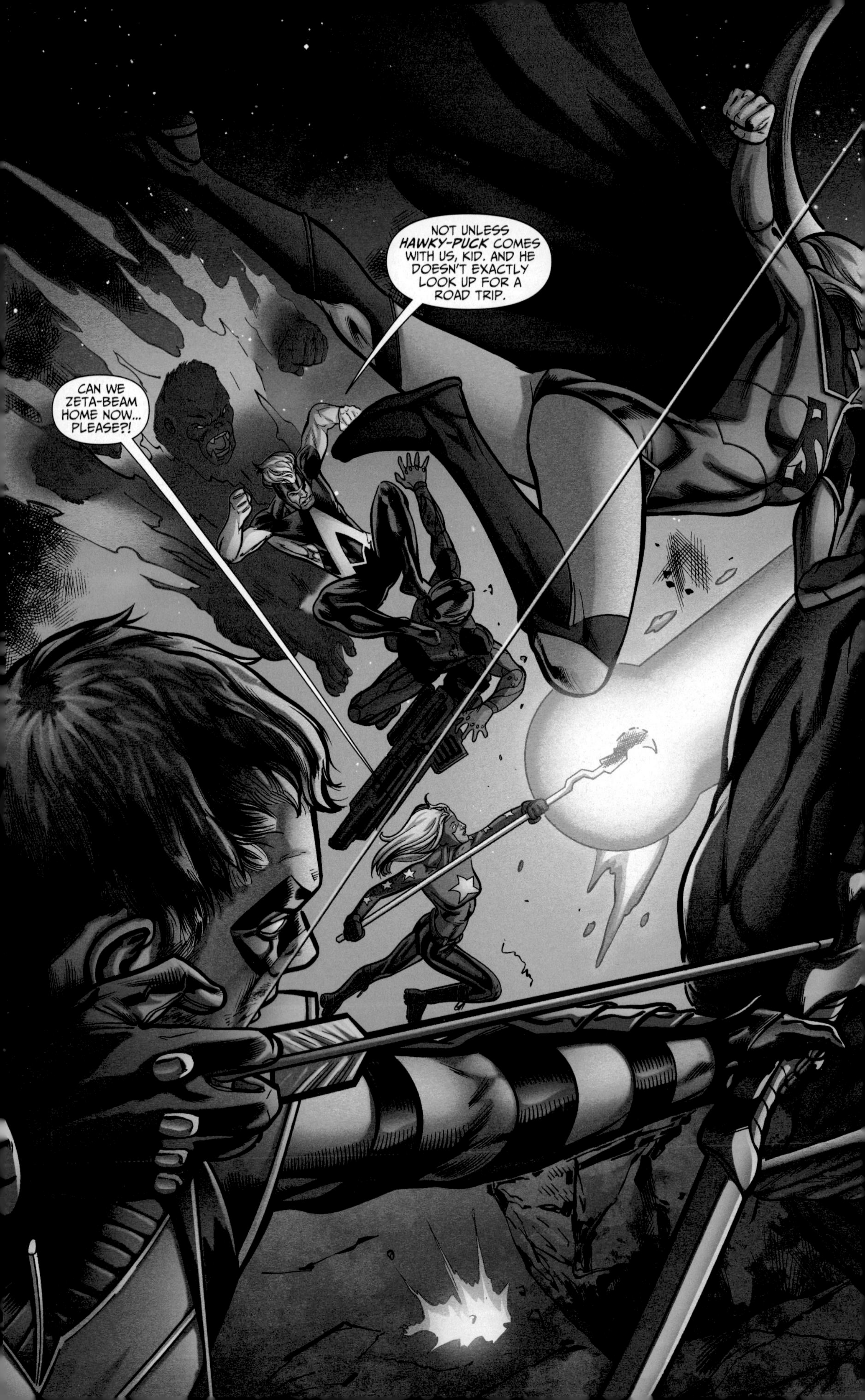
NOT UNLESS HAWKY-PUCK COMES WITH US, KID. AND HE DOESN'T EXACTLY LOOK UP FOR A ROAD TRIP.
CAN WE ZETA-BEAM HOME NOW... PLEASE?!

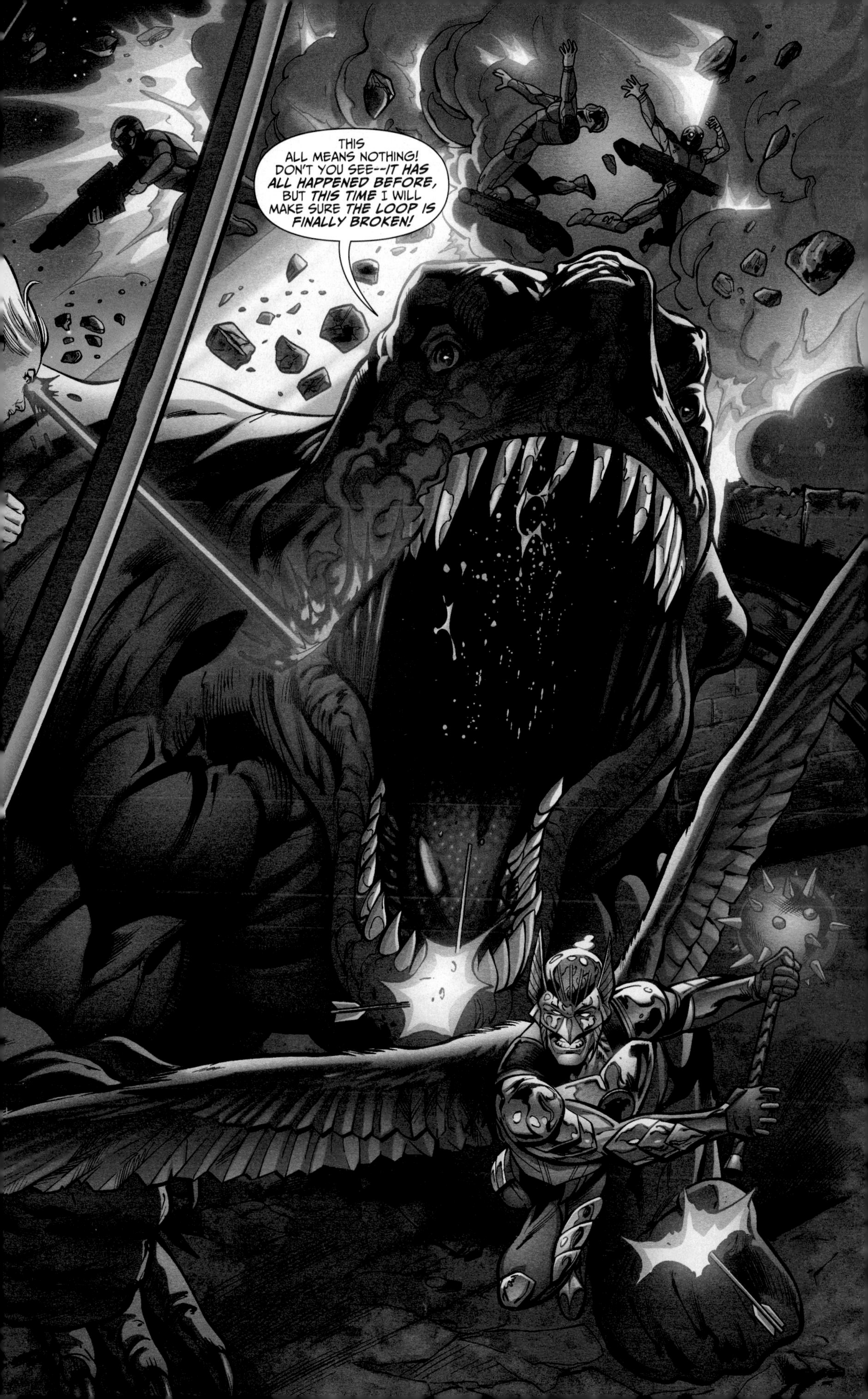
THIS ALL MEANS NOTHING! DON'T YOU SEE--*IT HAS ALL HAPPENED BEFORE*, BUT *THIS TIME* I WILL MAKE SURE *THE LOOP IS FINALLY BROKEN!*

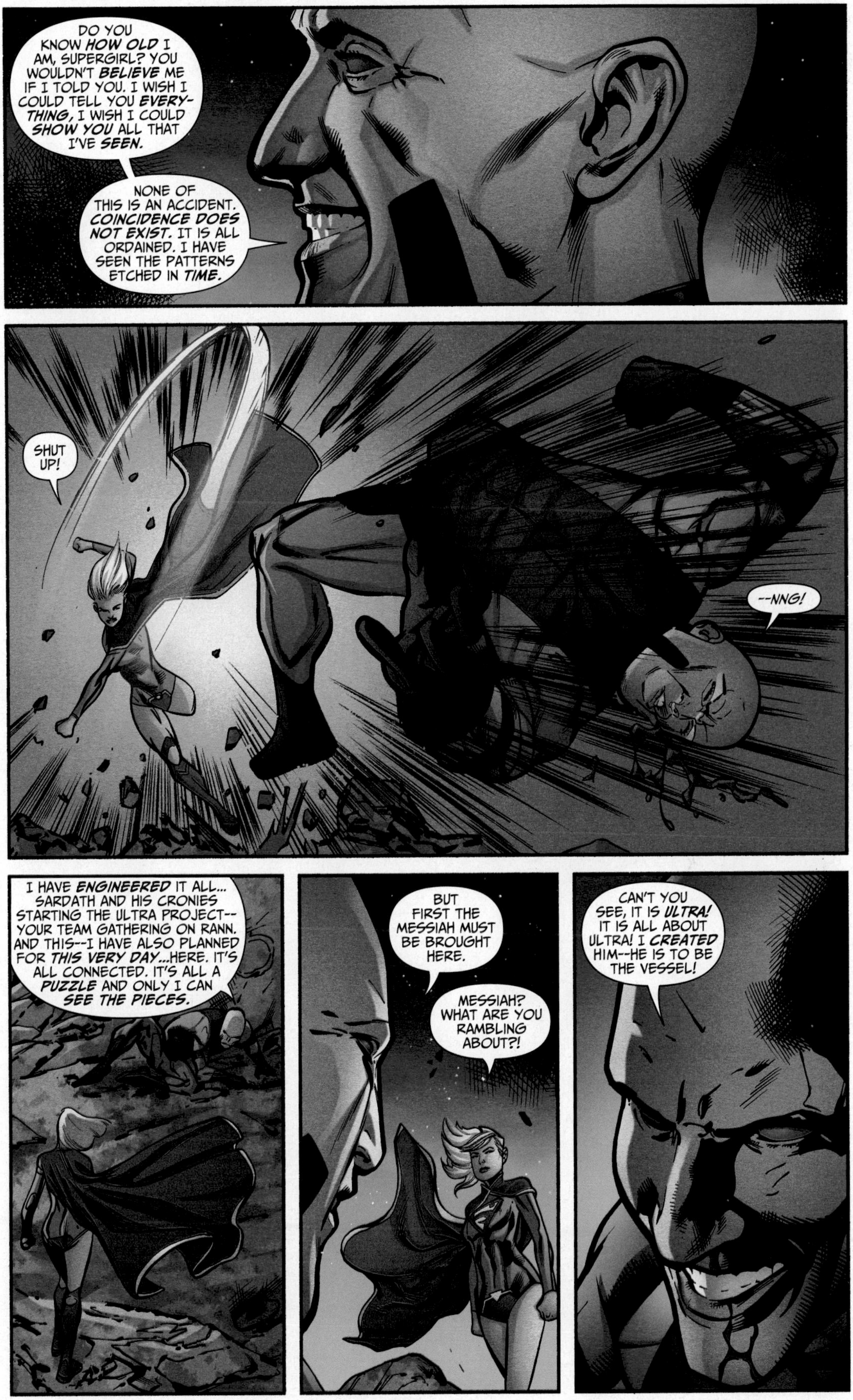
DO YOU KNOW HOW OLD I AM, SUPERGIRL? YOU WOULDN'T BELIEVE ME IF I TOLD YOU. I WISH I COULD TELL YOU EVERY-THING, I WISH I COULD SHOW YOU ALL THAT I'VE SEEN.
NONE OF THIS IS AN ACCIDENT. COINCIDENCE DOES NOT EXIST. IT IS ALL ORDAINED. I HAVE SEEN THE PATTERNS ETCHED IN TIME.
SHUT UP!
--NNG!
I HAVE ENGINEERED IT ALL... SARDATH AND HIS CRONIES STARTING THE ULTRA PROJECT--YOUR TEAM GATHERING ON RANN. AND THIS--I HAVE ALSO PLANNED FOR THIS VERY DAY...HERE. IT'S ALL CONNECTED. IT'S ALL A PUZZLE AND ONLY I CAN SEE THE PIECES.
BUT FIRST THE MESSIAH MUST BE BROUGHT HERE.
MESSIAH? WHAT ARE YOU RAMBLING ABOUT?!
CAN'T YOU SEE, IT IS ULTRA! IT IS ALL ABOUT ULTRA! I CREATED HIM--HE IS TO BE THE VESSEL!

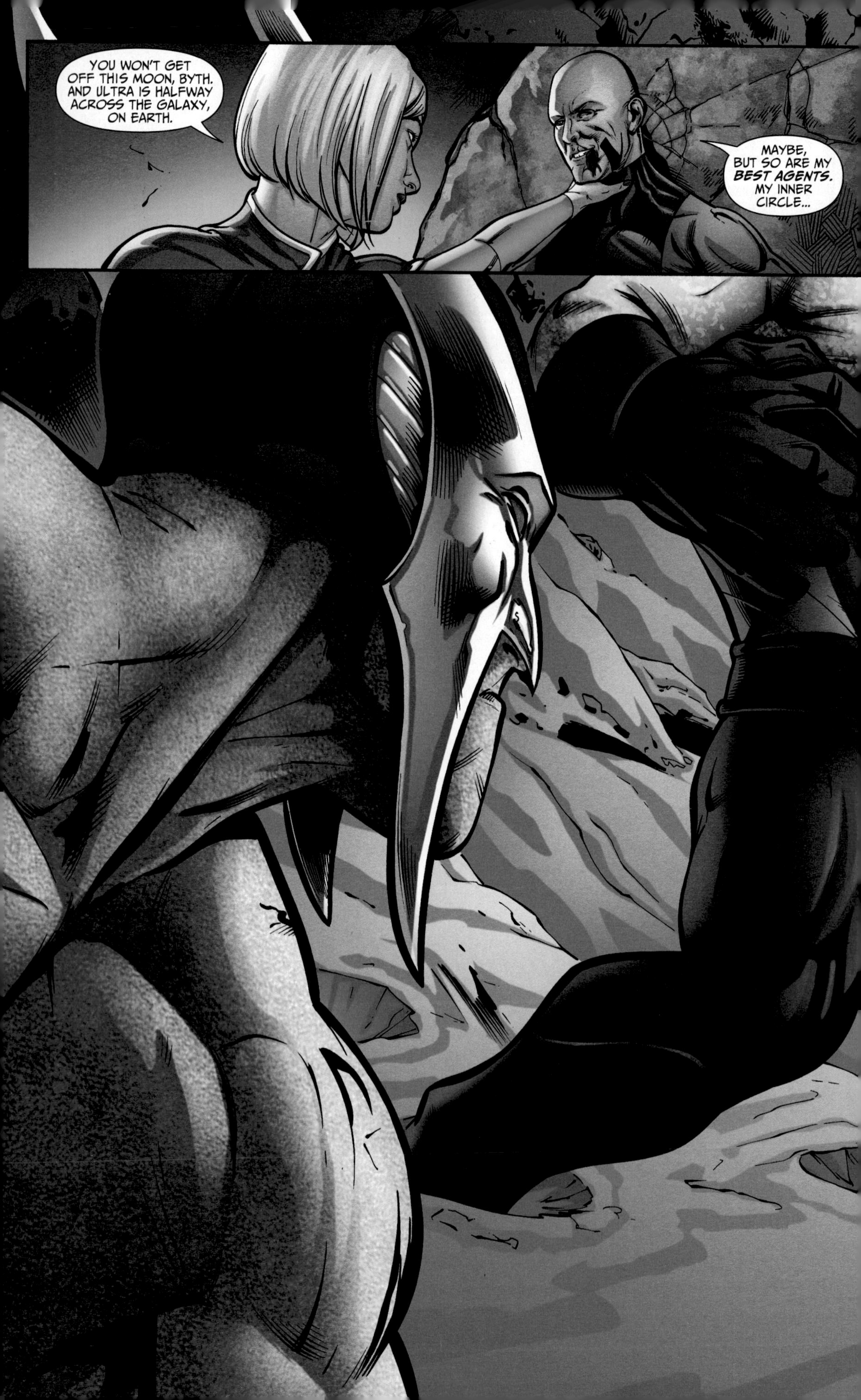
YOU WON'T GET OFF THIS MOON, BYTH. AND ULTRA IS HALFWAY ACROSS THE GALAXY, ON EARTH.
MAYBE, BUT SO ARE MY *BEST AGENTS.* MY INNER CIRCLE...

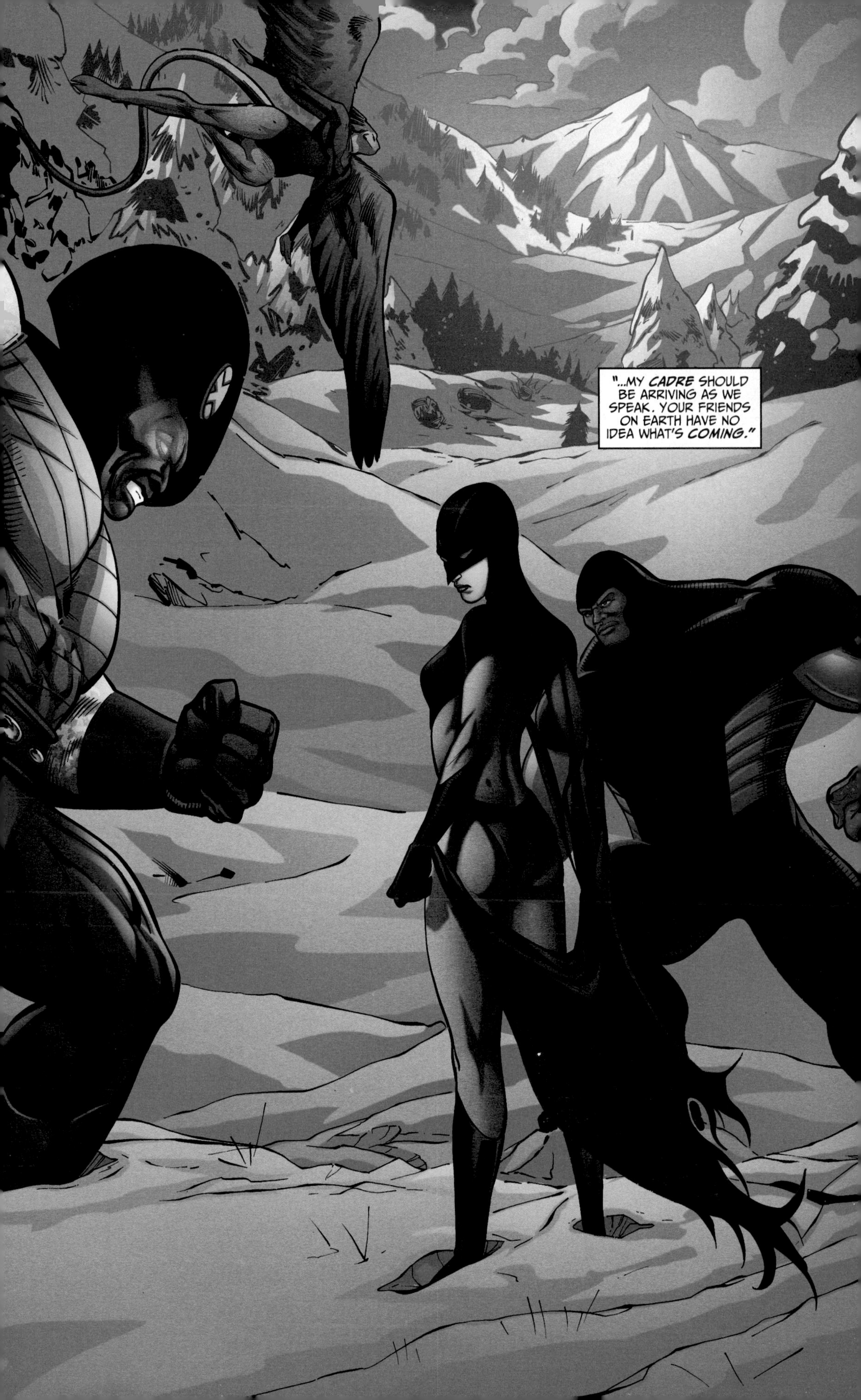
"...MY CADRE SHOULD BE ARRIVING AS WE SPEAK. YOUR FRIENDS ON EARTH HAVE NO IDEA WHAT'S COMING."

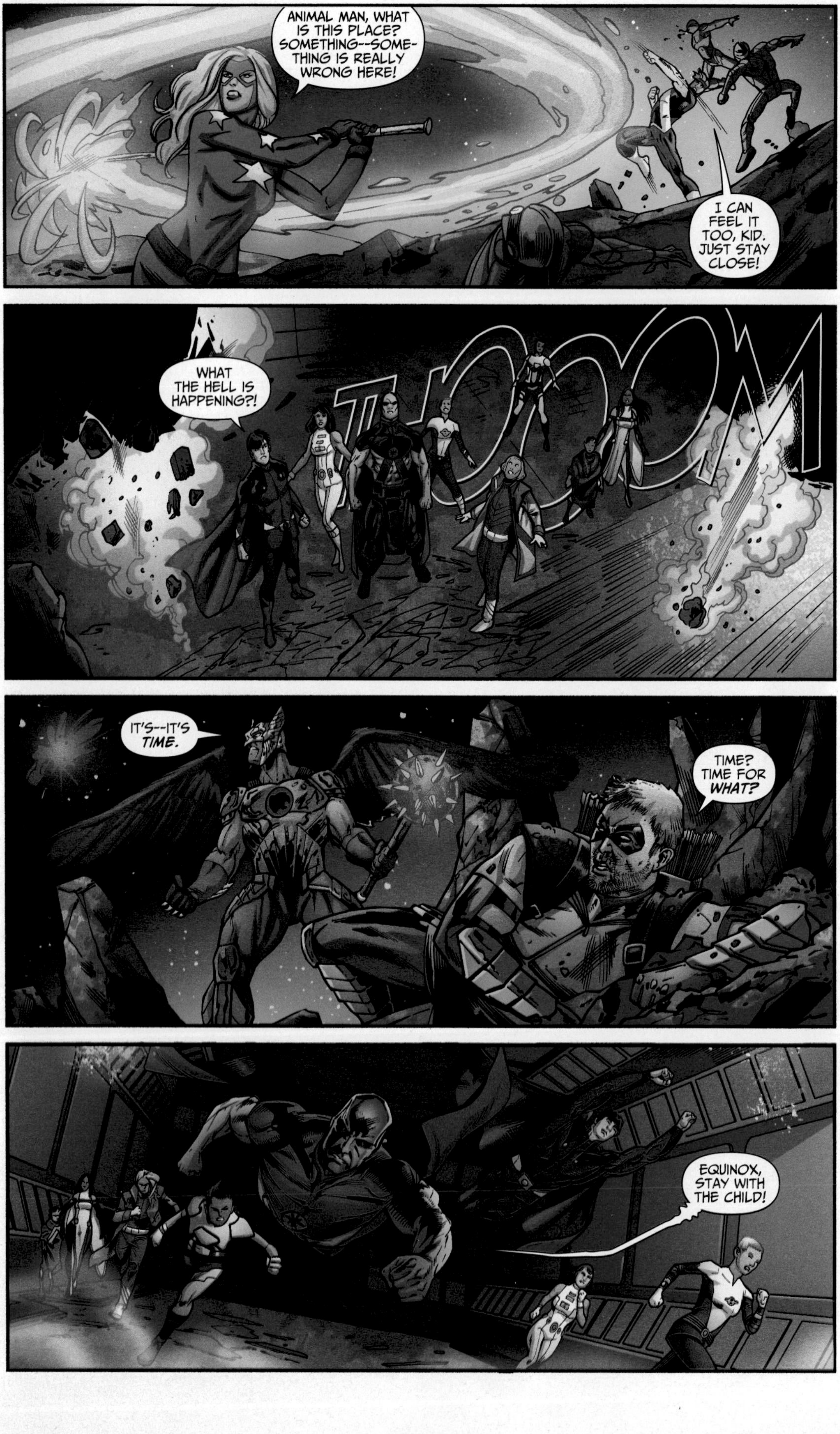
ANIMAL MAN, WHAT IS THIS PLACE? SOMETHING--SOME-THING IS REALLY WRONG HERE!
I CAN FEEL IT TOO, KID. JUST STAY CLOSE!
WHAT THE HELL IS HAPPENING?!
THOOOM
IT'S--IT'S *TIME.*
TIME? TIME FOR *WHAT?*
EQUINOX, STAY WITH THE CHILD!

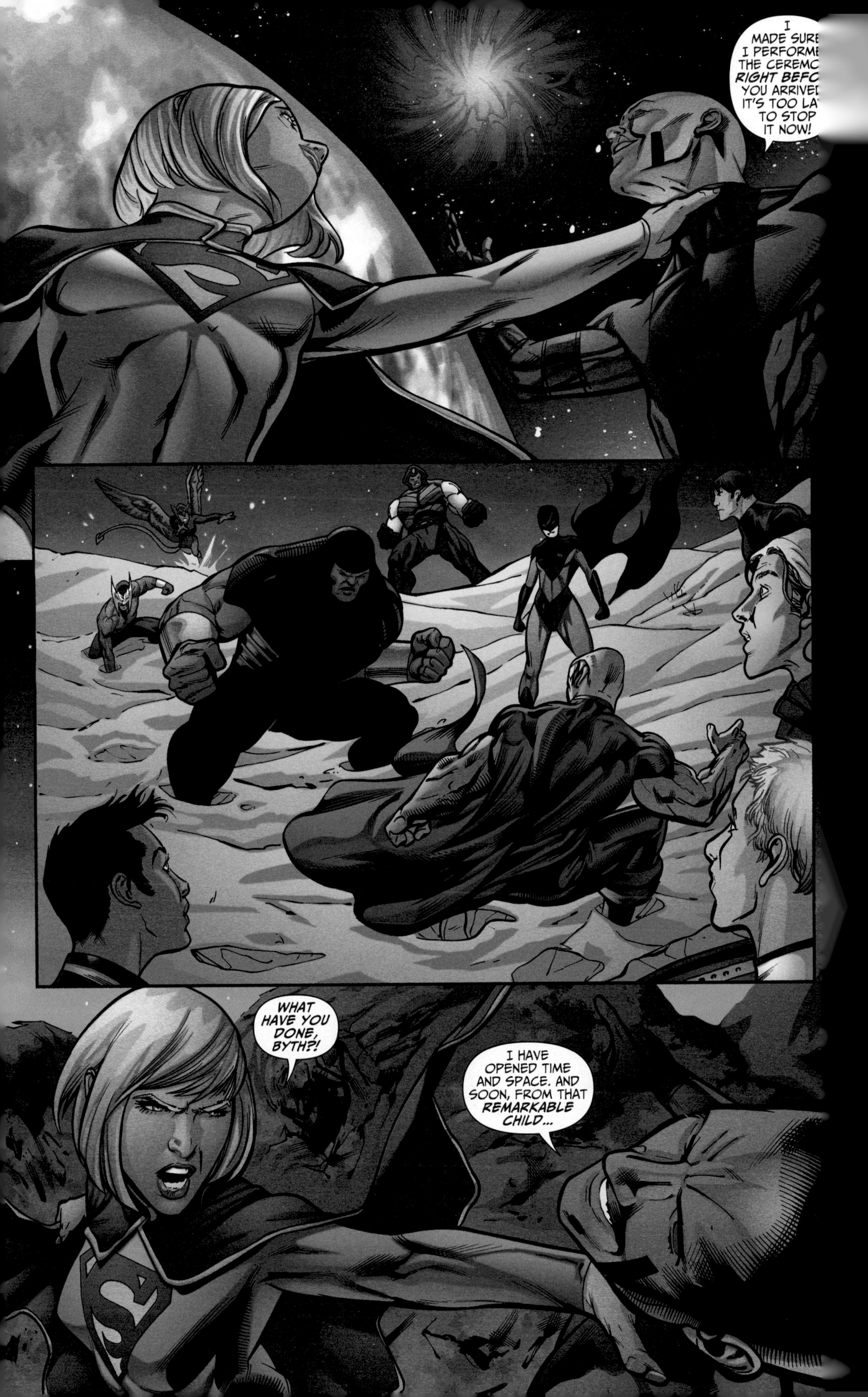

I MADE SURE I PERFORME THE CEREMO RIGHT BEFO YOU ARRIVED IT'S TOO LA TO STOP IT NOW!
WHAT HAVE YOU DONE, BYTH?!
I HAVE OPENED TIME AND SPACE. AND SOON, FROM THAT REMARKABLE CHILD...

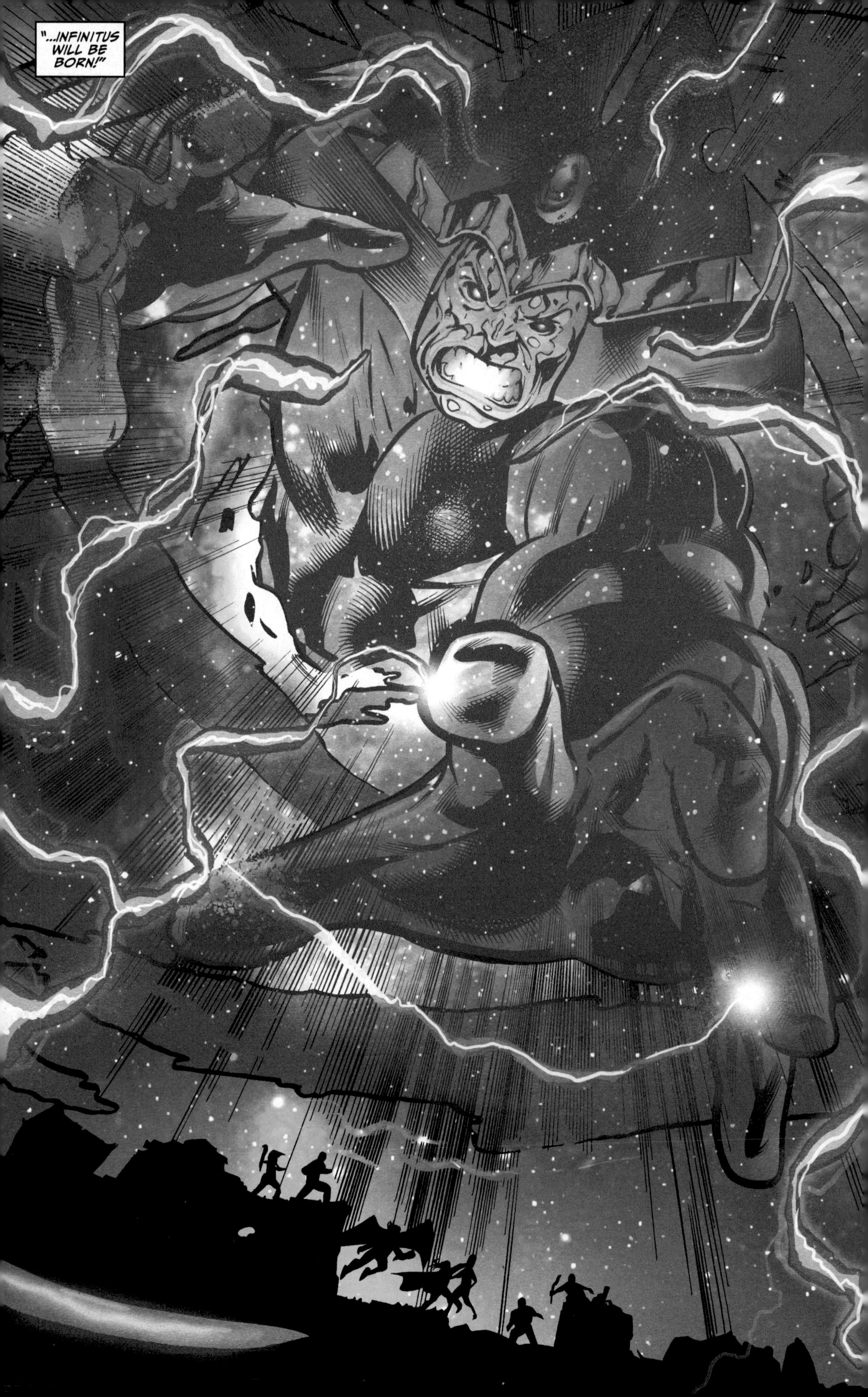
"...INFINITUS WILL BE BORN!"

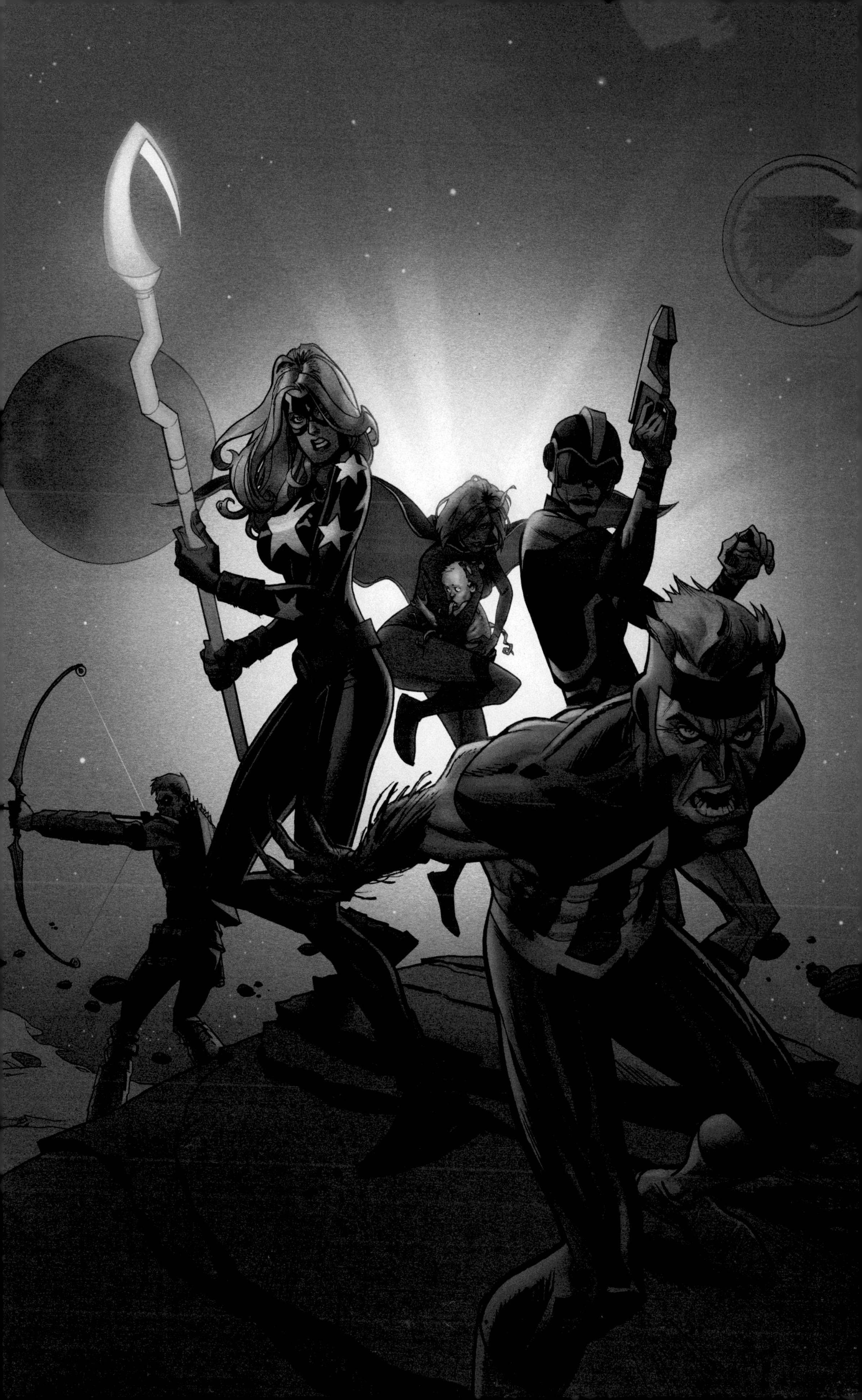

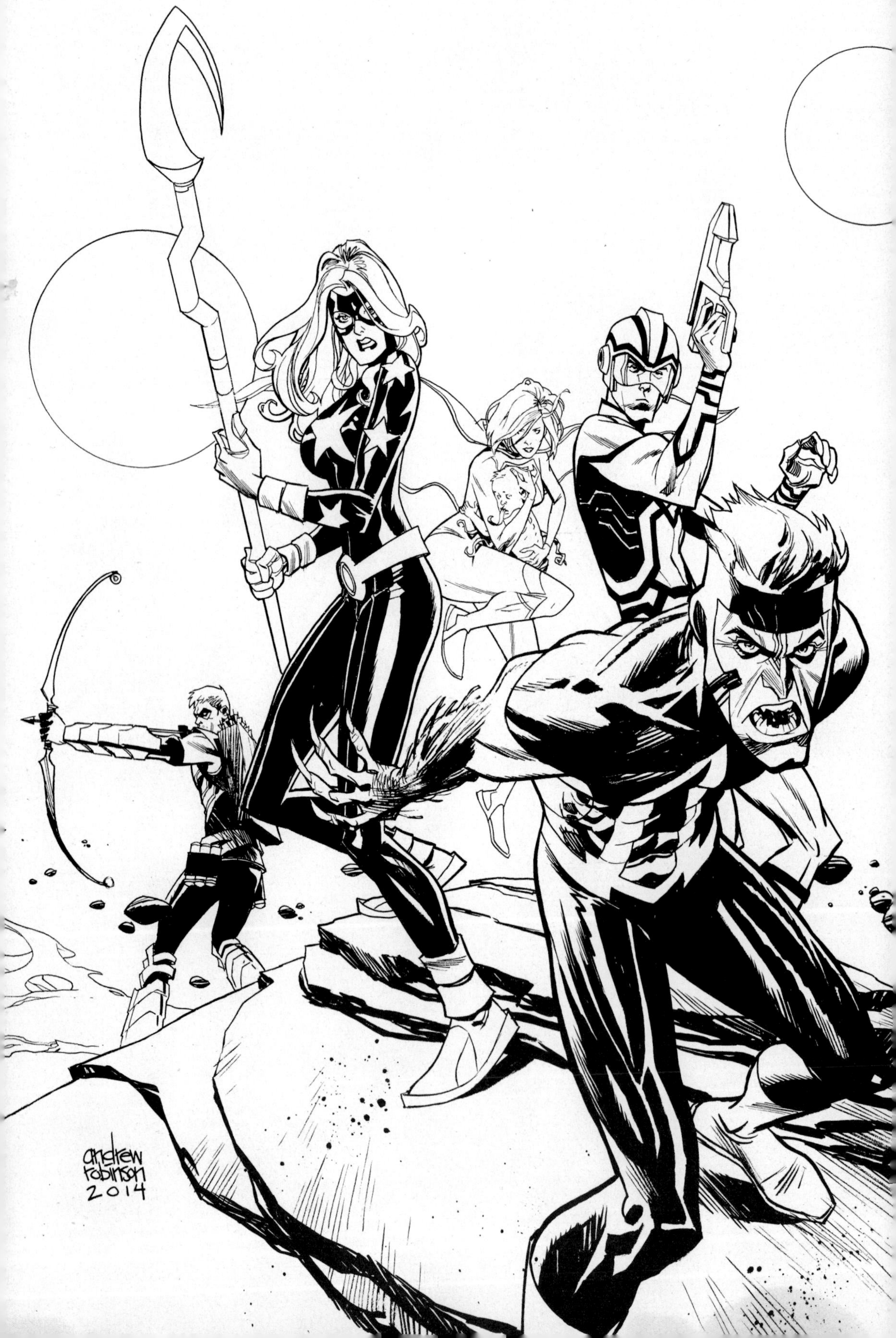
andrew
robinson
2014

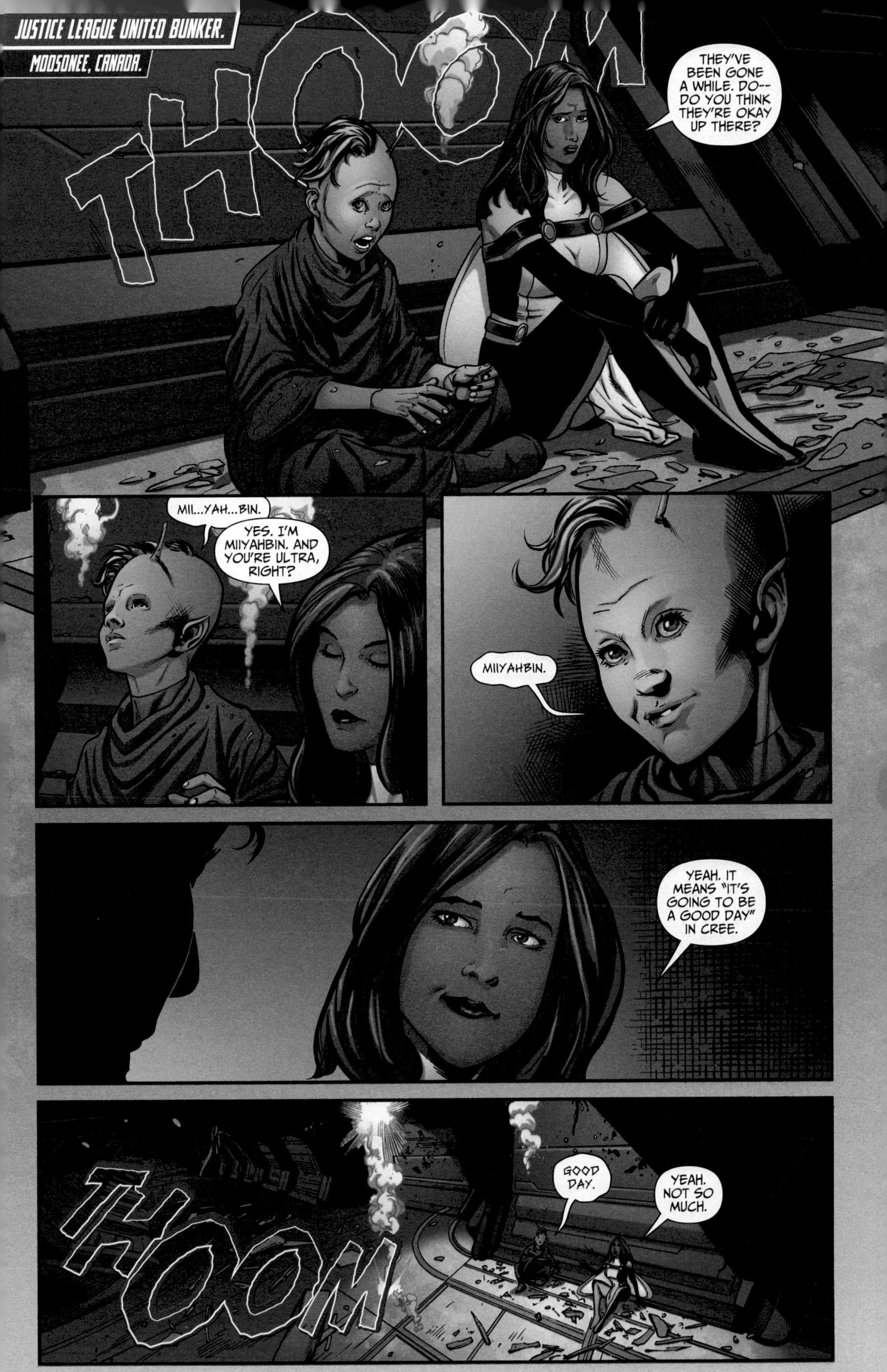
JUSTICE LEAGUE UNITED BUNKER.
MOOSONEE, CANADA.
THOOM
THEY'VE BEEN GONE A WHILE. DO-- DO YOU THINK THEY'RE OKAY UP THERE?
MII...YAH...BIN.
YES. I'M MIIYAHBIN. AND YOU'RE ULTRA, RIGHT?
MIIYAHBIN.
YEAH. IT MEANS "IT'S GOING TO BE A GOOD DAY" IN CREE.
THOOM
GOOD DAY.
YEAH. NOT SO MUCH.

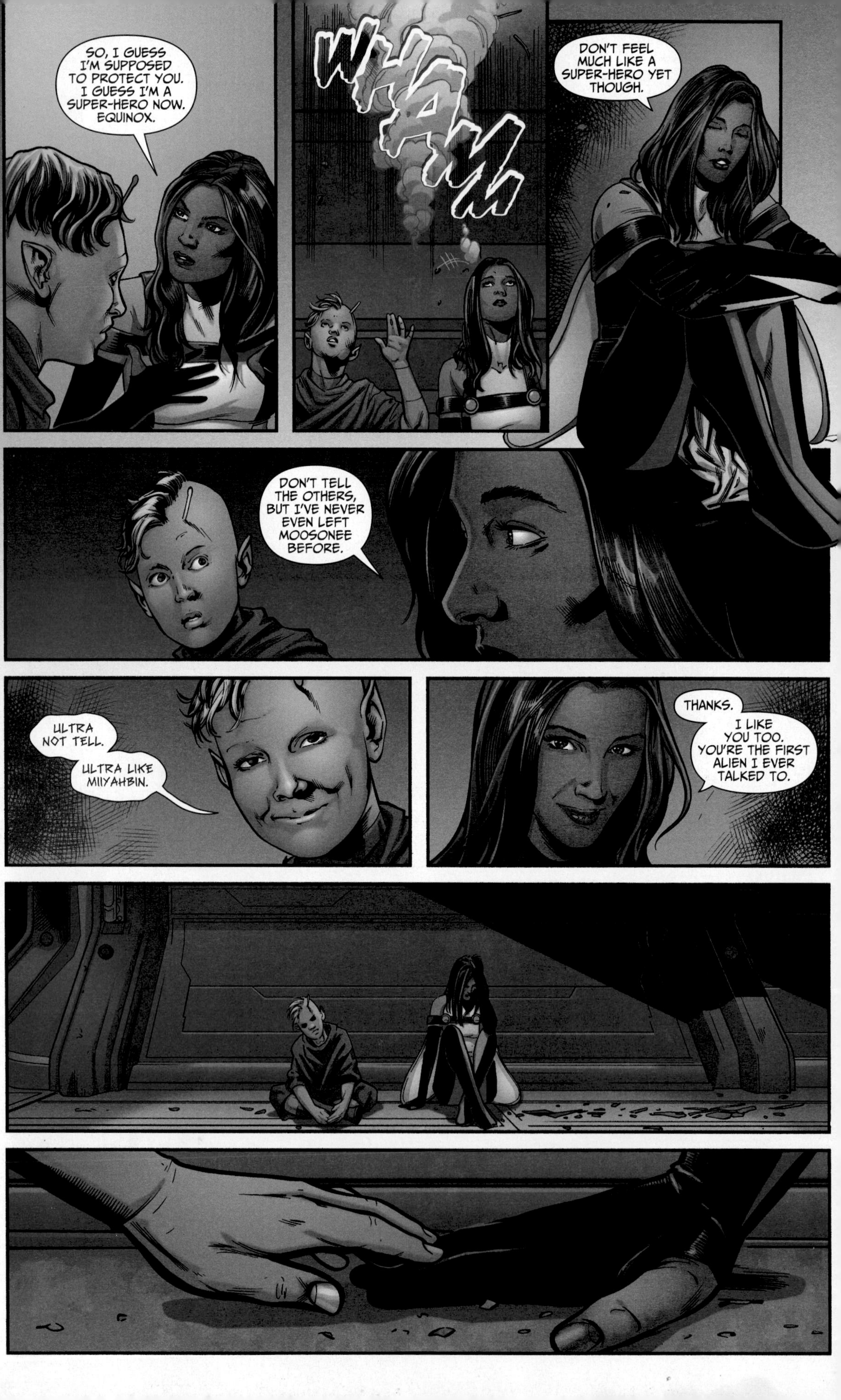
SO, I GUESS I'M SUPPOSED TO PROTECT YOU. I GUESS I'M A SUPER-HERO NOW. EQUINOX.
WHAM
DON'T FEEL MUCH LIKE A SUPER-HERO YET THOUGH.
DON'T TELL THE OTHERS, BUT I'VE NEVER EVEN LEFT MOOSONEE BEFORE.
ULTRA NOT TELL.
ULTRA LIKE MIIYAHBIN.
THANKS.
I LIKE YOU TOO. YOU'RE THE FIRST ALIEN I EVER TALKED TO.

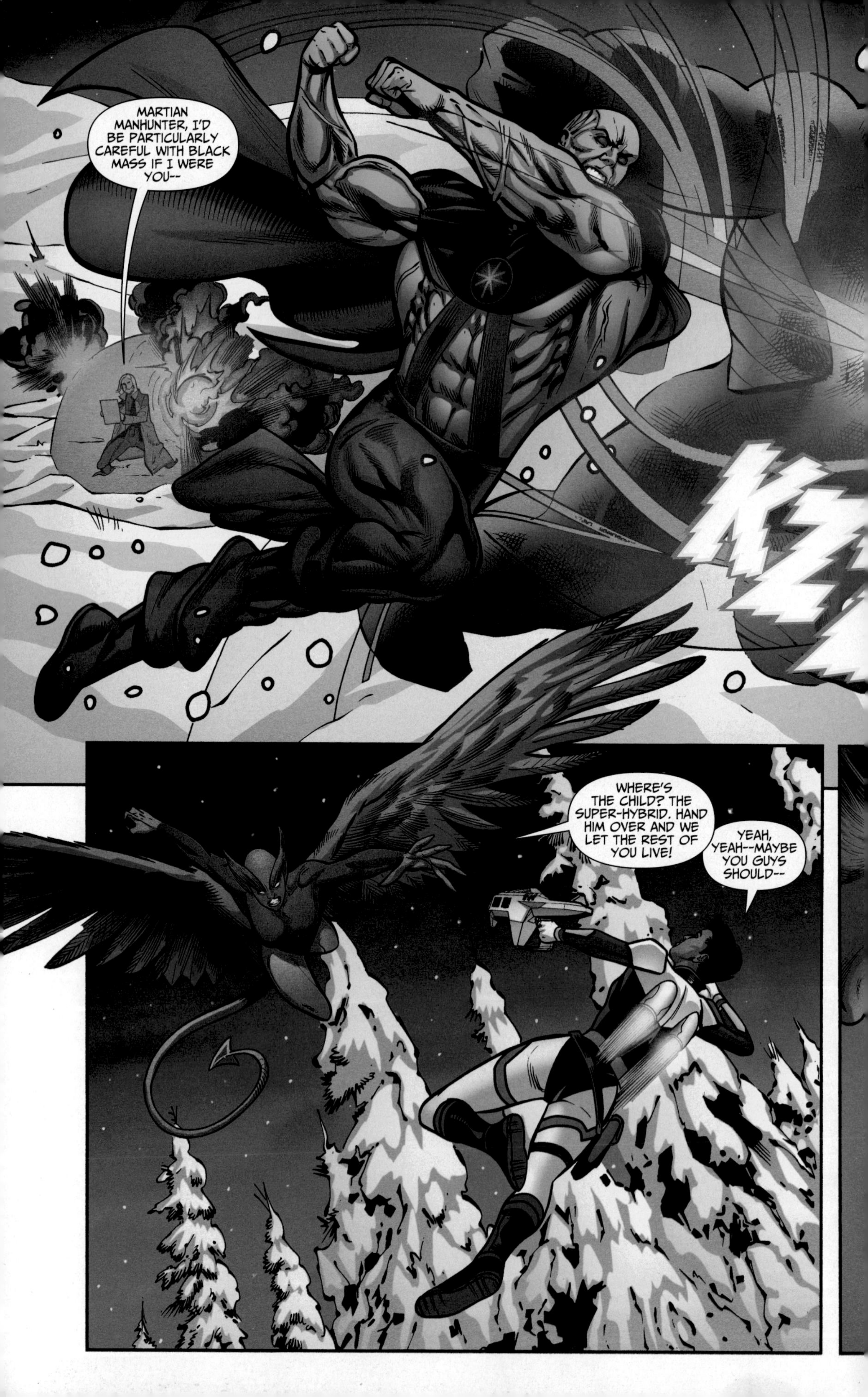
MARTIAN MANHUNTER, I'D BE PARTICULARLY CAREFUL WITH BLACK MASS IF I WERE YOU--
KZ
WHERE'S THE CHILD? THE SUPER-HYBRID. HAND HIM OVER AND WE LET THE REST OF YOU LIVE!
YEAH, YEAH--MAYBE YOU GUYS SHOULD--

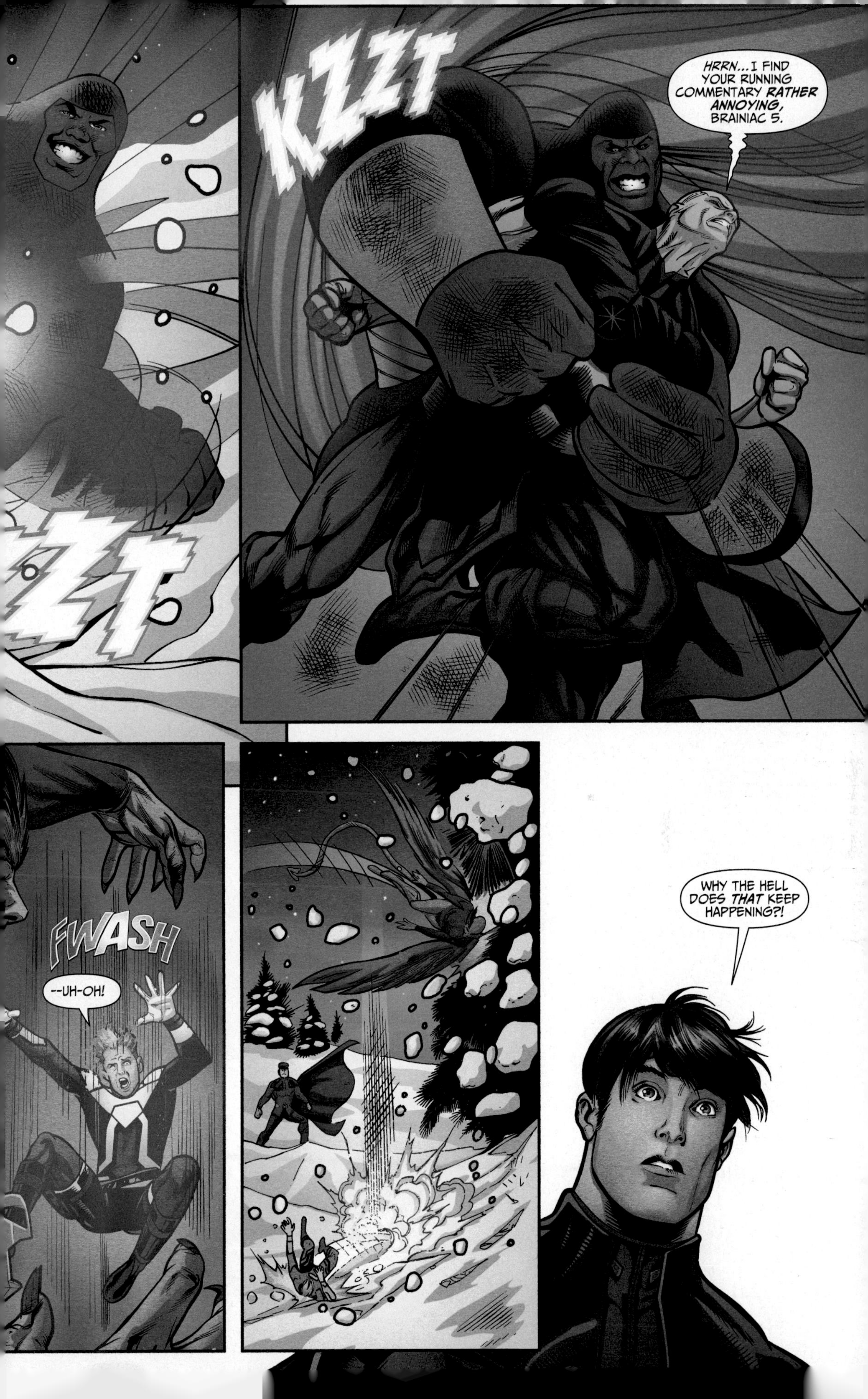
KZZZT
HRRN...I FIND YOUR RUNNING COMMENTARY RATHER ANNOYING, BRAINIAC 5.
FWASH
--UH-OH!
WHY THE HELL DOES THAT KEEP HAPPENING?!

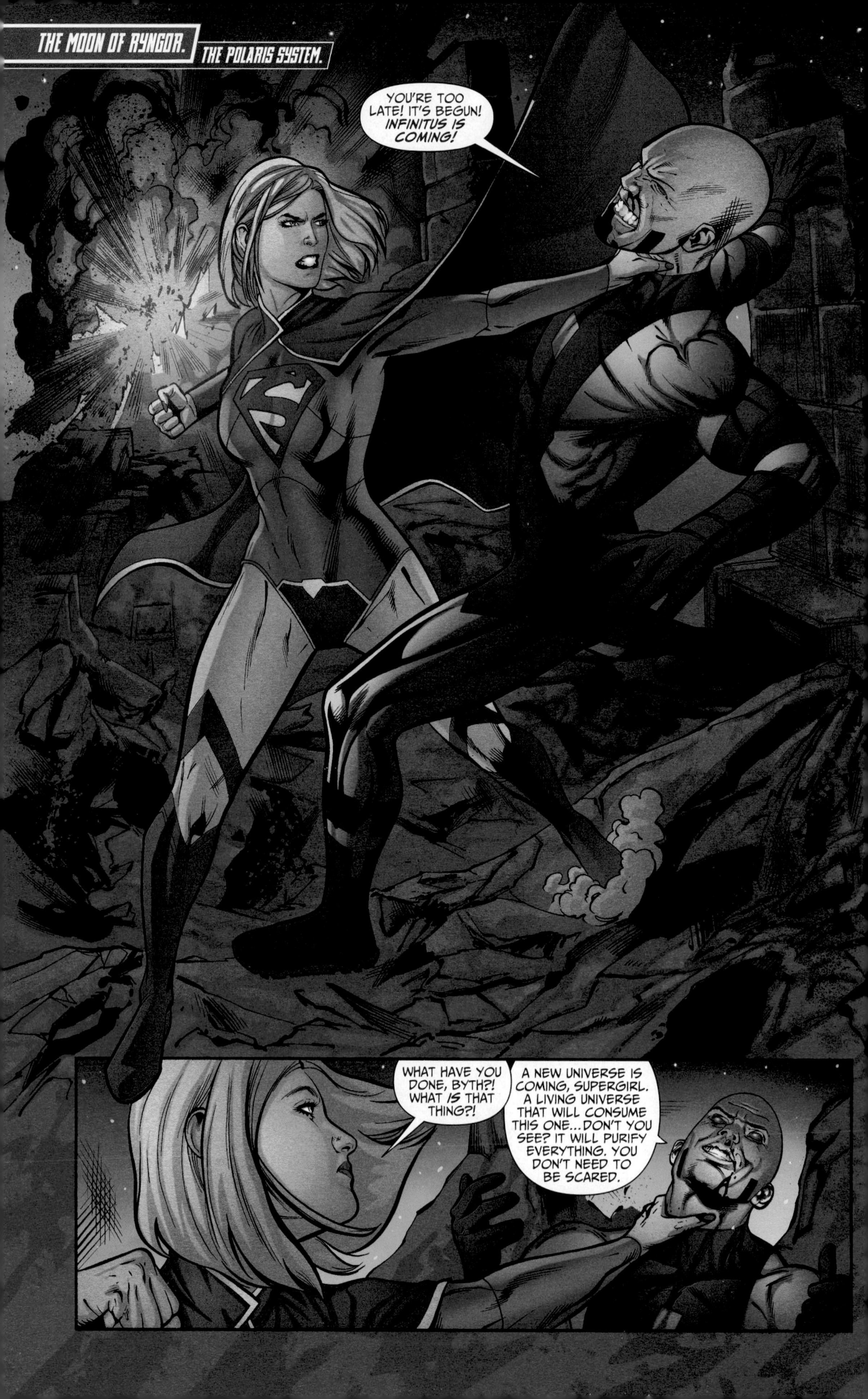
THE MOON OF RYNGOR.
THE POLARIS SYSTEM.
YOU'RE TOO LATE! IT'S BEGUN! INFINITUS IS COMING!
WHAT HAVE YOU DONE, BYTH?! WHAT IS THAT THING?!
A NEW UNIVERSE IS COMING, SUPERGIRL. A LIVING UNIVERSE THAT WILL CONSUME THIS ONE... DON'T YOU SEE? IT WILL PURIFY EVERYTHING. YOU DON'T NEED TO BE SCARED.

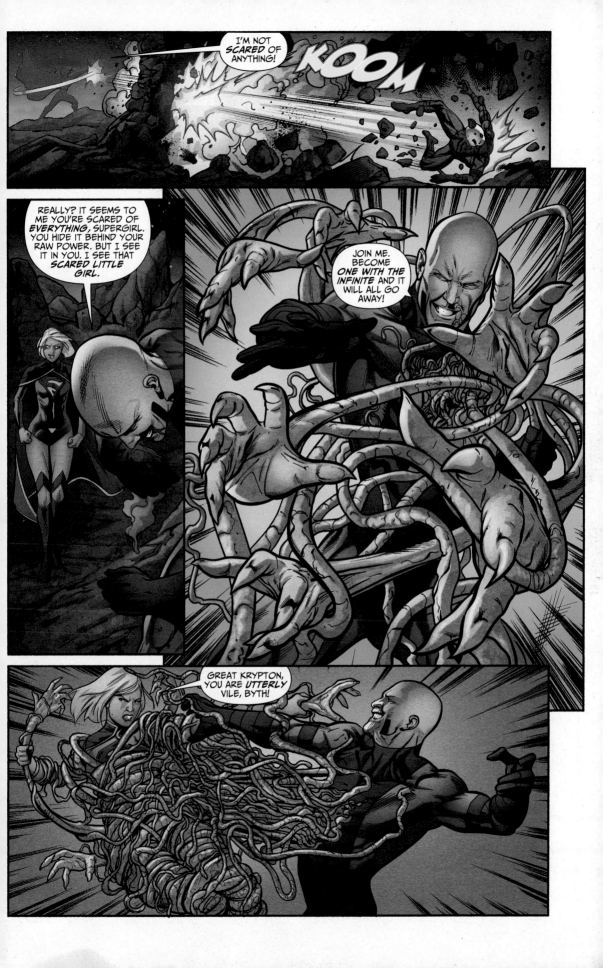

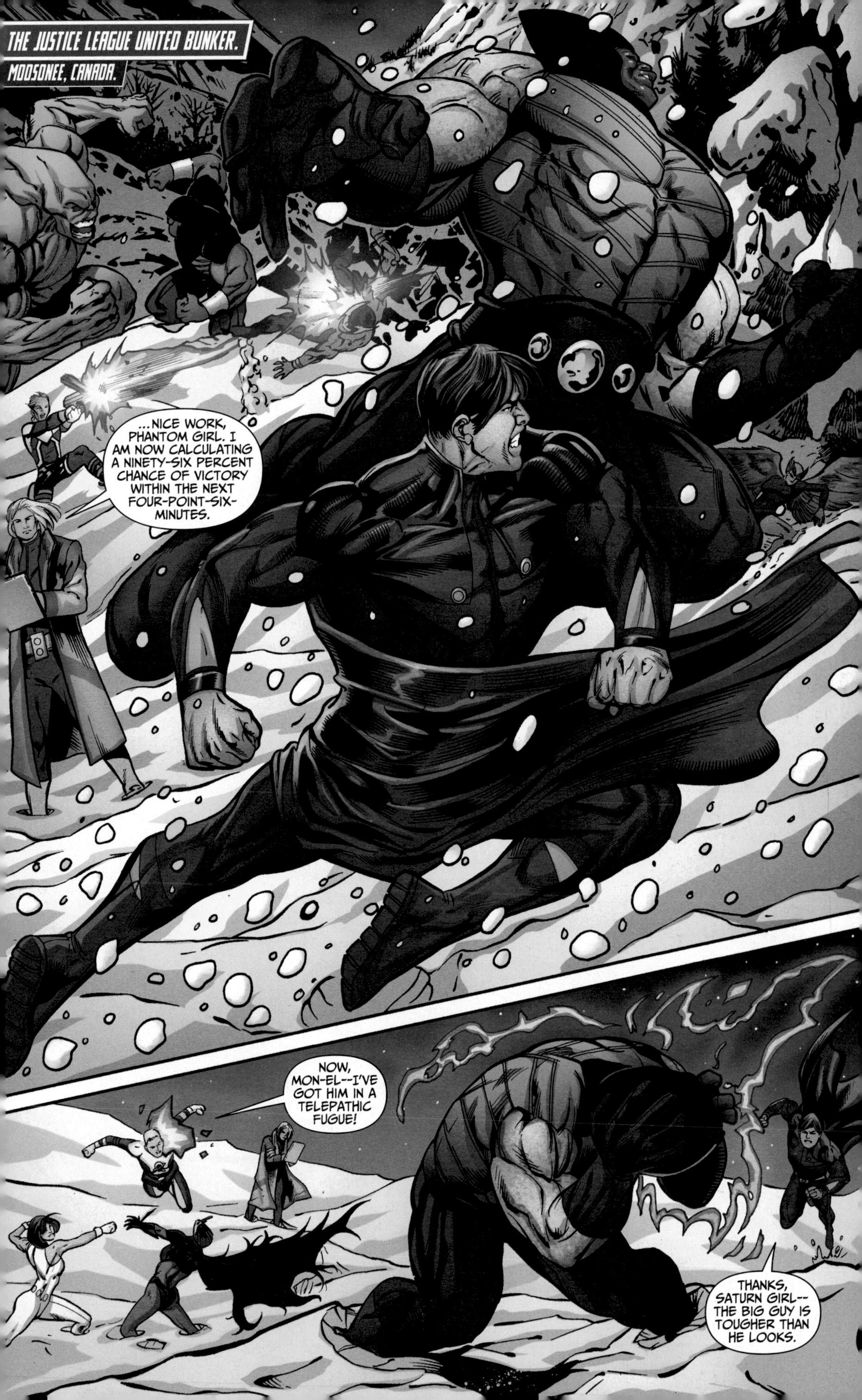
THE JUSTICE LEAGUE UNITED BUNKER.
MOOSONEE, CANADA.
...NICE WORK, PHANTOM GIRL. I AM NOW CALCULATING A NINETY-SIX PERCENT CHANCE OF VICTORY WITHIN THE NEXT FOUR-POINT-SIX-MINUTES.
NOW, MON-EL--I'VE GOT HIM IN A TELEPATHIC FUGUE!
THANKS, SATURN GIRL-- THE BIG GUY IS TOUGHER THAN HE LOOKS.

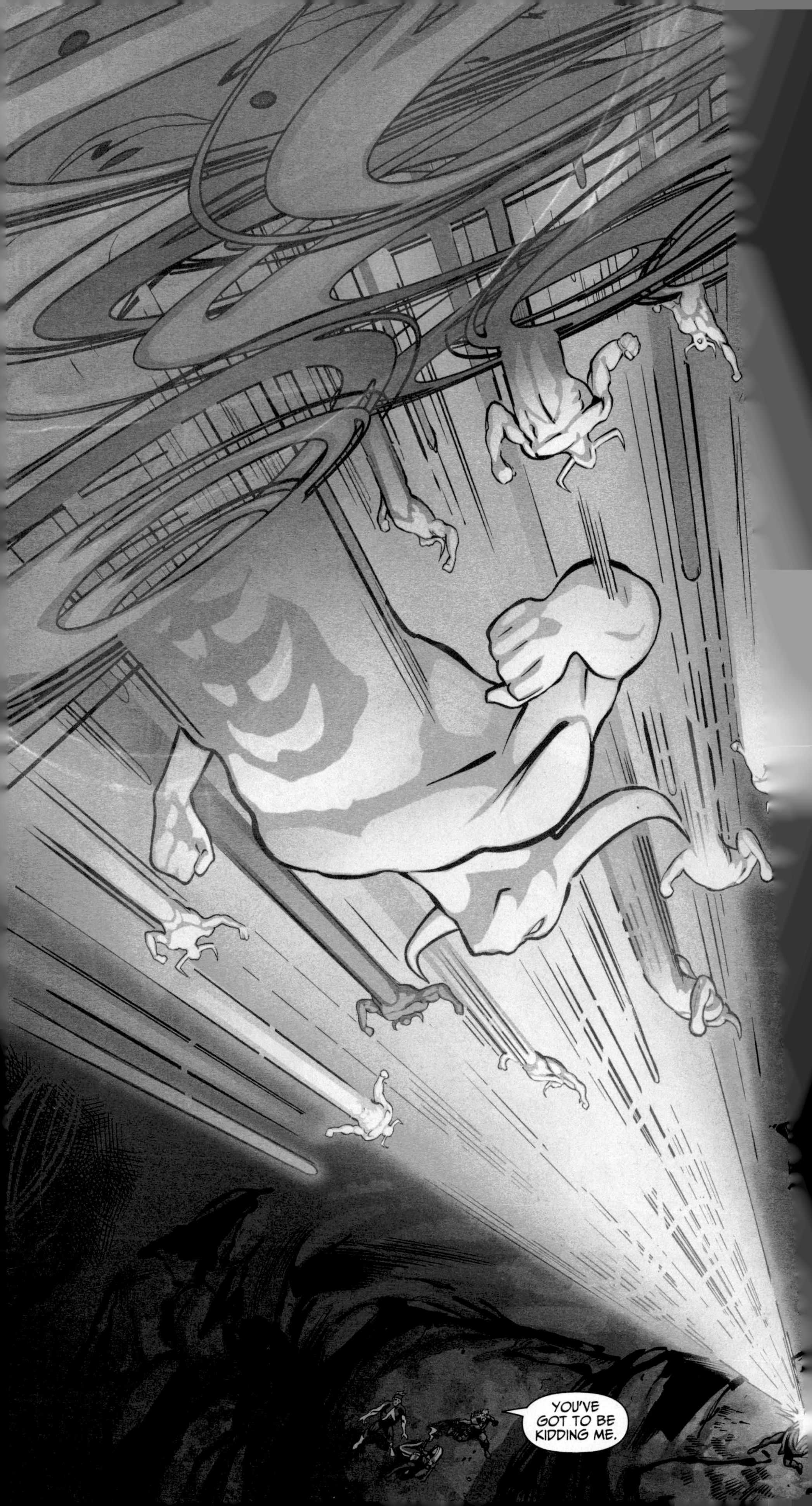
YOU'VE GOT TO BE KIDDING ME.

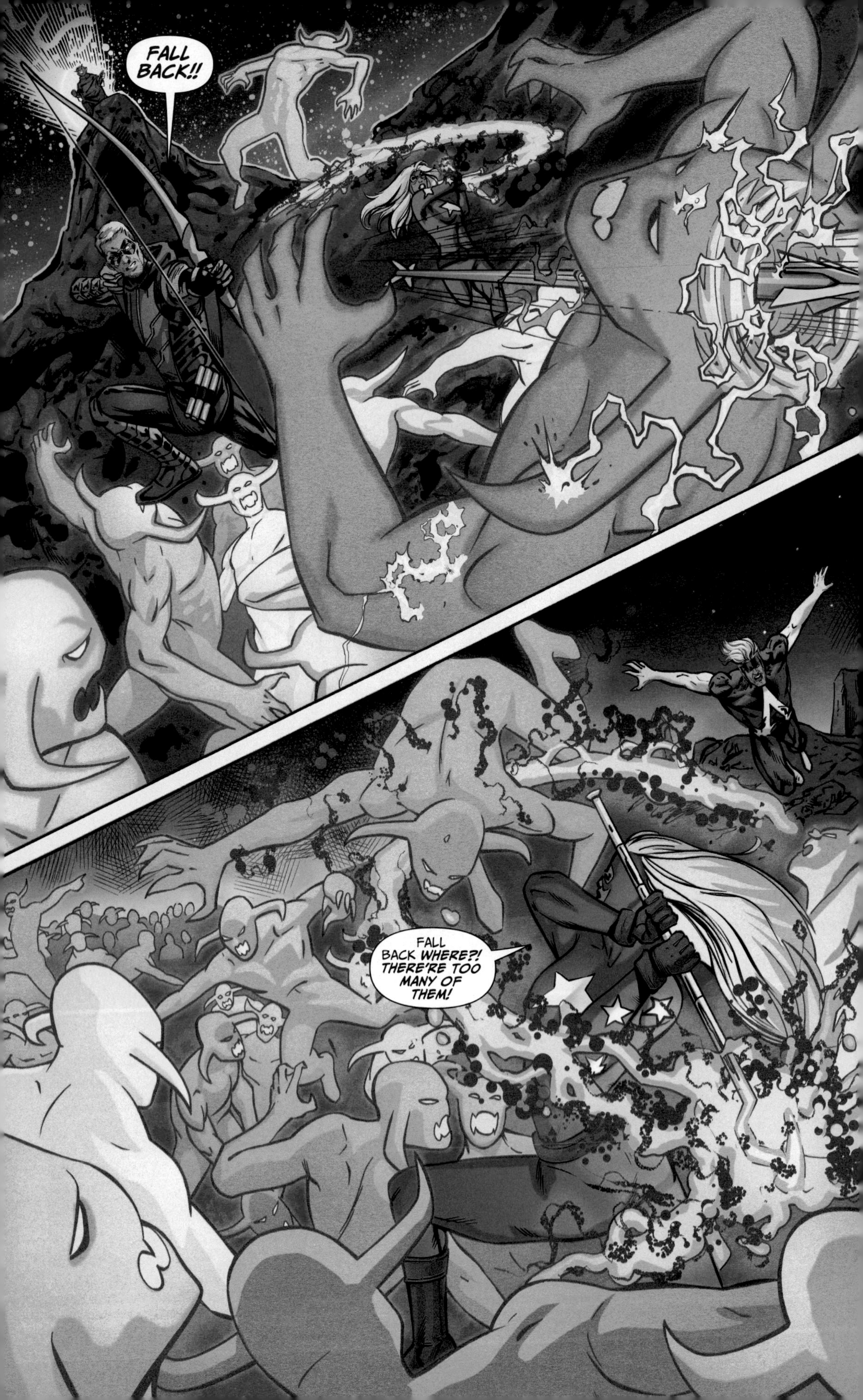
FALL BACK!!
FALL BACK WHERE?! THERE'RE TOO MANY OF THEM!

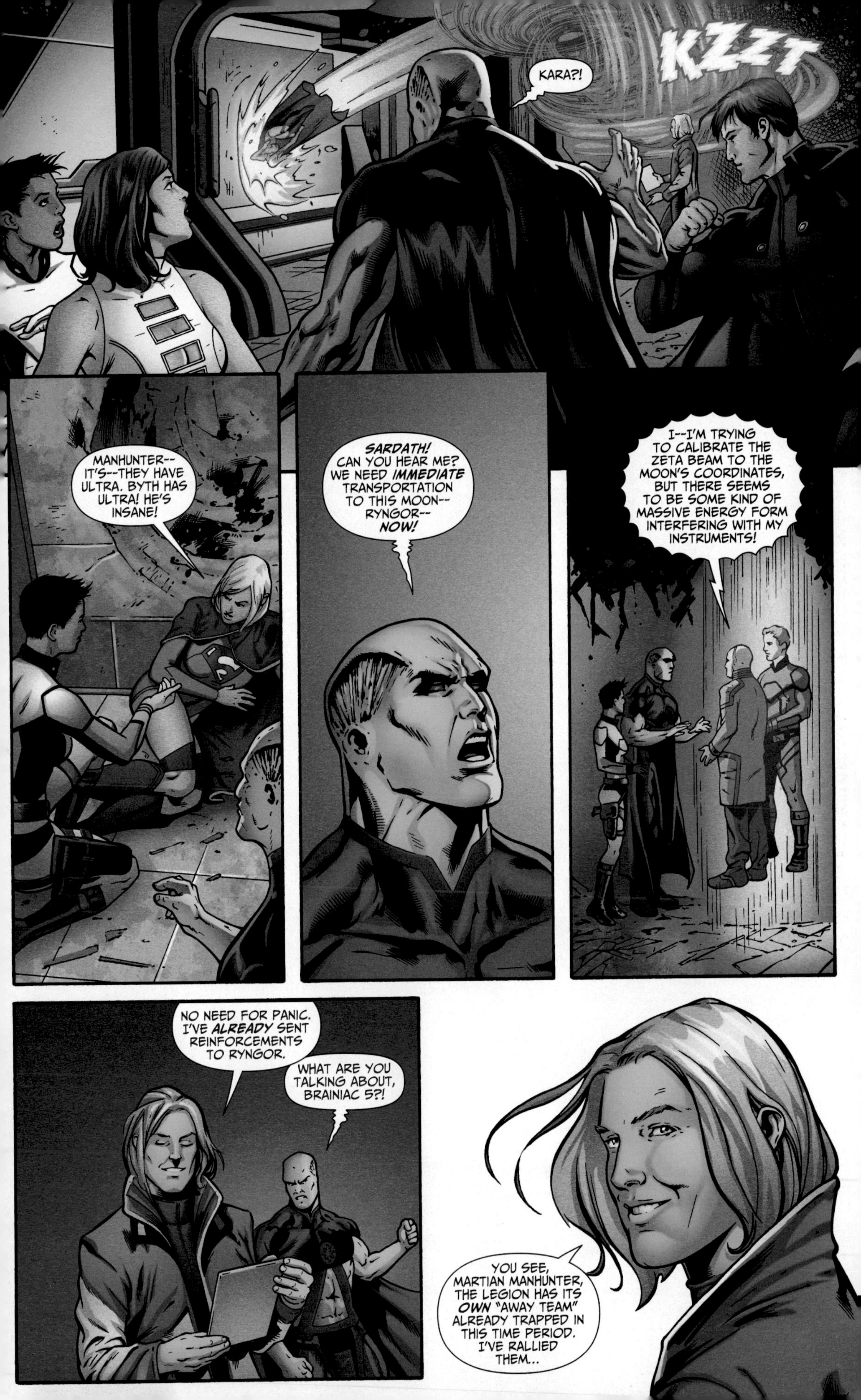
KZZT
KARA?!
MANHUNTER-- IT'S--THEY HAVE ULTRA. BYTH HAS ULTRA! HE'S INSANE!
SARDATH! CAN YOU HEAR ME? WE NEED IMMEDIATE TRANSPORTATION TO THIS MOON-- RYNGOR-- NOW!
I--I'M TRYING TO CALIBRATE THE ZETA BEAM TO THE MOON'S COORDINATES, BUT THERE SEEMS TO BE SOME KIND OF MASSIVE ENERGY FORM INTERFERING WITH MY INSTRUMENTS!
NO NEED FOR PANIC. I'VE ALREADY SENT REINFORCEMENTS TO RYNGOR.
WHAT ARE YOU TALKING ABOUT, BRAINIAC 5?!
YOU SEE, MARTIAN MANHUNTER, THE LEGION HAS ITS OWN "AWAY TEAM" ALREADY TRAPPED IN THIS TIME PERIOD. I'VE RALLIED THEM...

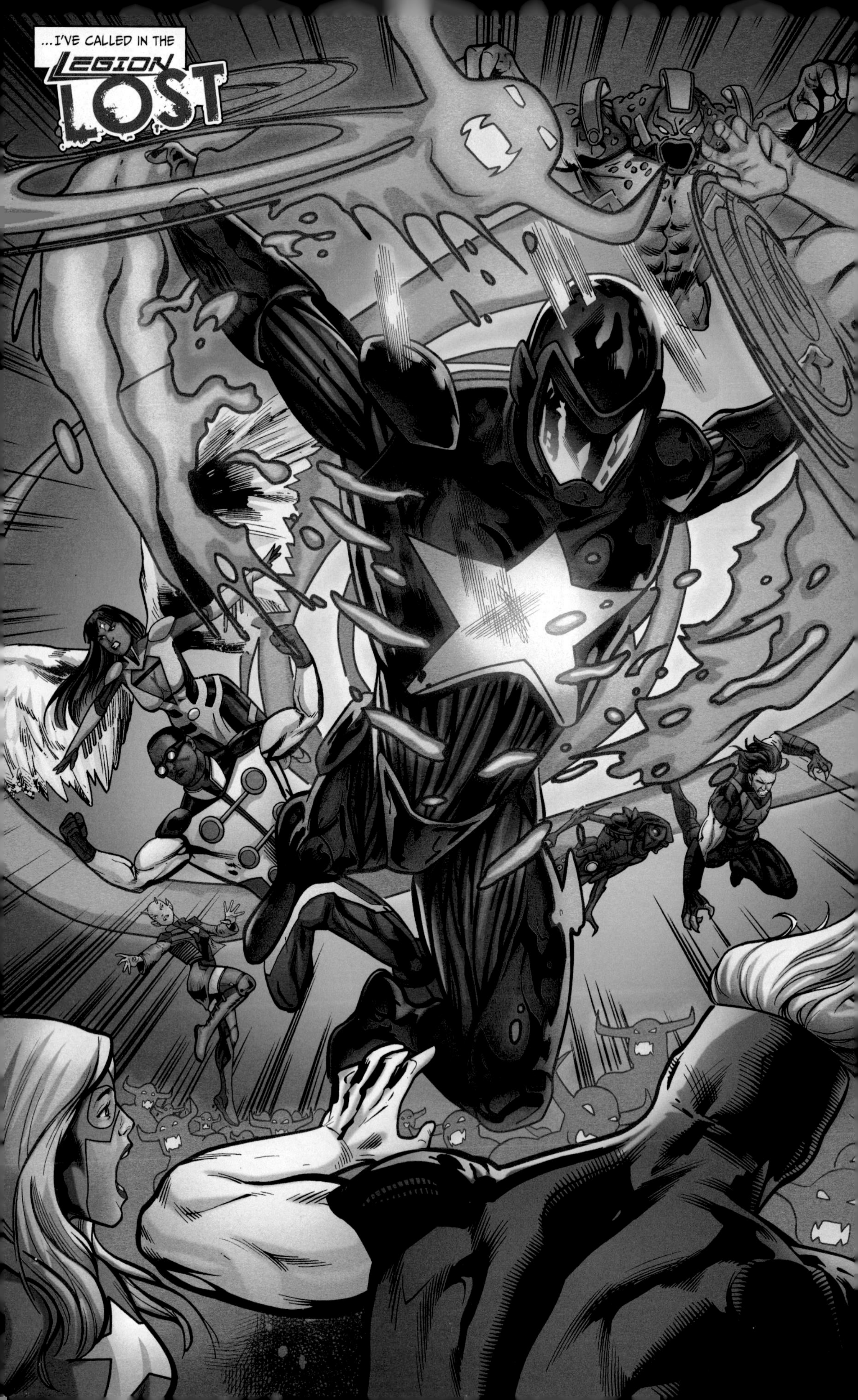
...I'VE CALLED IN THE
LEGION LOST

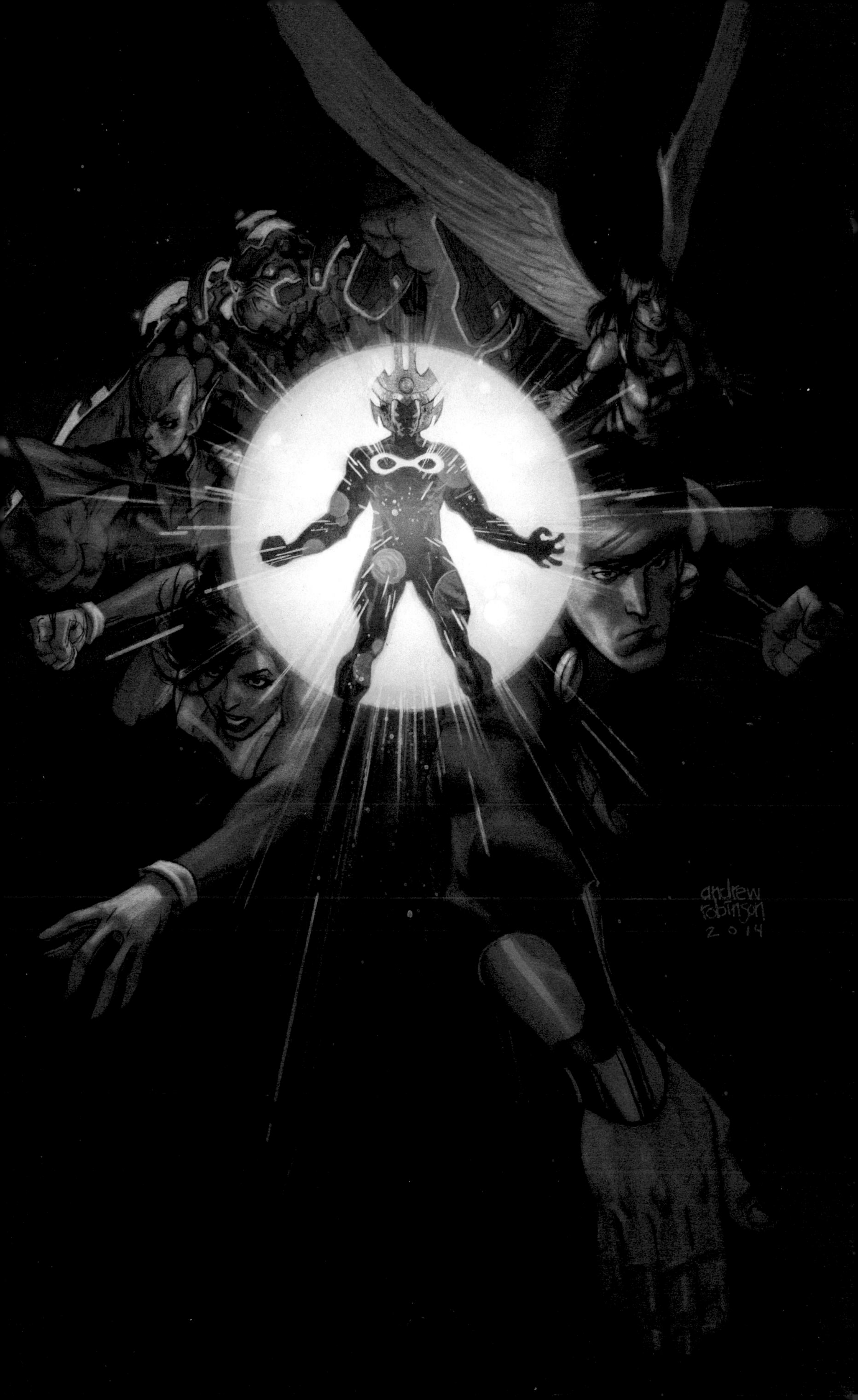
andrew robinson
2014

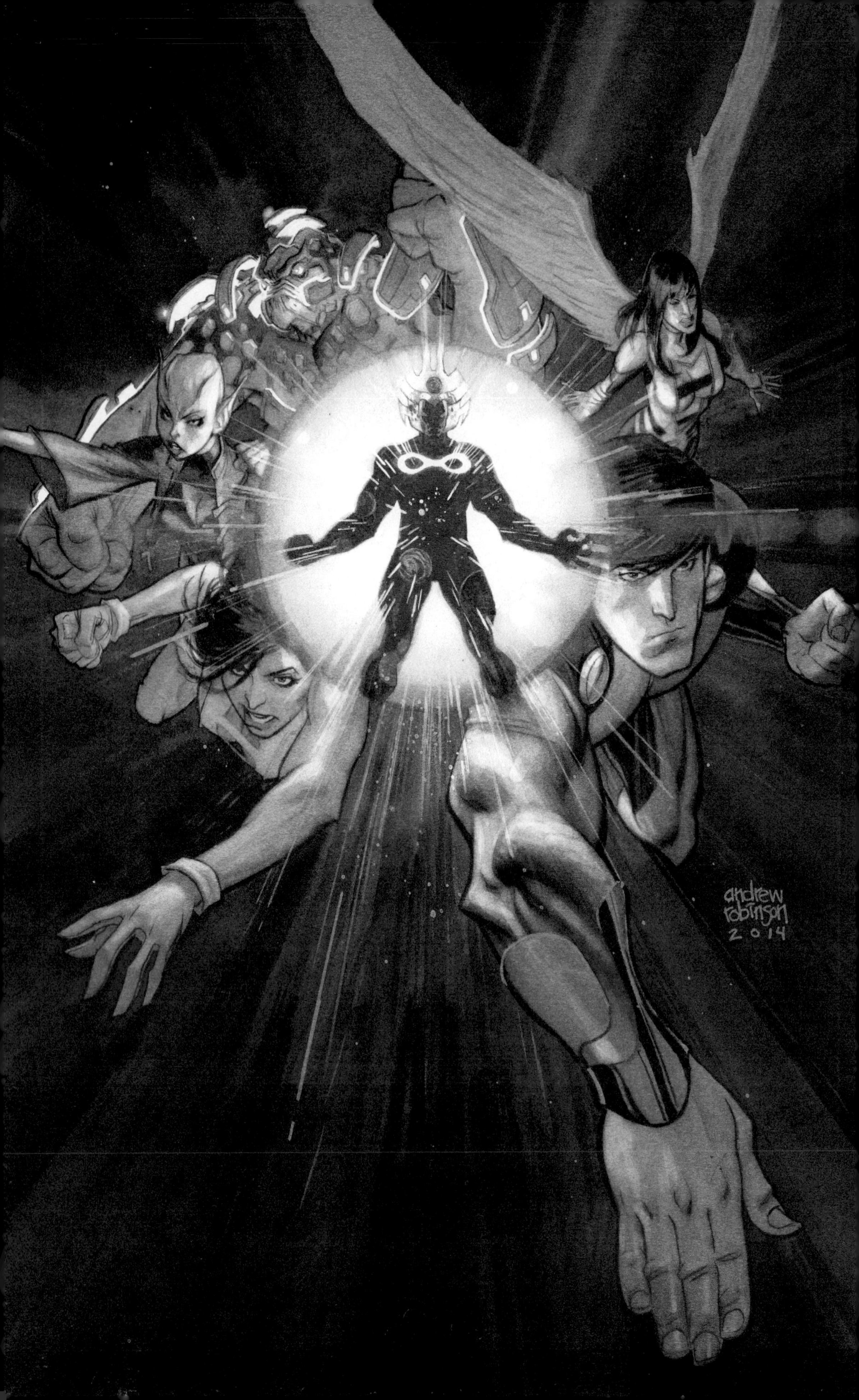
andrew robinson 2014

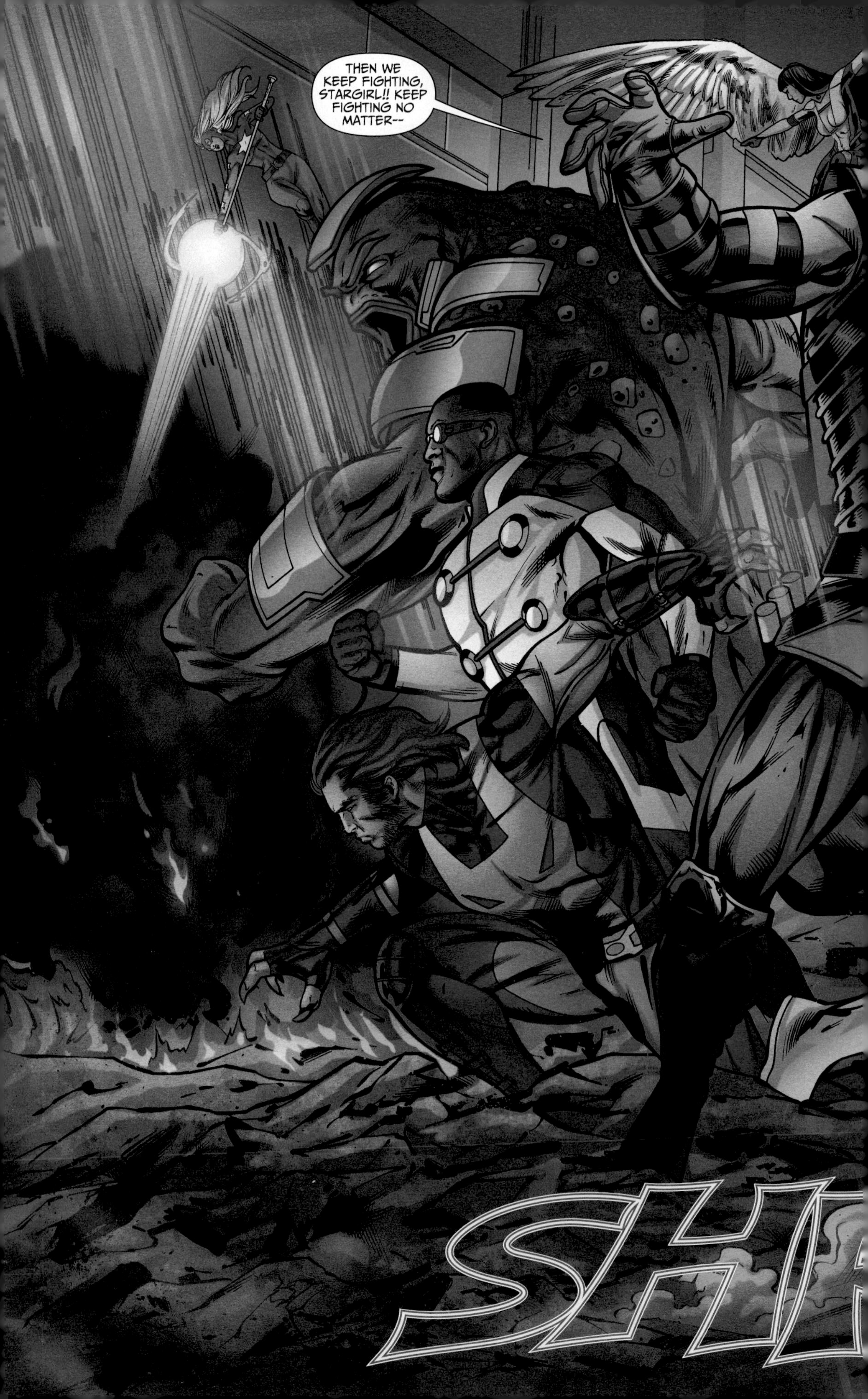
THEN WE KEEP FIGHTING, STARGIRL!! KEEP FIGHTING NO MATTER--
SHI

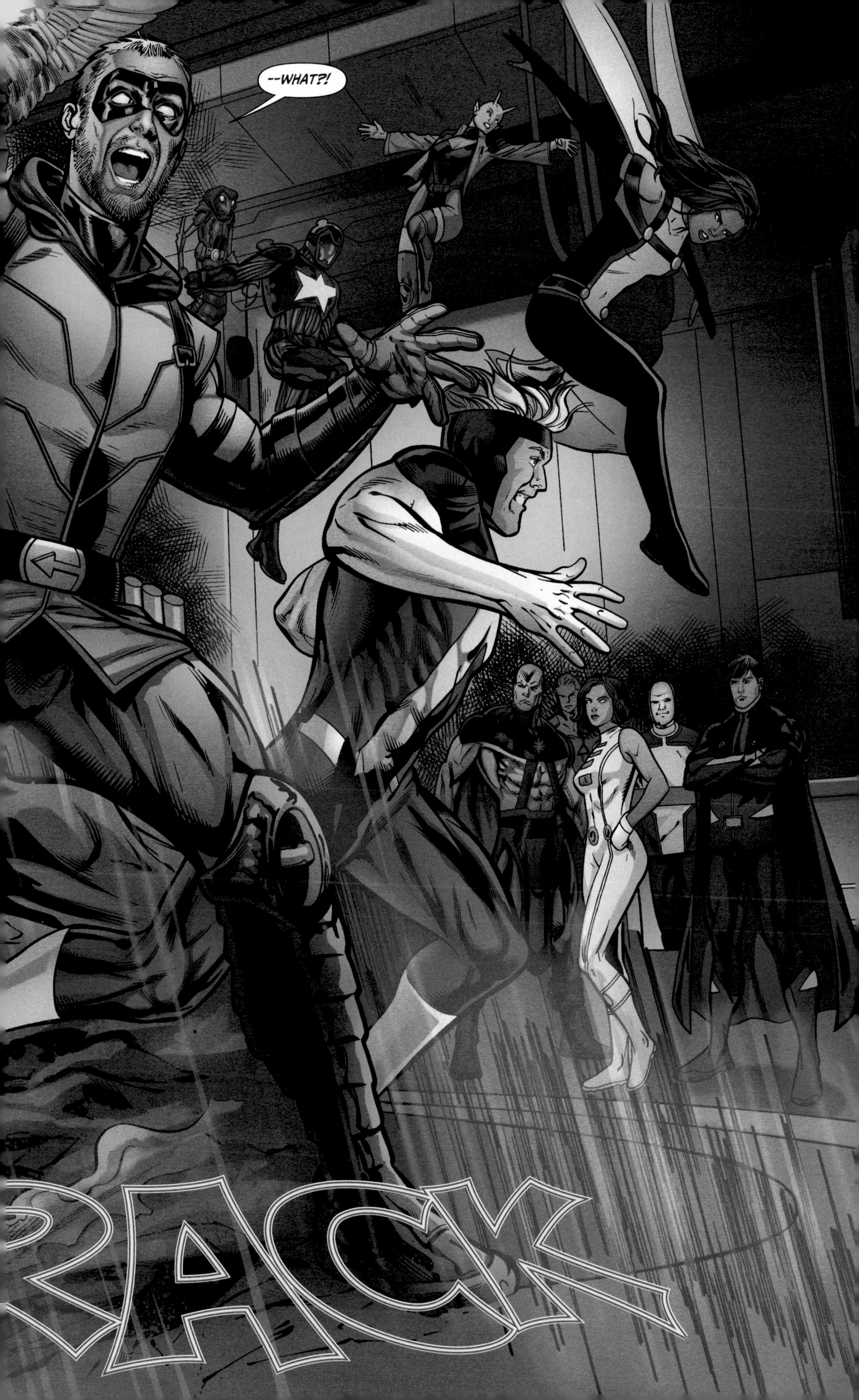
--WHAT?!
RACK

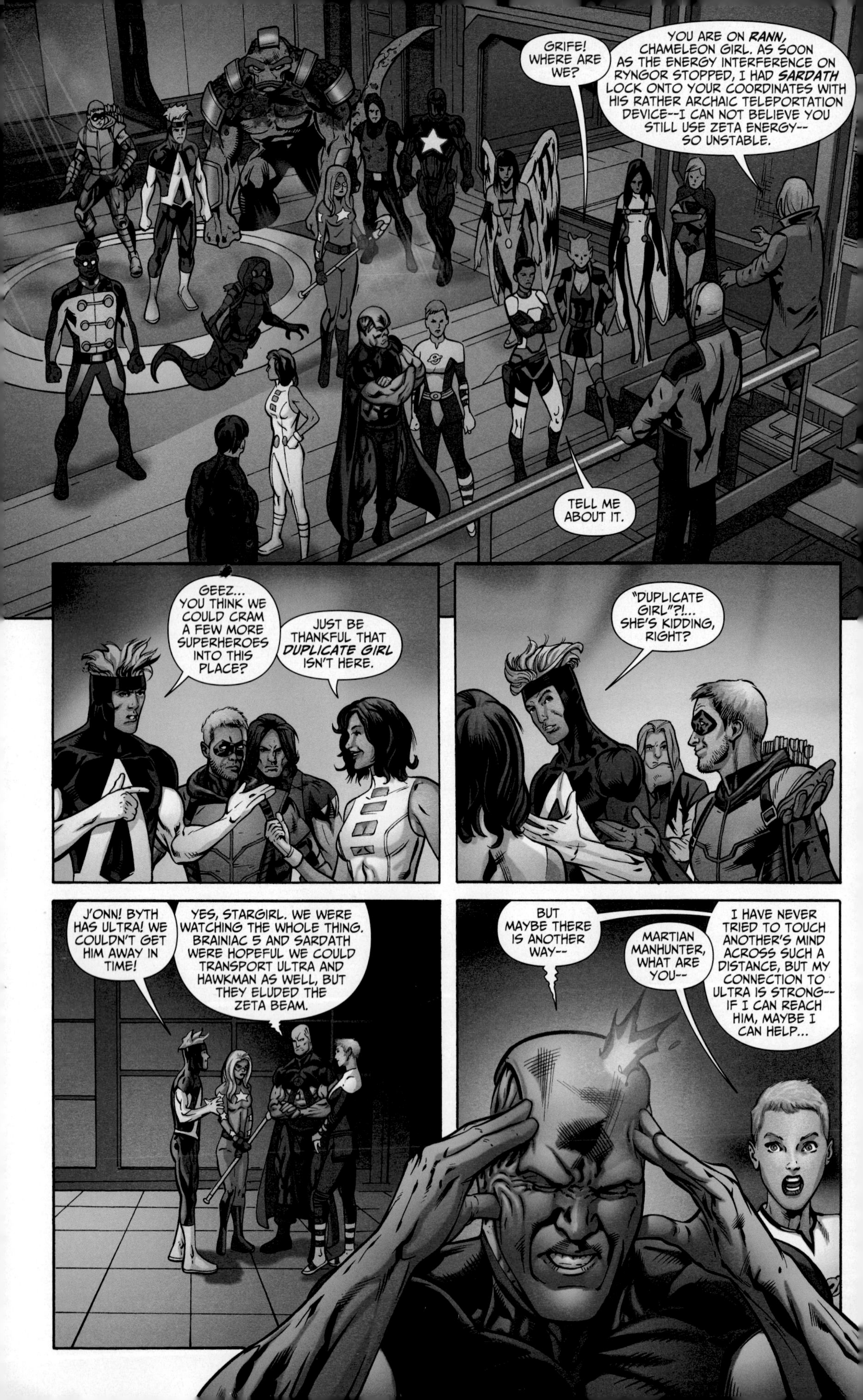
GRIFE! WHERE ARE WE?
YOU ARE ON RANN, CHAMELEON GIRL. AS SOON AS THE ENERGY INTERFERENCE ON RYNGOR STOPPED, I HAD SARDATH LOCK ONTO YOUR COORDINATES WITH HIS RATHER ARCHAIC TELEPORTATION DEVICE--I CAN NOT BELIEVE YOU STILL USE ZETA ENERGY-- SO UNSTABLE.
TELL ME ABOUT IT.
GEEZ... YOU THINK WE COULD CRAM A FEW MORE SUPERHEROES INTO THIS PLACE?
JUST BE THANKFUL THAT DUPLICATE GIRL ISN'T HERE.
"DUPLICATE GIRL"?!... SHE'S KIDDING, RIGHT?
J'ONN! BYTH HAS ULTRA! WE COULDN'T GET HIM AWAY IN TIME!
YES, STARGIRL. WE WERE WATCHING THE WHOLE THING. BRAINIAC 5 AND SARDATH WERE HOPEFUL WE COULD TRANSPORT ULTRA AND HAWKMAN AS WELL, BUT THEY ELUDED THE ZETA BEAM.
BUT MAYBE THERE IS ANOTHER WAY--
MARTIAN MANHUNTER, WHAT ARE YOU--
I HAVE NEVER TRIED TO TOUCH ANOTHER'S MIND ACROSS SUCH A DISTANCE, BUT MY CONNECTION TO ULTRA IS STRONG-- IF I CAN REACH HIM, MAYBE I CAN HELP...

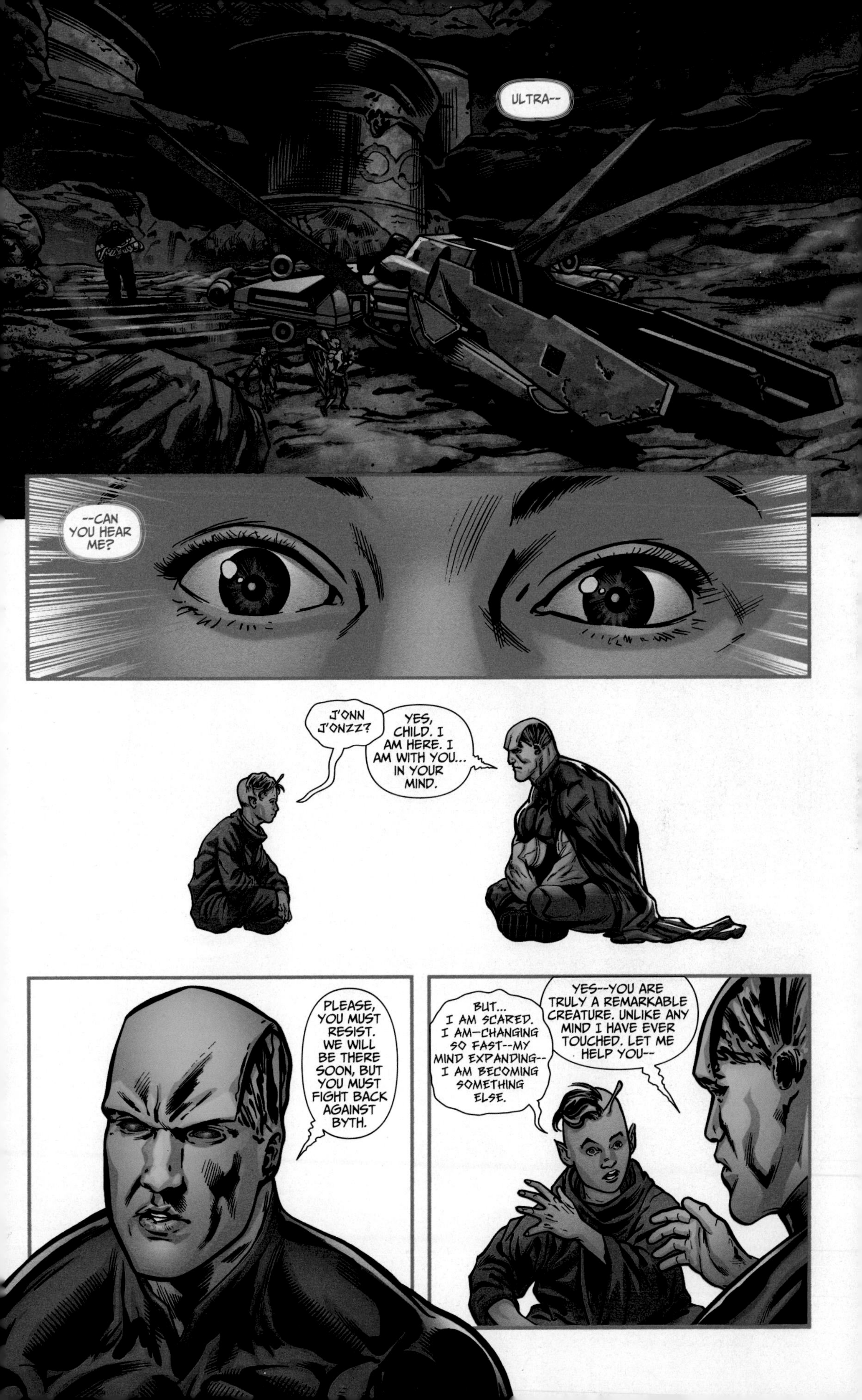
ULTRA--
--CAN YOU HEAR ME?
J'ONN J'ONZZ?
YES, CHILD. I AM HERE. I AM WITH YOU... IN YOUR MIND.
PLEASE, YOU MUST RESIST. WE WILL BE THERE SOON, BUT YOU MUST FIGHT BACK AGAINST BYTH.
BUT... I AM SCARED. I AM--CHANGING SO FAST--MY MIND EXPANDING-- I AM BECOMING SOMETHING ELSE.
YES--YOU ARE TRULY A REMARKABLE CREATURE. UNLIKE ANY MIND I HAVE EVER TOUCHED. LET ME HELP YOU--

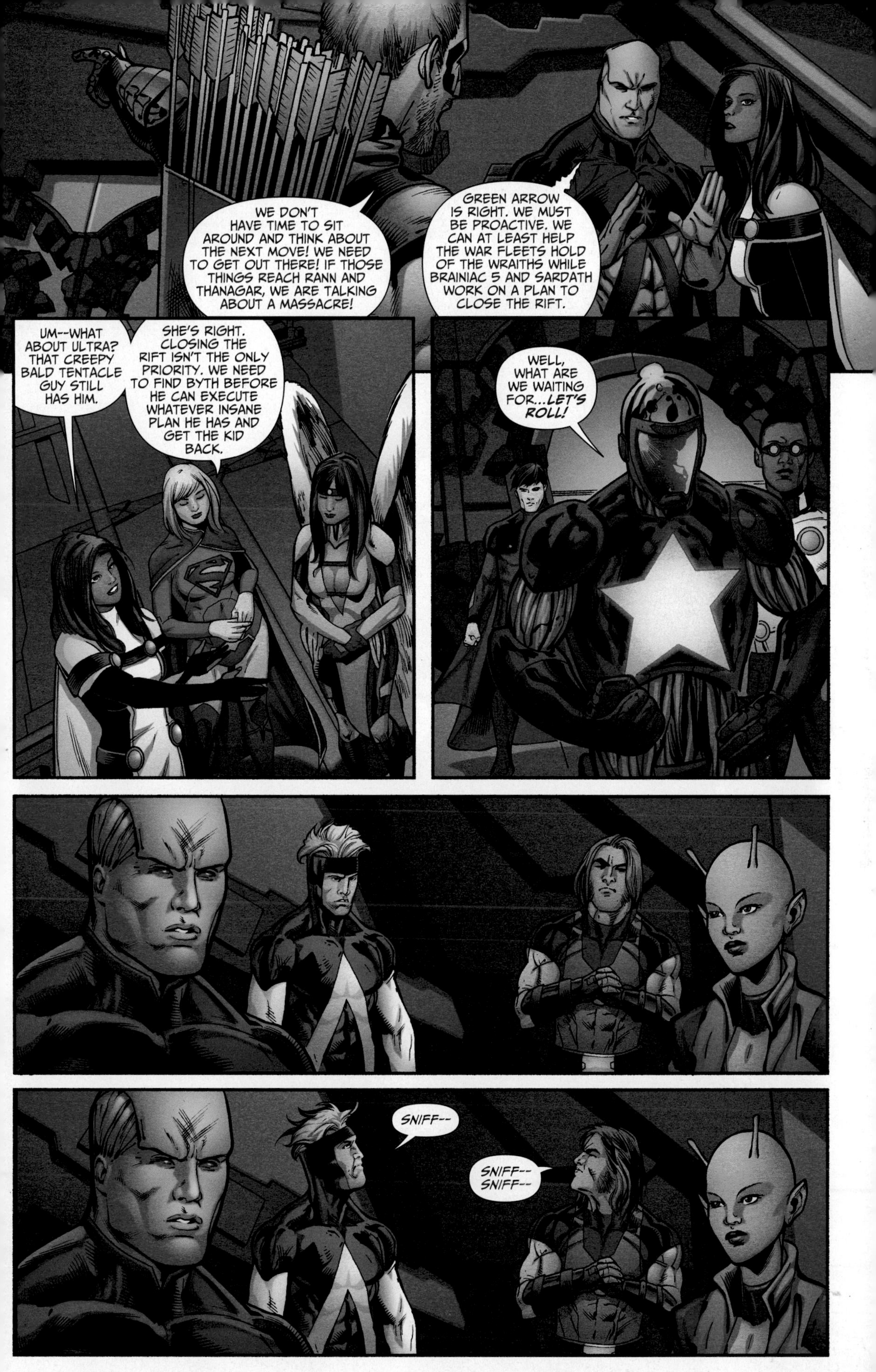
WE DON'T HAVE TIME TO SIT AROUND AND THINK ABOUT THE NEXT MOVE! WE NEED TO GET OUT THERE! IF THOSE THINGS REACH RANN AND THANAGAR, WE ARE TALKING ABOUT A MASSACRE!
GREEN ARROW IS RIGHT. WE MUST BE PROACTIVE. WE CAN AT LEAST HELP THE WAR FLEETS HOLD OF THE WRAITHS WHILE BRAINIAC 5 AND SARDATH WORK ON A PLAN TO CLOSE THE RIFT.
UM--WHAT ABOUT ULTRA? THAT CREEPY BALD TENTACLE GUY STILL HAS HIM.
SHE'S RIGHT. CLOSING THE RIFT ISN'T THE ONLY PRIORITY. WE NEED TO FIND BYTH BEFORE HE CAN EXECUTE WHATEVER INSANE PLAN HE HAS AND GET THE KID BACK.
WELL, WHAT ARE WE WAITING FOR...LET'S ROLL!
SNIFF--
SNIFF-- SNIFF--

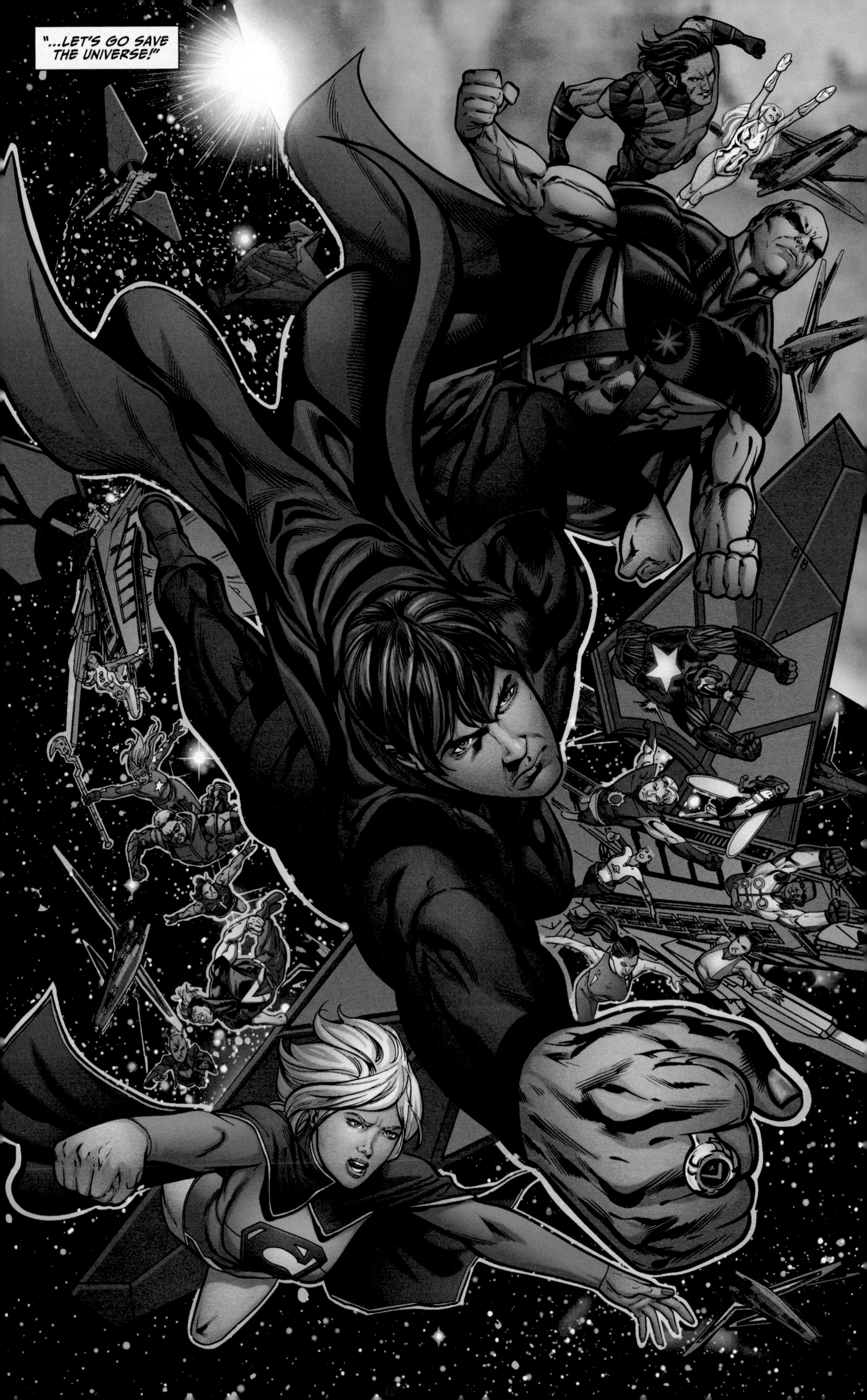
"...LET'S GO SAVE THE UNIVERSE!"

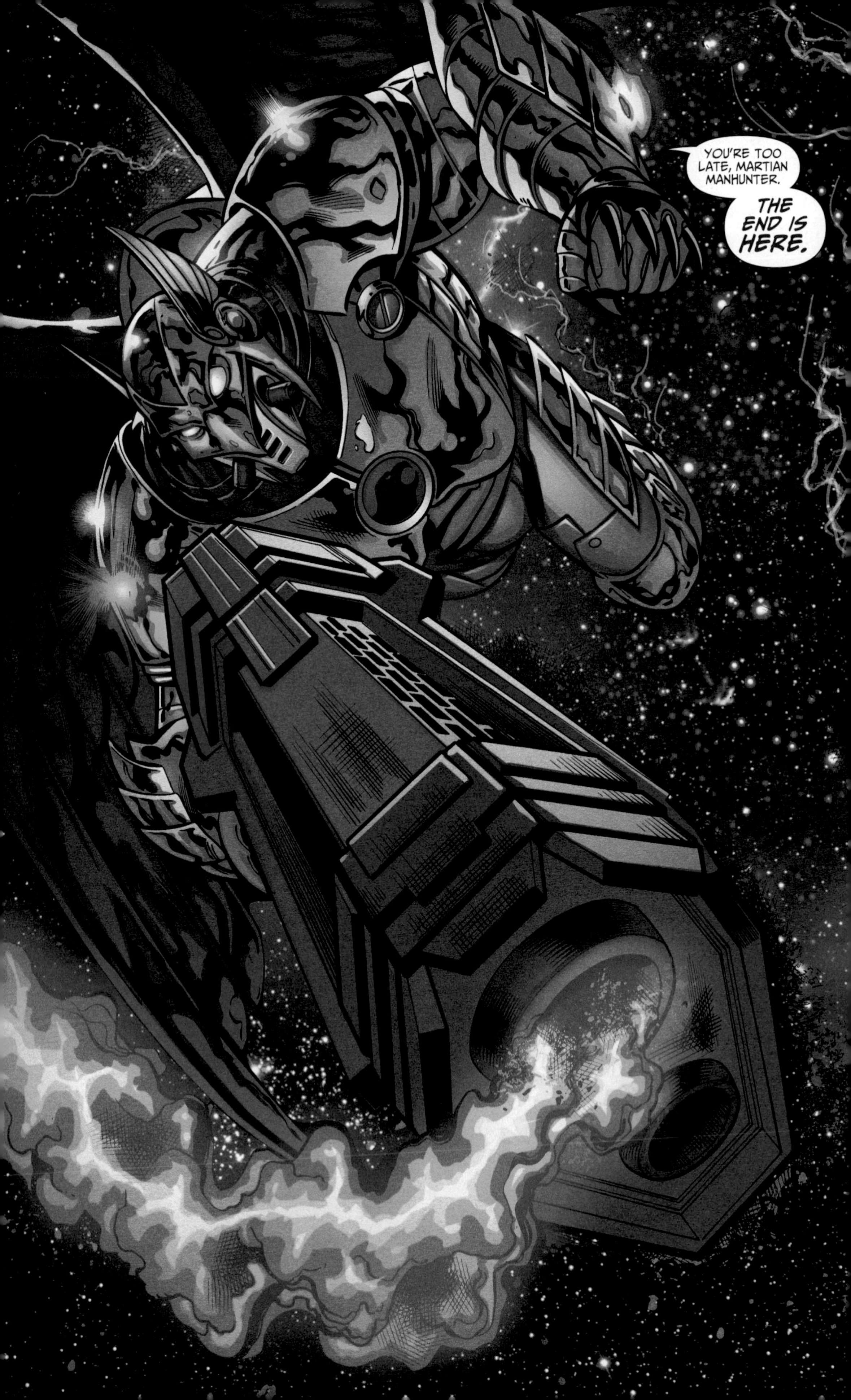
YOU'RE TOO LATE, MARTIAN MANHUNTER.
THE END IS HERE.

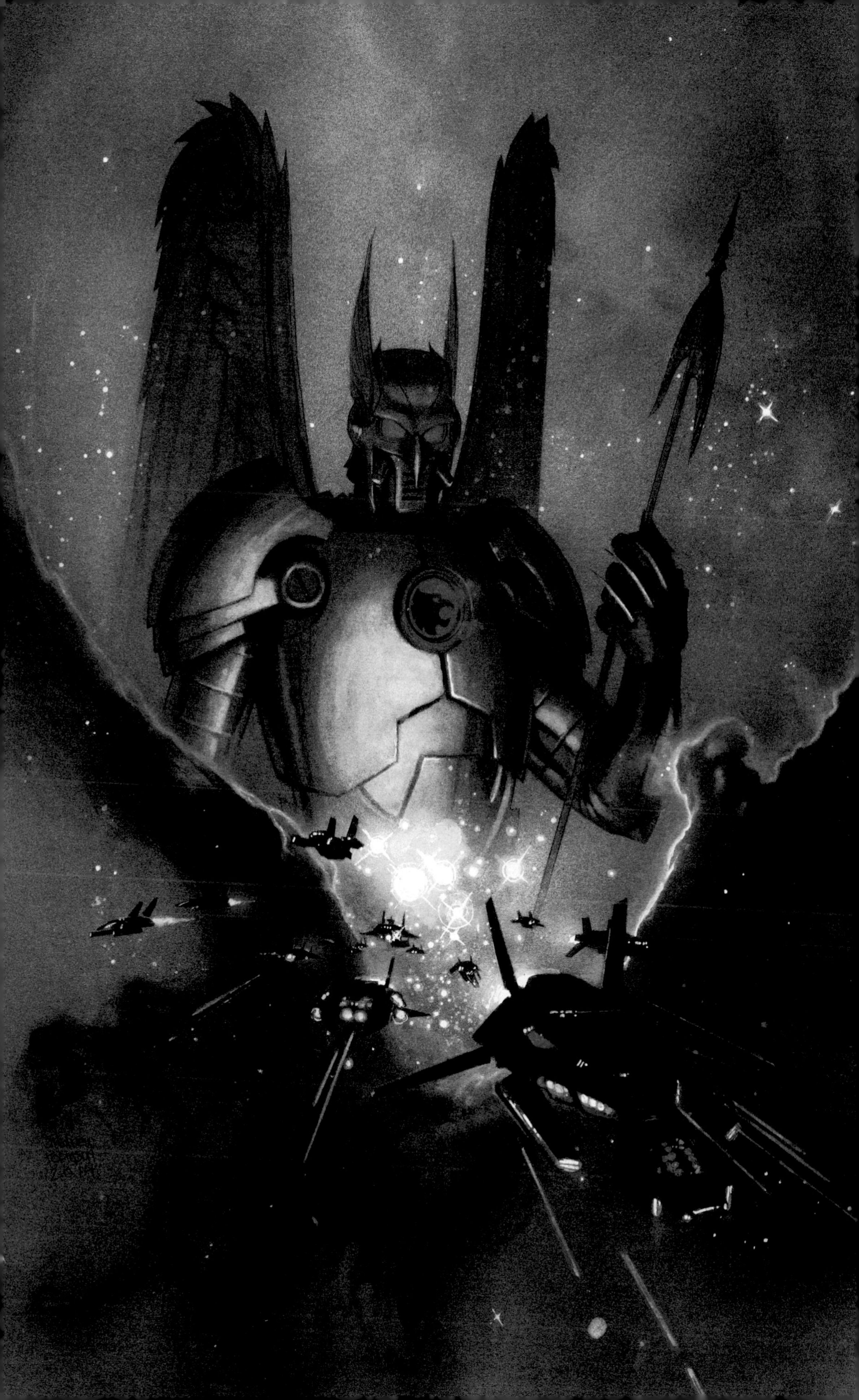

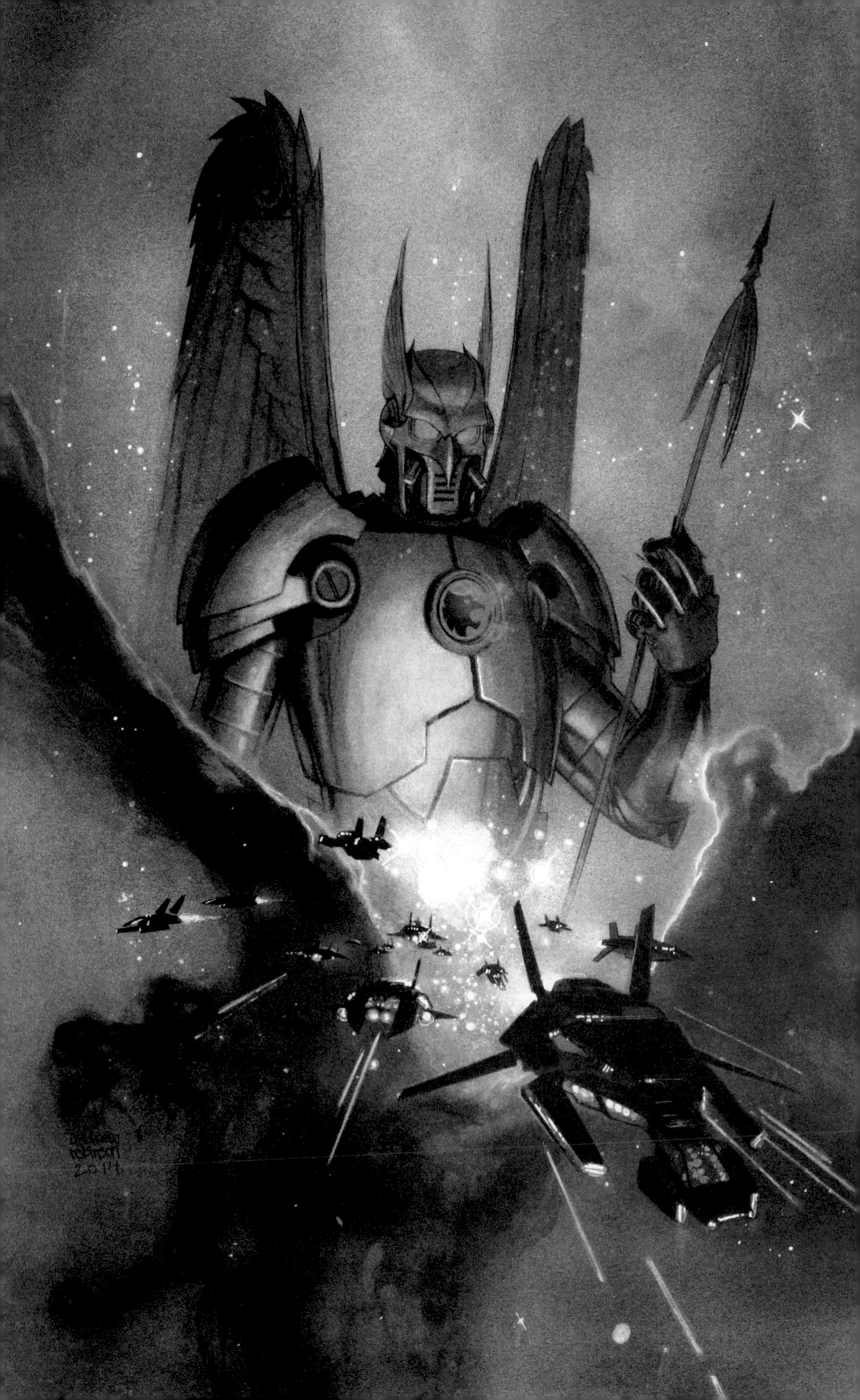

IT ALL STARTED WITH A DREAM...

ONE MAN--INTERGALACTIC INDUSTRIALIST R.J. BRANDE--HAD A DREAM OF CREATING A TEAM OF YOUNG HEROES MADE UP OF EVERY RACE IN THE UNITED PLANETS.

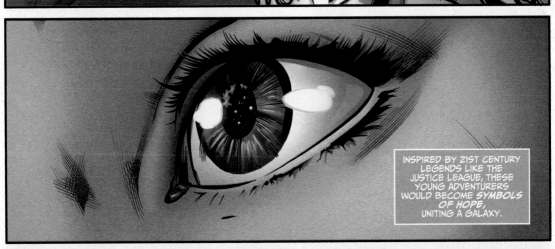

INSPIRED BY 21ST CENTURY LEGENDS LIKE THE JUSTICE LEAGUE, THESE YOUNG ADVENTURERS WOULD BECOME *SYMBOLS OF HOPE,* UNITING A GALAXY.

TAKING NAMES LIKE COSMIC BOY, LIGHTNING LAD AND SATURN GIRL, *THE LEGION OF SUPER-HEROES* WAS BORN.

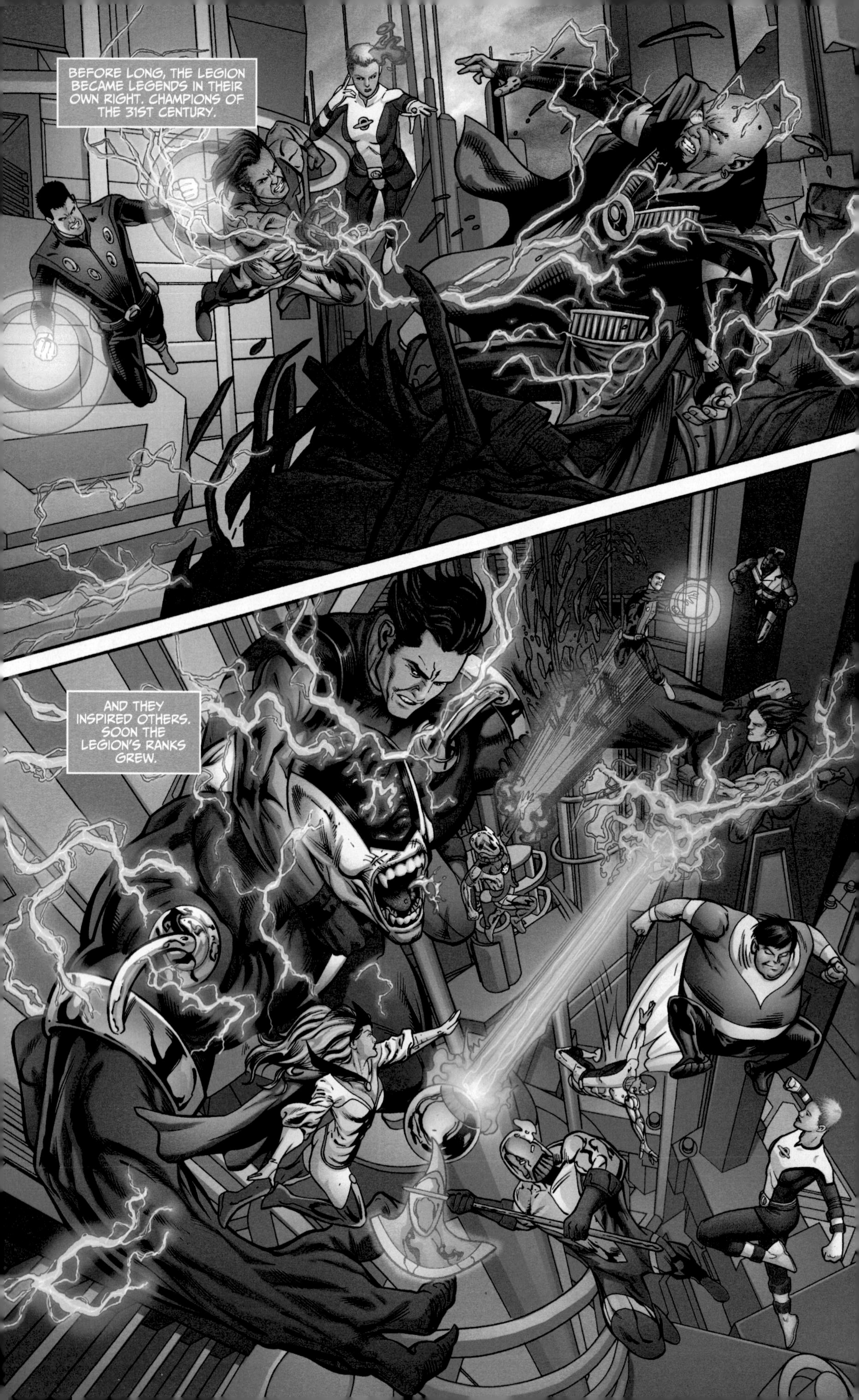
BEFORE LONG, THE LEGION BECAME LEGENDS IN THEIR OWN RIGHT. CHAMPIONS OF THE 31ST CENTURY.
AND THEY INSPIRED OTHERS. SOON THE LEGION'S RANKS GREW.

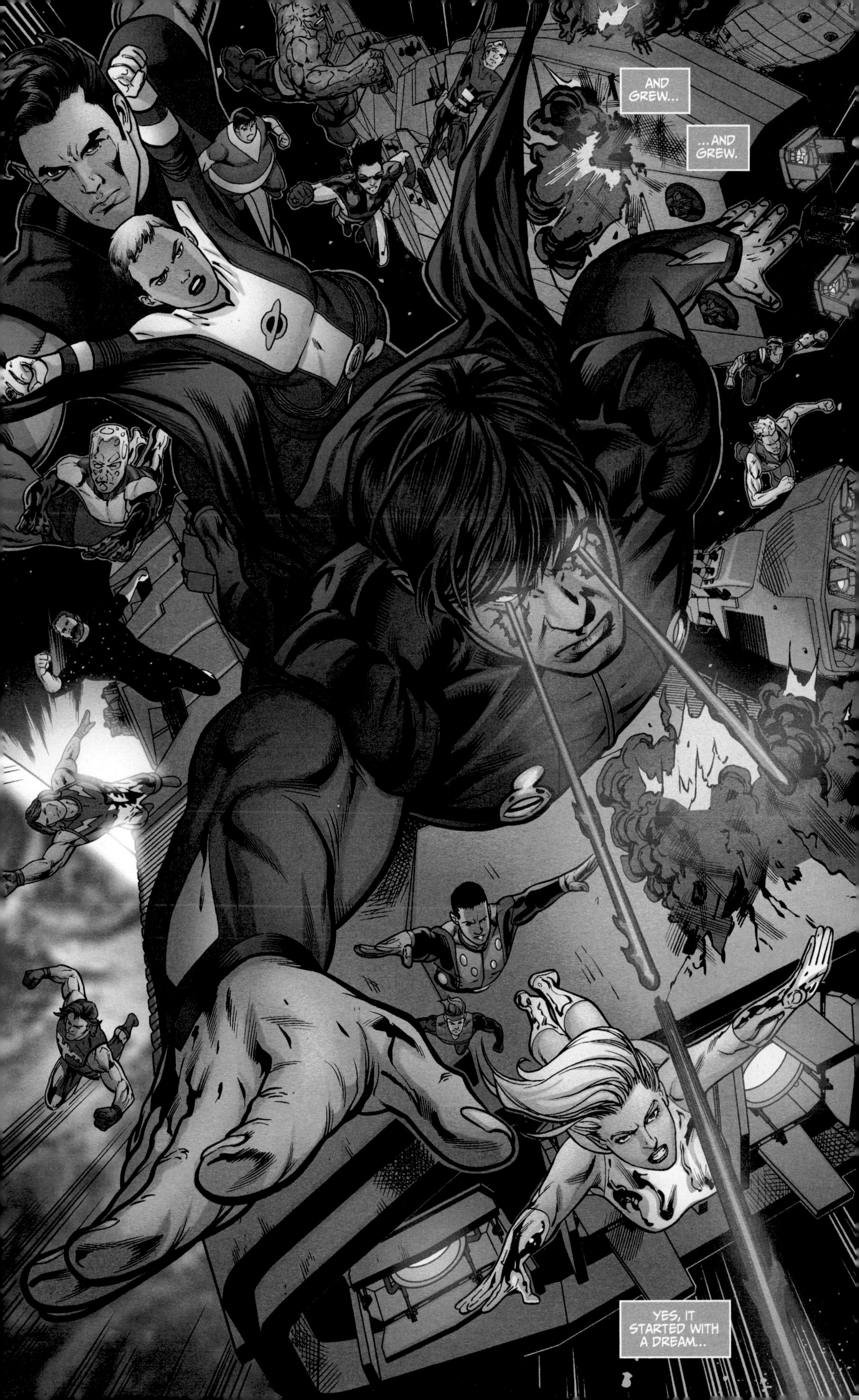
AND GREW...
...AND GREW.
YES, IT STARTED WITH A DREAM...

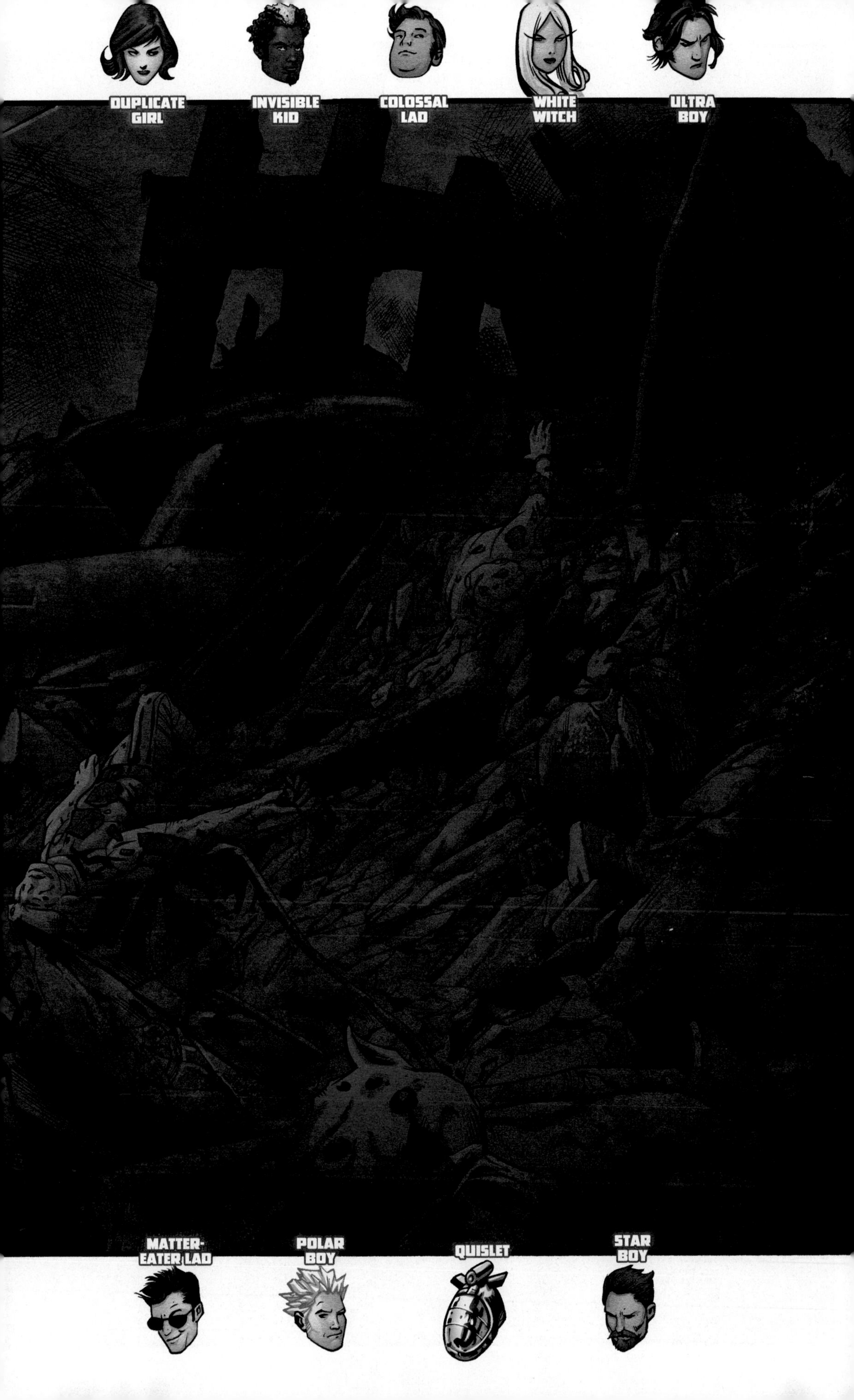

DUPLICATE GIRL
INVISIBLE KID
COLOSSAL LAD
WHITE WITCH
ULTRA BOY
MATTER-EATER LAD
POLAR BOY
QUISLET
STAR BOY

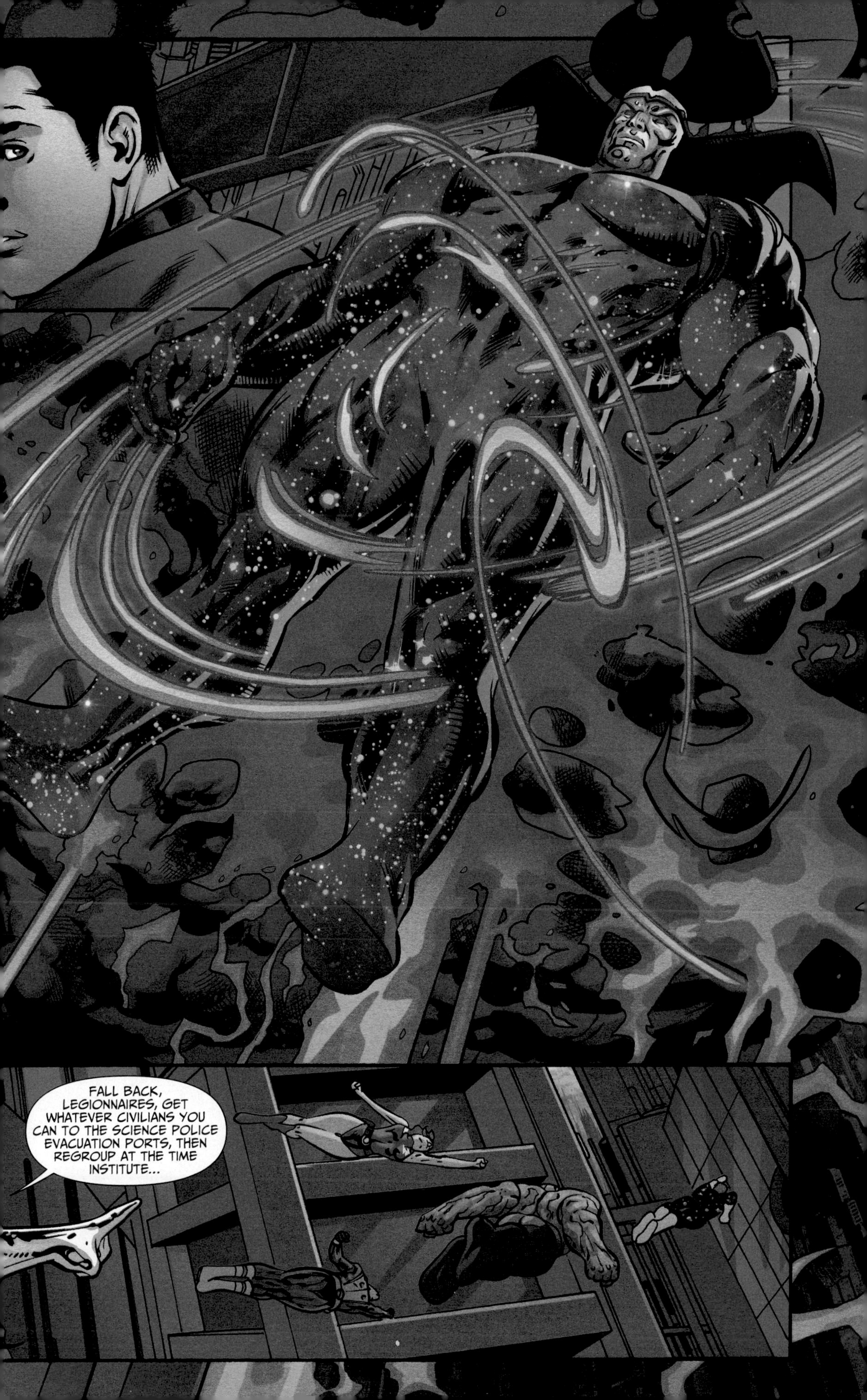
FALL BACK, LEGIONNAIRES, GET WHATEVER CIVILIANS YOU CAN TO THE SCIENCE POLICE EVACUATION PORTS, THEN REGROUP AT THE TIME INSTITUTE...

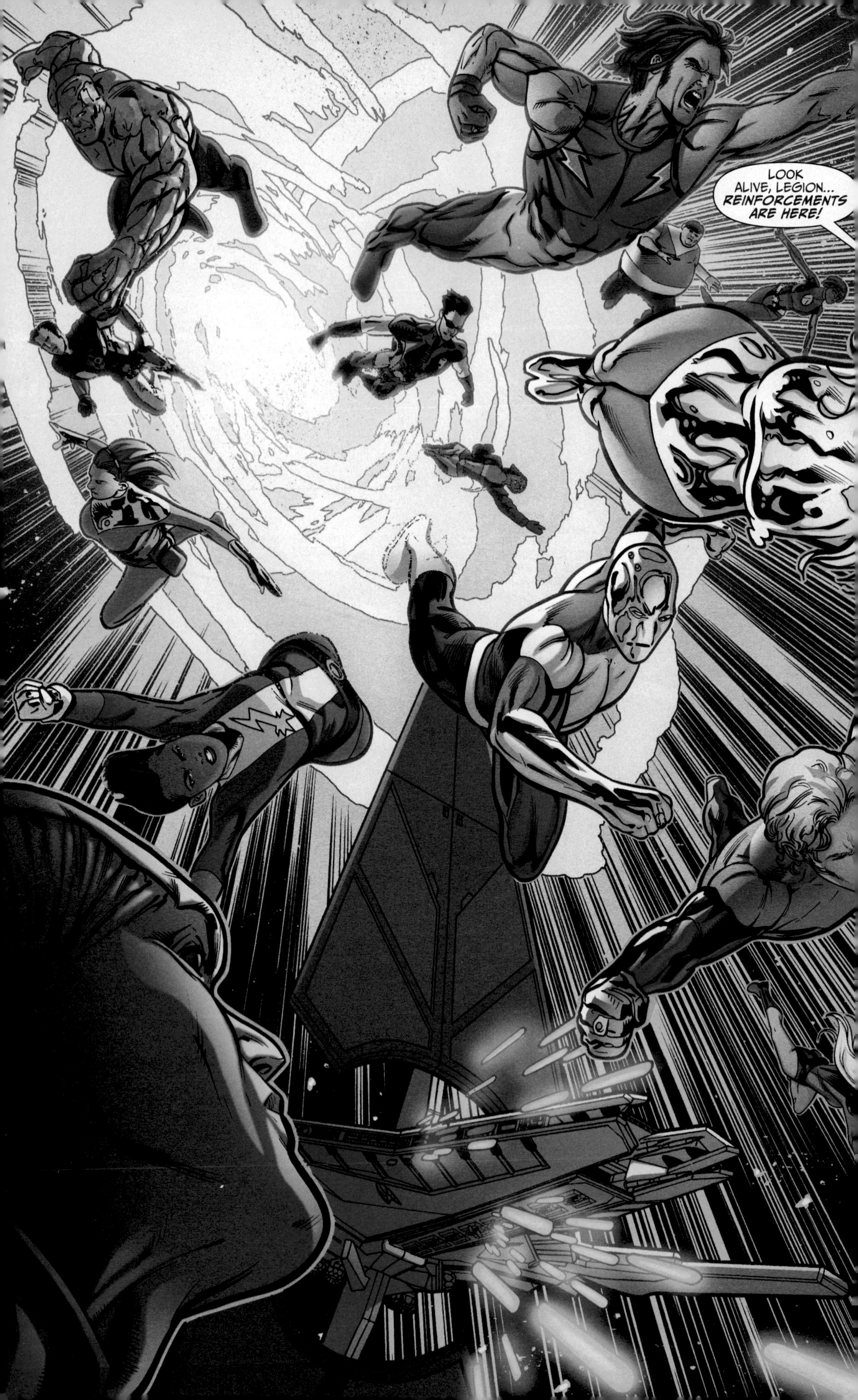
LOOK ALIVE, LEGION... REINFORCEMENTS ARE HERE!

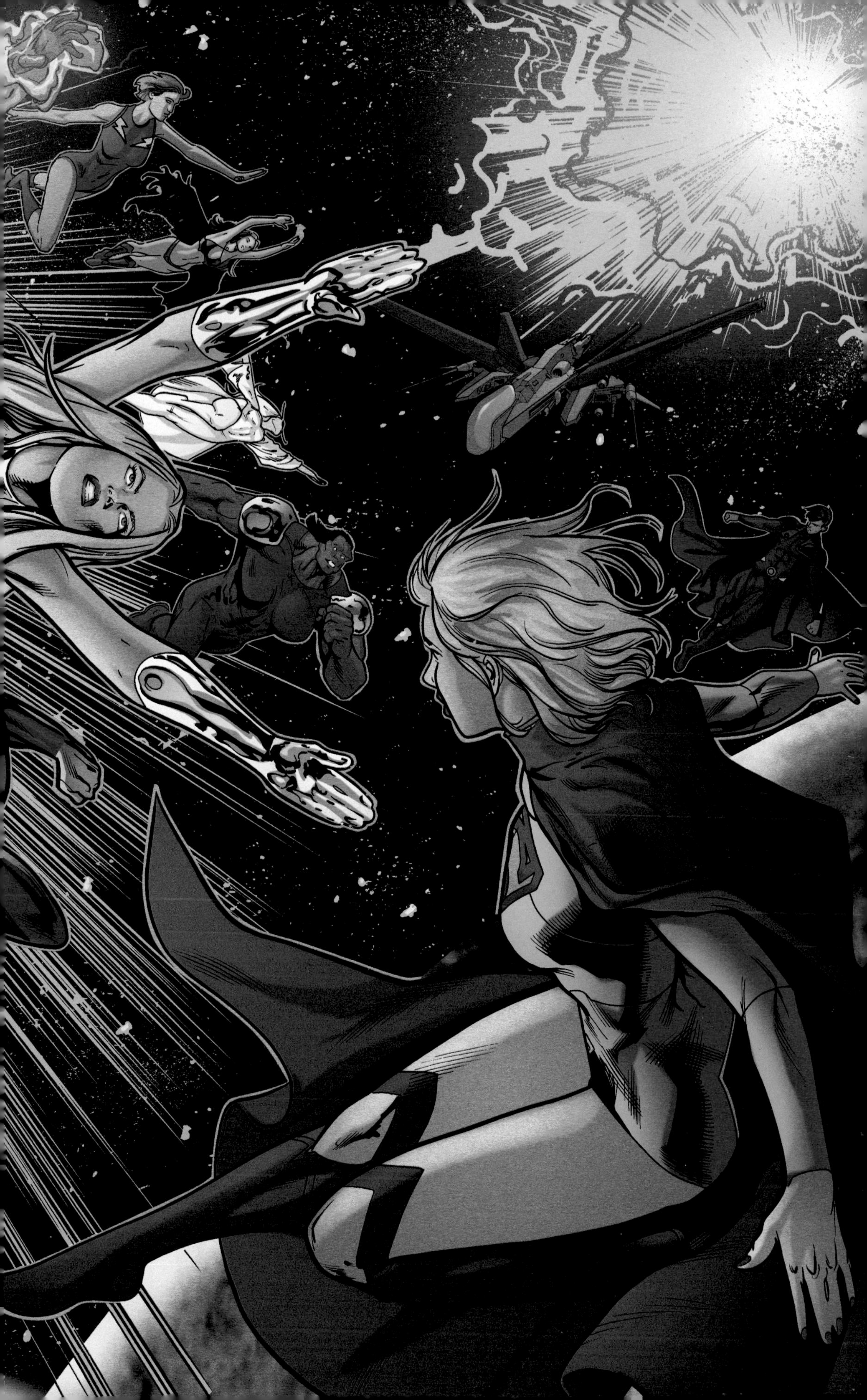

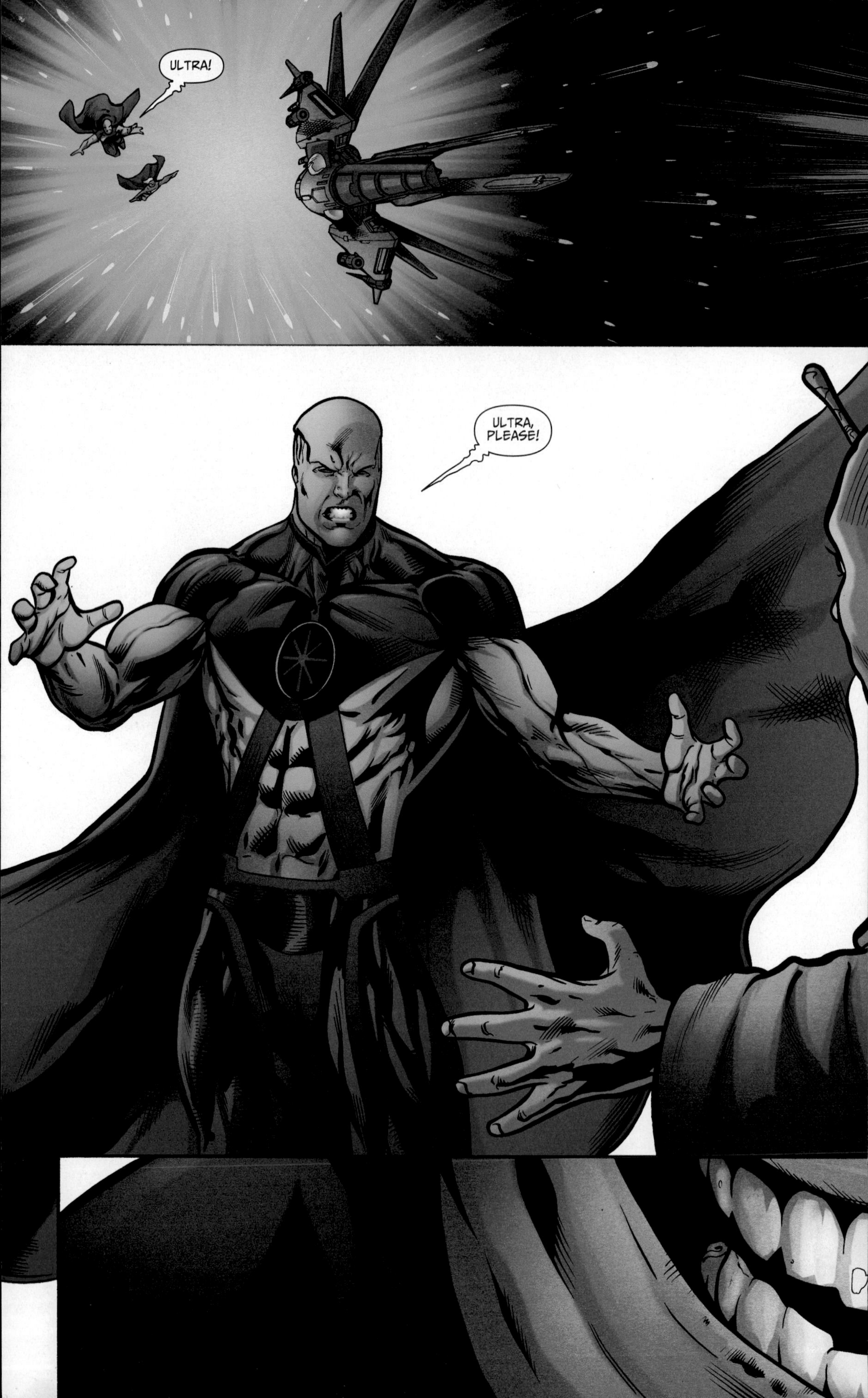
ULTRA!
ULTRA, PLEASE!

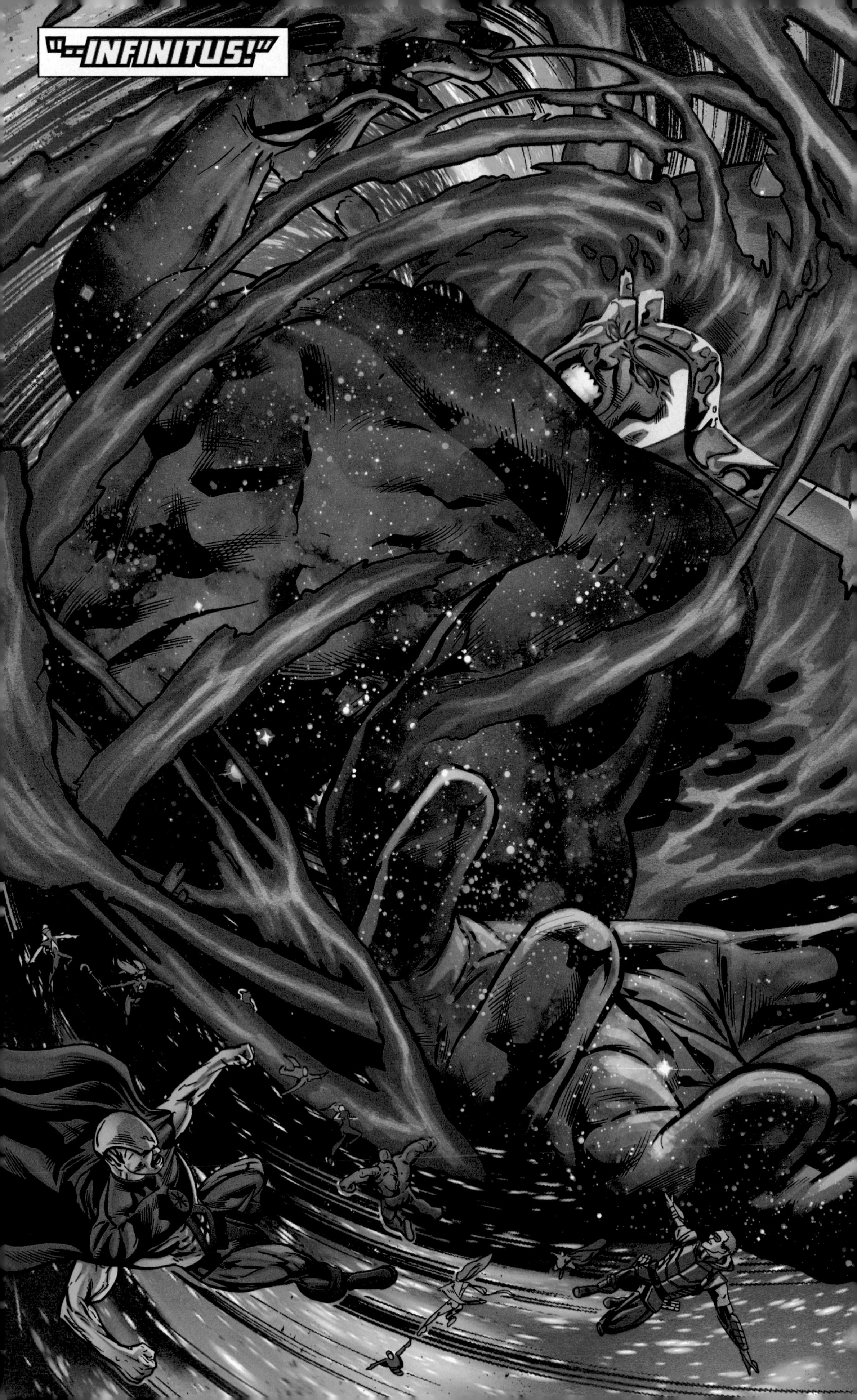
"--INFINITUS!"

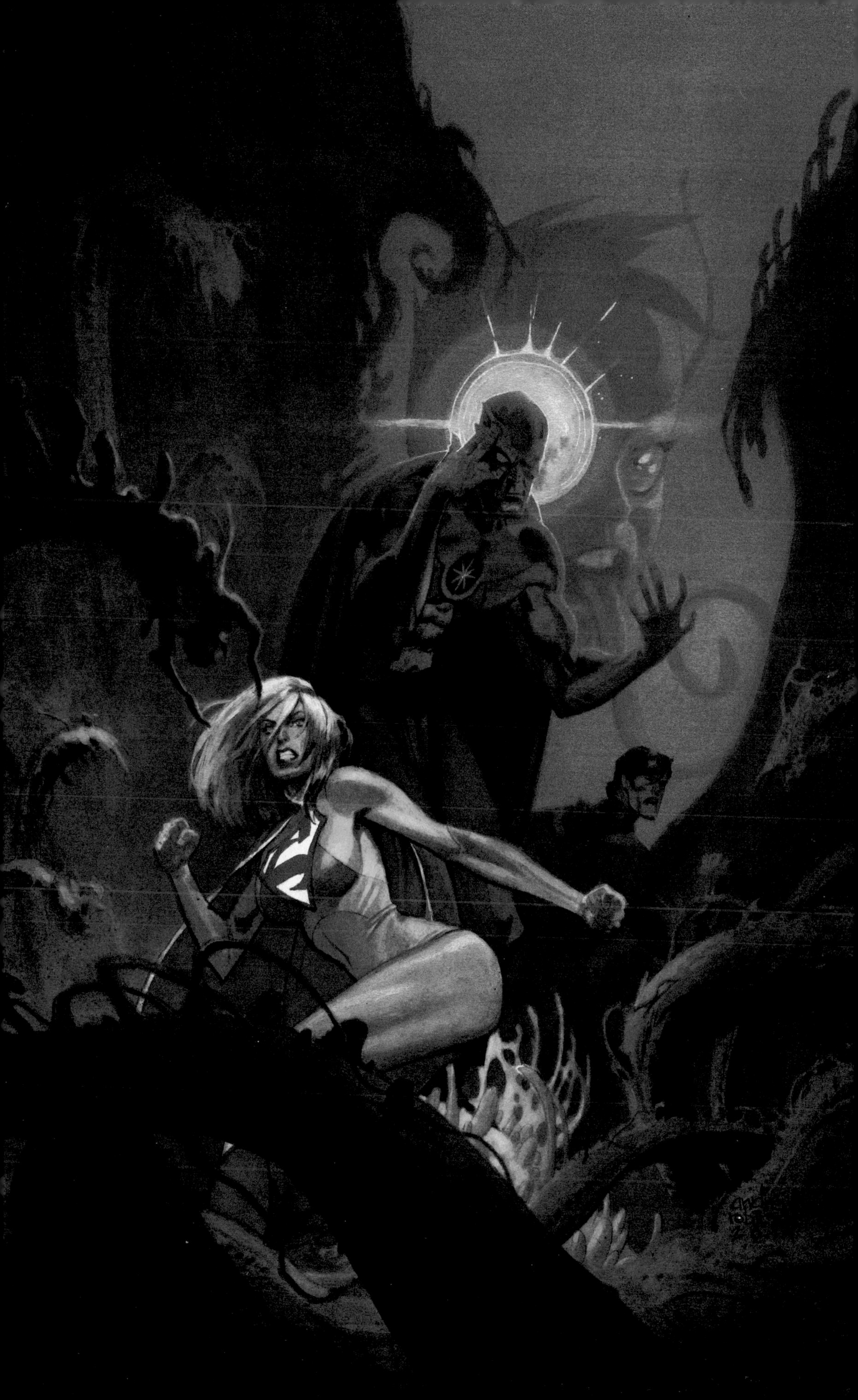

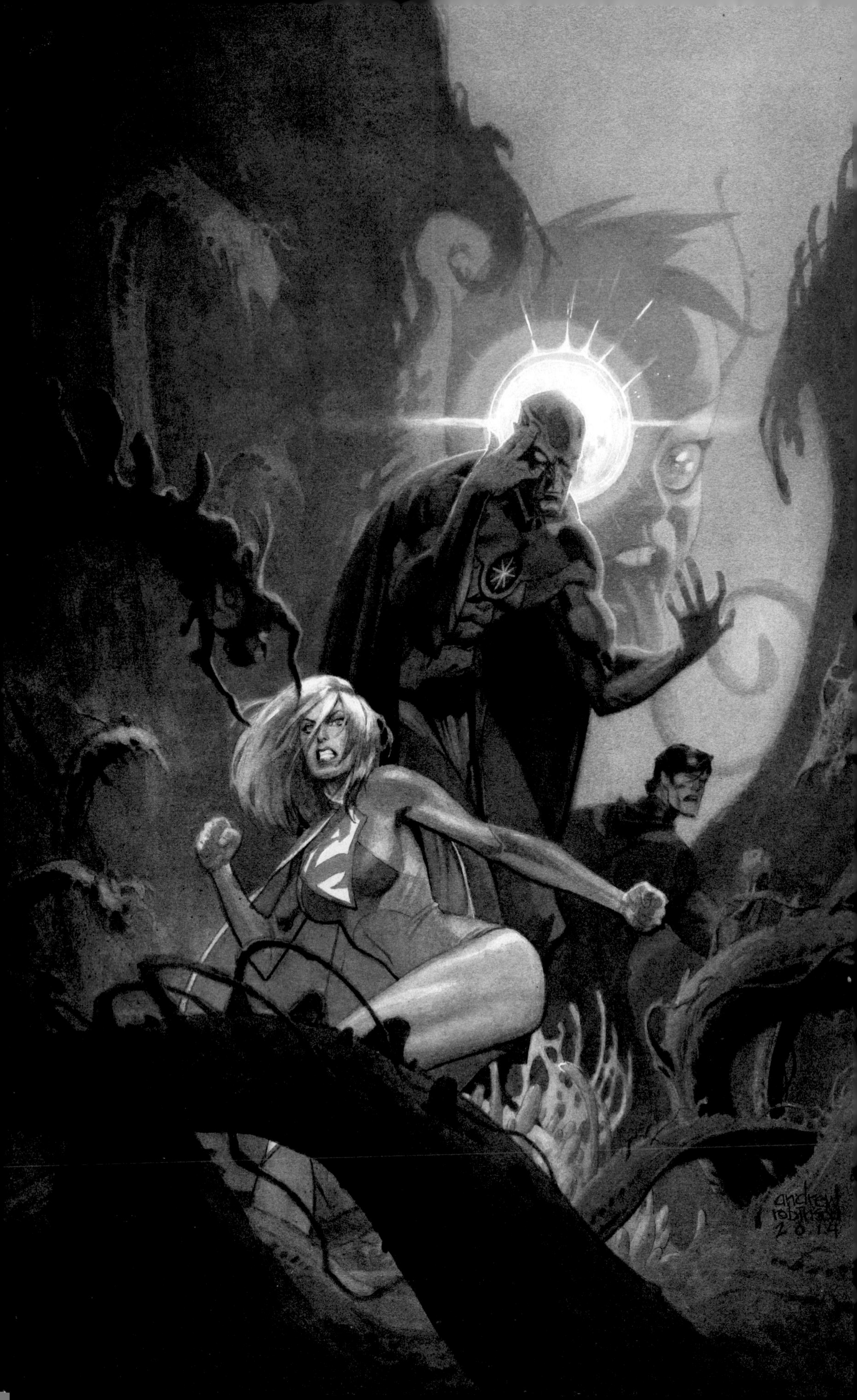
andrew robinson 2014

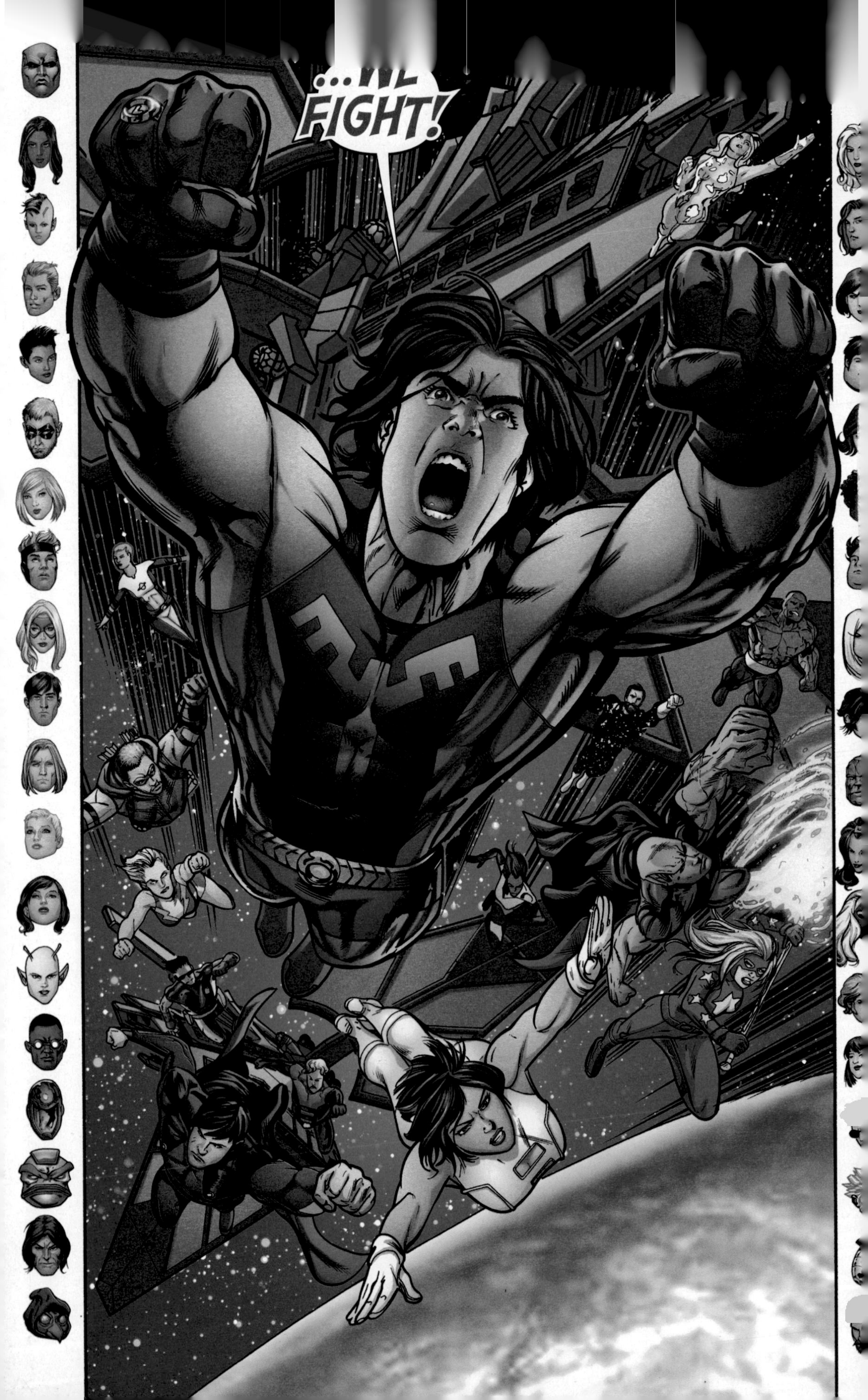
FIGHT!

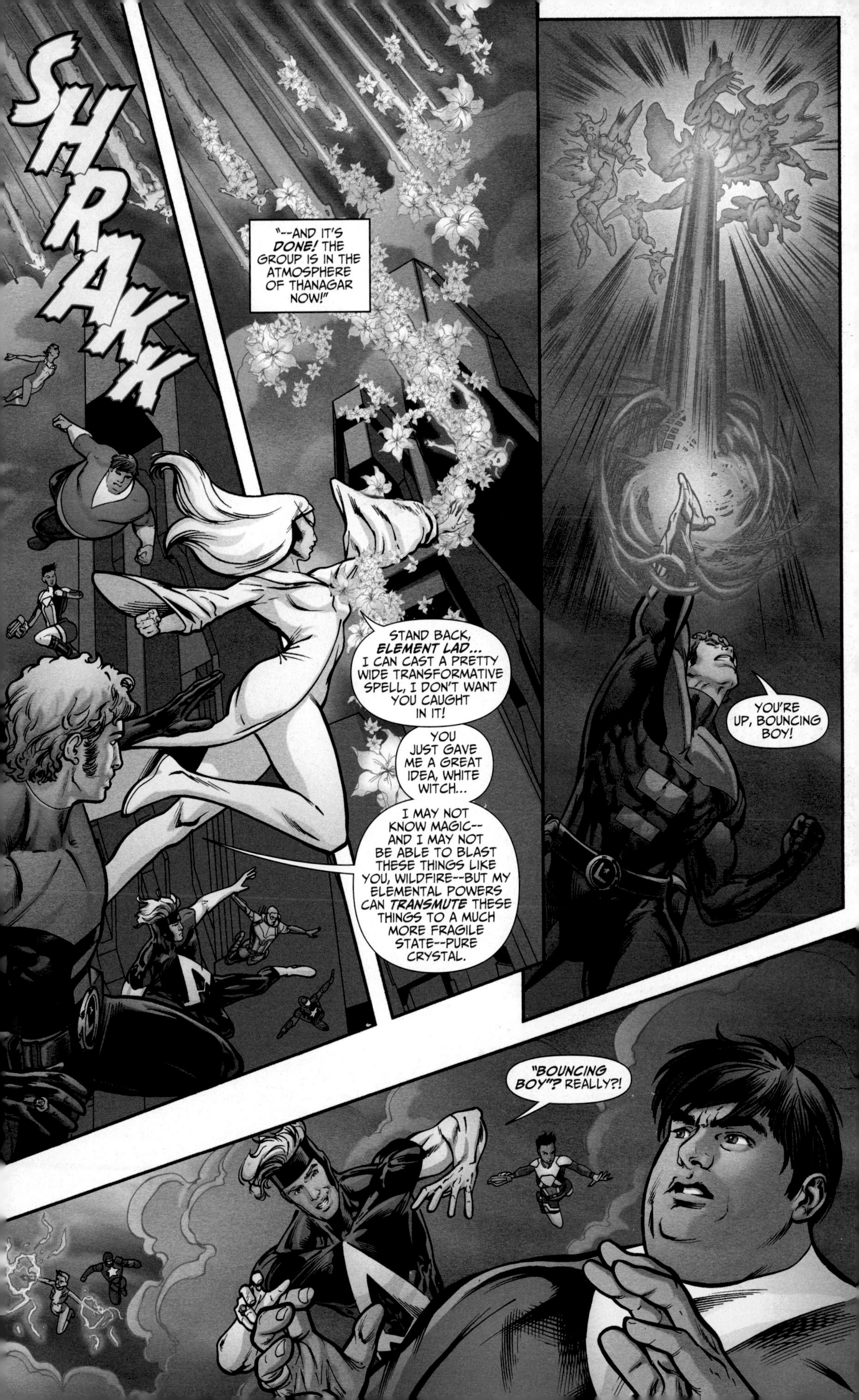
SHRAKK
"--AND IT'S DONE! THE GROUP IS IN THE ATMOSPHERE OF THANAGAR NOW!"
STAND BACK, ELEMENT LAD... I CAN CAST A PRETTY WIDE TRANSFORMATIVE SPELL, I DON'T WANT YOU CAUGHT IN IT!
YOU JUST GAVE ME A GREAT IDEA, WHITE WITCH...
I MAY NOT KNOW MAGIC-- AND I MAY NOT BE ABLE TO BLAST THESE THINGS LIKE YOU, WILDFIRE--BUT MY ELEMENTAL POWERS CAN TRANSMUTE THESE THINGS TO A MUCH MORE FRAGILE STATE--PURE CRYSTAL.
YOU'RE UP, BOUNCING BOY!
"BOUNCING BOY"? REALLY?!

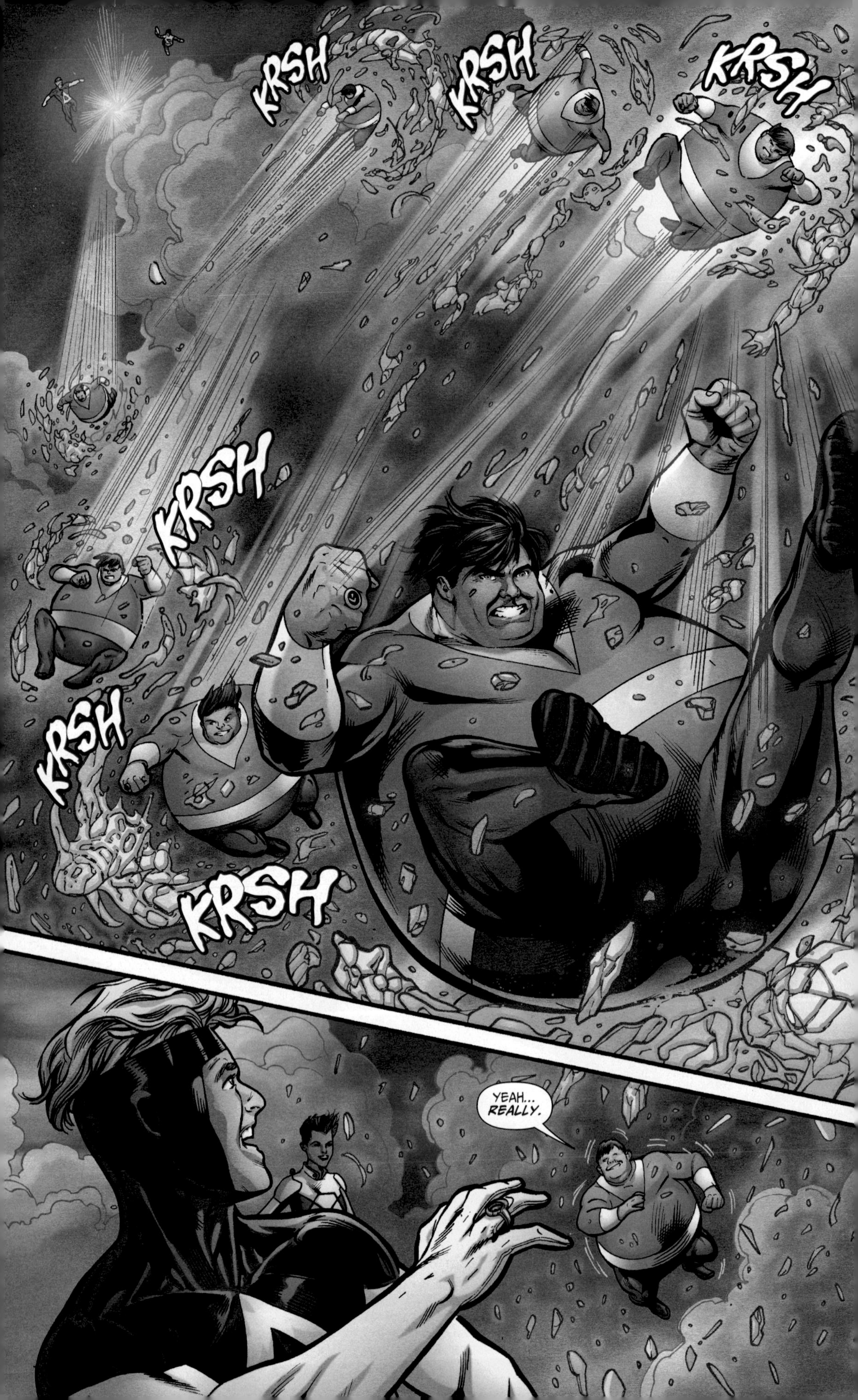
KRSH
KRSH
KRSH
KRSH
KRSH
KRSH
YEAH... REALLY.

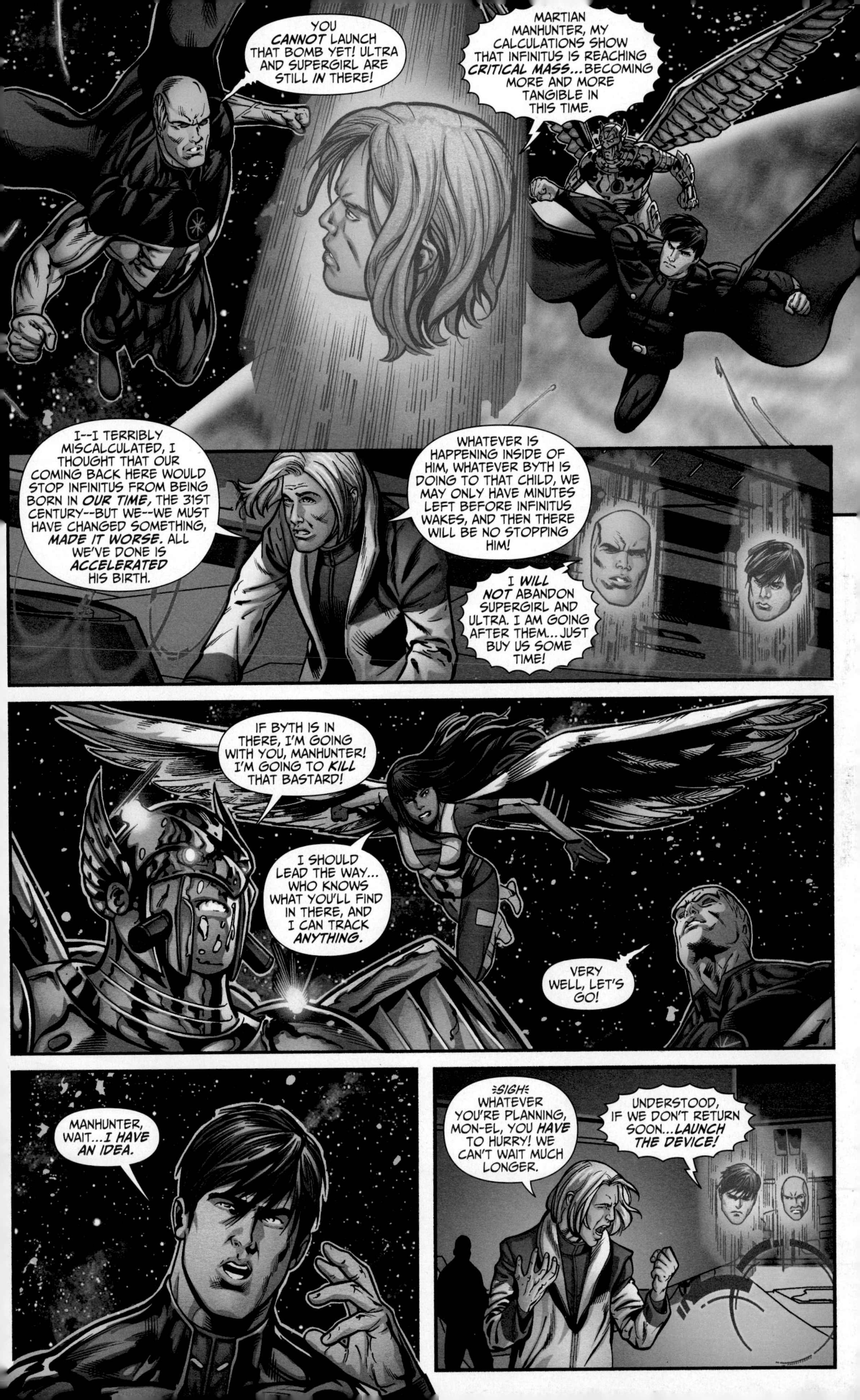
YOU CANNOT LAUNCH THAT BOMB YET! ULTRA AND SUPERGIRL ARE STILL IN THERE!
MARTIAN MANHUNTER, MY CALCULATIONS SHOW THAT INFINITUS IS REACHING CRITICAL MASS...BECOMING MORE AND MORE TANGIBLE IN THIS TIME.
I--I TERRIBLY MISCALCULATED, I THOUGHT THAT OUR COMING BACK HERE WOULD STOP INFINITUS FROM BEING BORN IN OUR TIME, THE 31ST CENTURY--BUT WE--WE MUST HAVE CHANGED SOMETHING, MADE IT WORSE. ALL WE'VE DONE IS ACCELERATED HIS BIRTH.
WHATEVER IS HAPPENING INSIDE OF HIM, WHATEVER BYTH IS DOING TO THAT CHILD, WE MAY ONLY HAVE MINUTES LEFT BEFORE INFINITUS WAKES, AND THEN THERE WILL BE NO STOPPING HIM!
I WILL NOT ABANDON SUPERGIRL AND ULTRA. I AM GOING AFTER THEM...JUST BUY US SOME TIME!
IF BYTH IS IN THERE, I'M GOING WITH YOU, MANHUNTER! I'M GOING TO KILL THAT BASTARD!
I SHOULD LEAD THE WAY... WHO KNOWS WHAT YOU'LL FIND IN THERE, AND I CAN TRACK ANYTHING.
VERY WELL, LET'S GO!
MANHUNTER, WAIT...I HAVE AN IDEA.
SIGH WHATEVER YOU'RE PLANNING, MON-EL, YOU HAVE TO HURRY! WE CAN'T WAIT MUCH LONGER.
UNDERSTOOD, IF WE DON'T RETURN SOON...LAUNCH THE DEVICE!

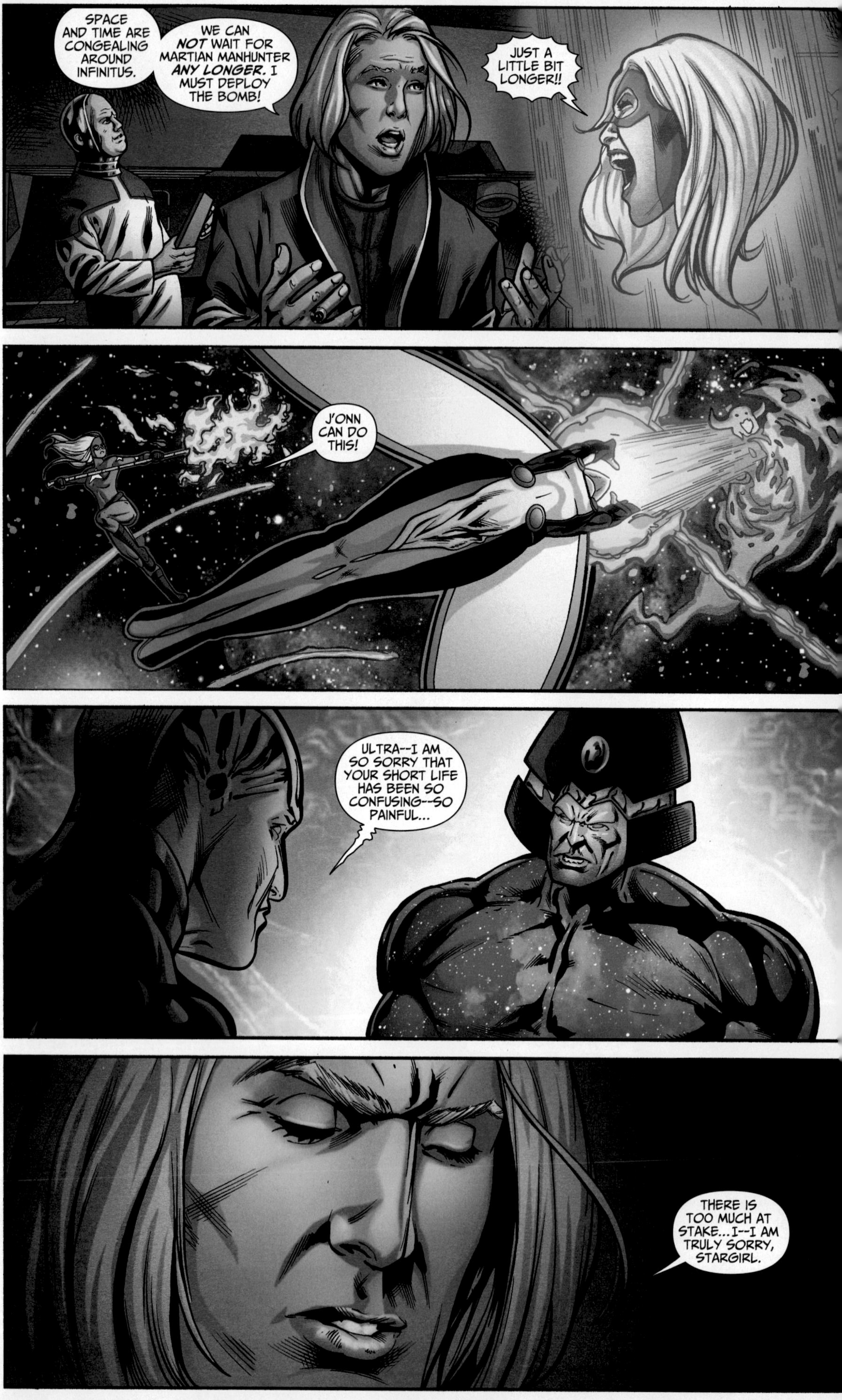
SPACE AND TIME ARE CONGEALING AROUND INFINITUS.
WE CAN NOT WAIT FOR MARTIAN MANHUNTER ANY LONGER. I MUST DEPLOY THE BOMB!
JUST A LITTLE BIT LONGER!!
J'ONN CAN DO THIS!
ULTRA--I AM SO SORRY THAT YOUR SHORT LIFE HAS BEEN SO CONFUSING--SO PAINFUL...
THERE IS TOO MUCH AT STAKE... I--I AM TRULY SORRY, STARGIRL.

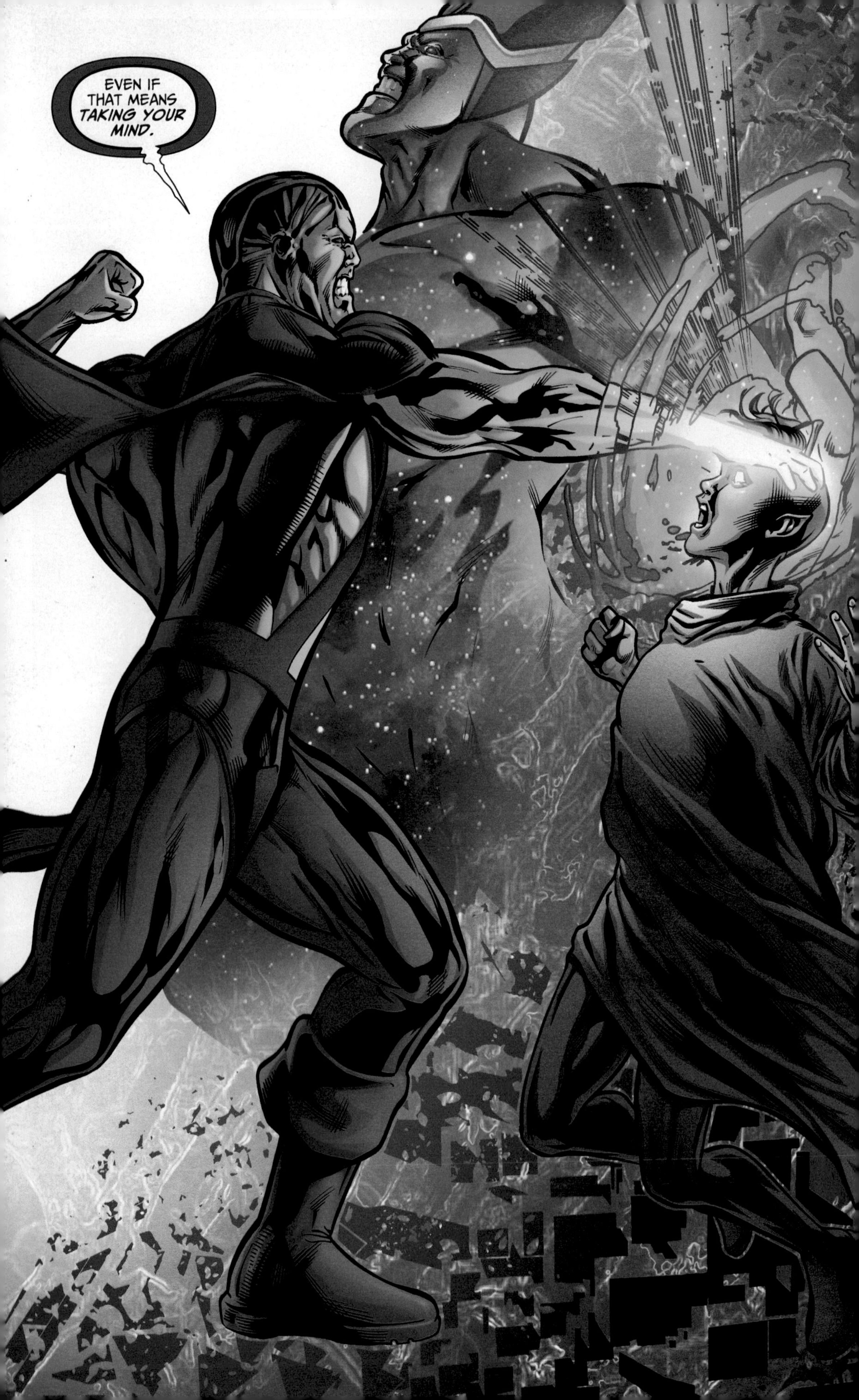
EVEN IF THAT MEANS *TAKING YOUR MIND.*

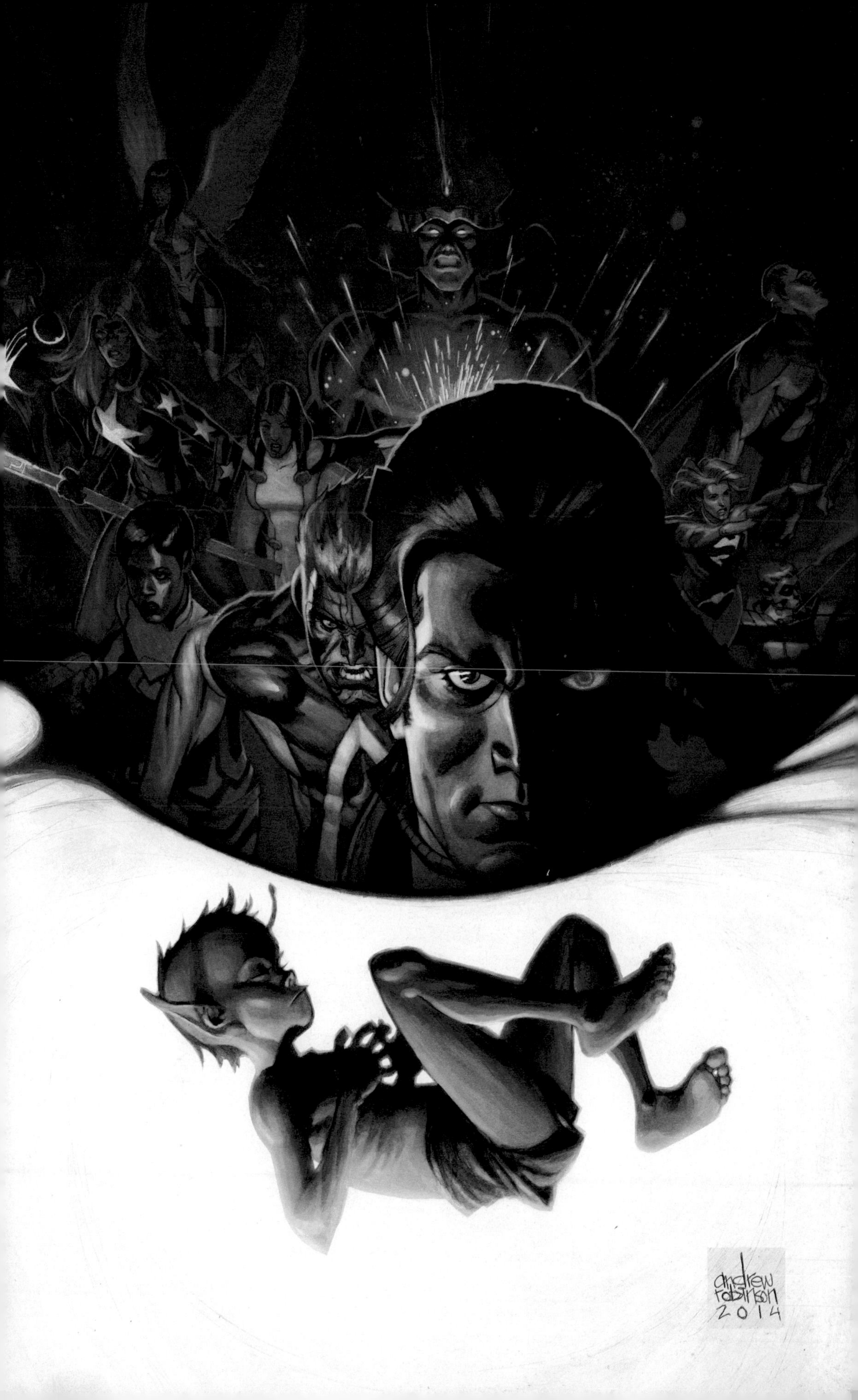
andrew robinson
2014

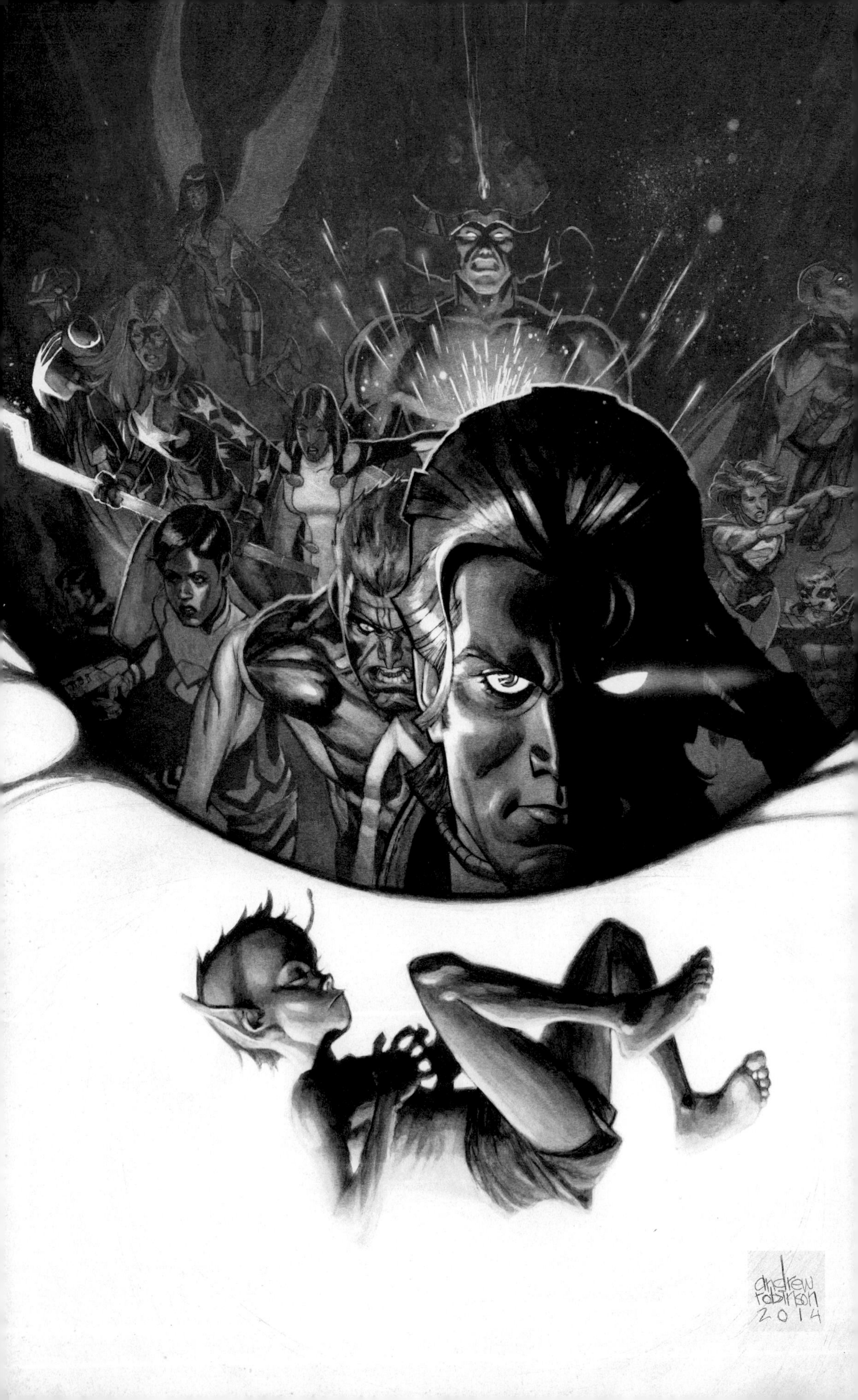
andrew robinson 2014

MOVE THE PLANET?! THAT'S *ABSURD*.

YOU ARE CORRECT, MARTIAN MANHUNTER. THAT *IS* ABSURD--

MAYBE NOT.

WHAT DO YOU MEAN?

I *MEAN*, THE *ZETA BEAM*. HOW MUCH MORE OBVIOUS COULD IT BE, SARDATH?

BUT THE ZETA BEAM ISN'T POWERFUL ENOUGH TO--

SHHH! I'M WORKING--

DON'T SHUSH ME!

HOW MANY SHIPS DOES RANN HAVE THAT ARE EQUIPPED WITH ZETA-TECH!?

SEVERAL THOUSAND THROUGHOUT THE GALAXY, BUT--

WE NEED THEM ALL HERE *NOW*. HAVE HALF OF THEM ZETA-BEAM IN ORBIT ABOVE THANAGAR'S NORTH POLE, THE OTHER HALF ABOVE THE SOUTH POLE!

BUT EVEN THAT WOULDN'T--

SNAP

NOW! THE BLACK HOLE IS GROWING! DON'T YOU SEE--THIS IS MY FAULT! I HAVE TO FIX THIS!

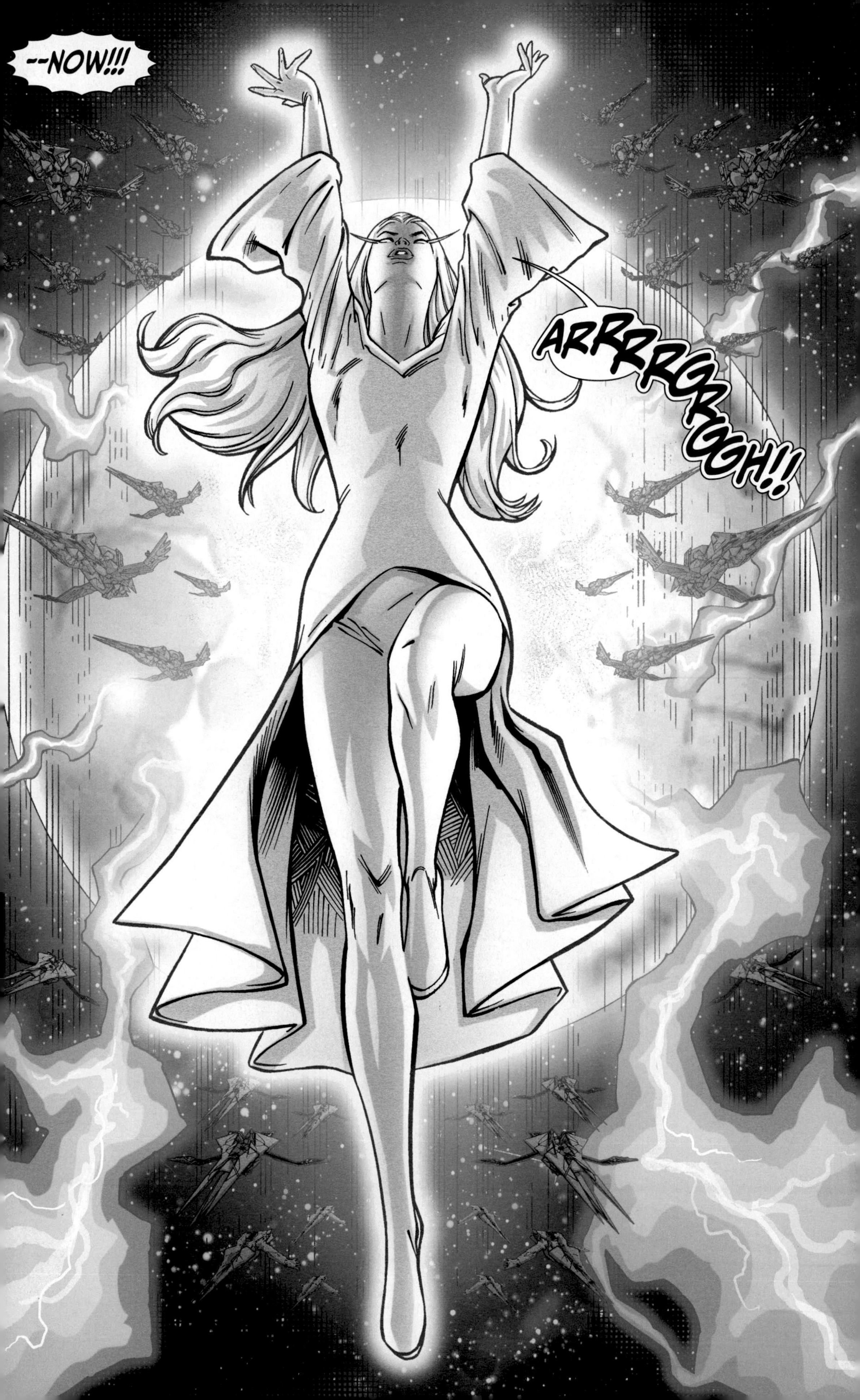
--NOW!!!
ARRRRRGRRGGH!!

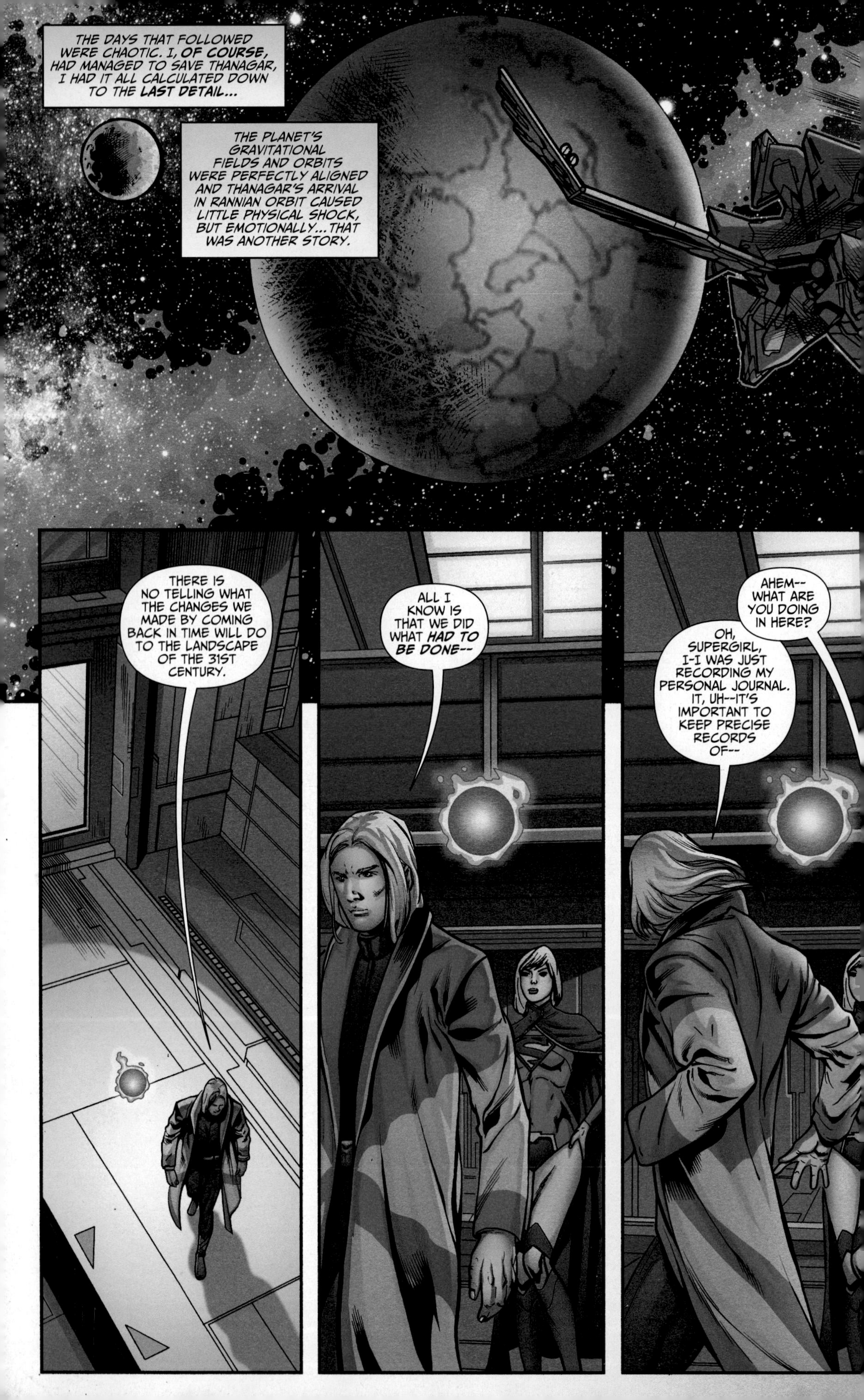
THE DAYS THAT FOLLOWED WERE CHAOTIC. I, OF COURSE, HAD MANAGED TO SAVE THANAGAR, I HAD IT ALL CALCULATED DOWN TO THE LAST DETAIL...
THE PLANET'S GRAVITATIONAL FIELDS AND ORBITS WERE PERFECTLY ALIGNED AND THANAGAR'S ARRIVAL IN RANNIAN ORBIT CAUSED LITTLE PHYSICAL SHOCK, BUT EMOTIONALLY...THAT WAS ANOTHER STORY.
THERE IS NO TELLING WHAT THE CHANGES WE MADE BY COMING BACK IN TIME WILL DO TO THE LANDSCAPE OF THE 31ST CENTURY.
ALL I KNOW IS THAT WE DID WHAT HAD TO BE DONE--
AHEM--WHAT ARE YOU DOING IN HERE?
OH, SUPERGIRL, I-I WAS JUST RECORDING MY PERSONAL JOURNAL. IT, UH--IT'S IMPORTANT TO KEEP PRECISE RECORDS OF--

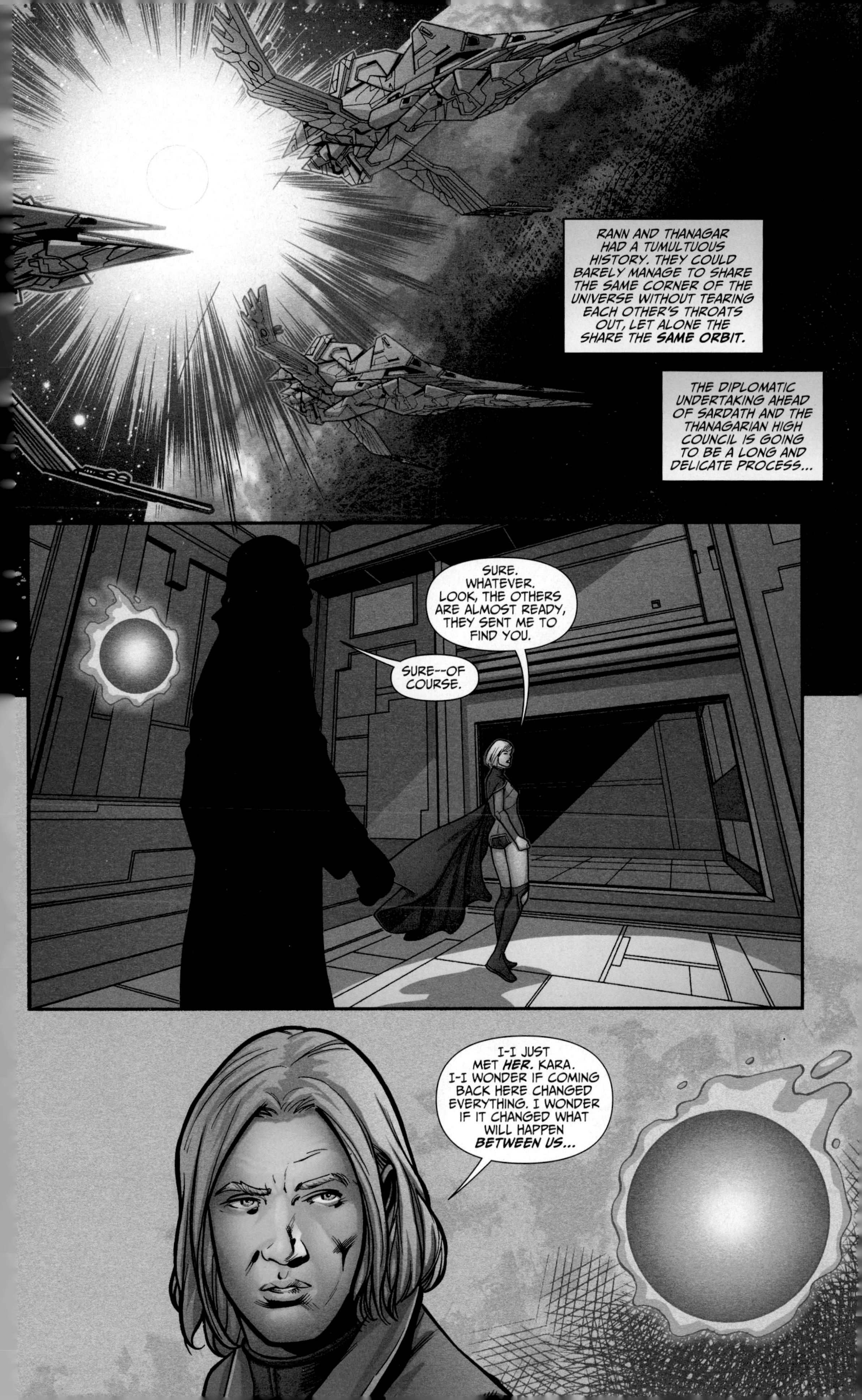
RANN AND THANAGAR HAD A TUMULTUOUS HISTORY. THEY COULD BARELY MANAGE TO SHARE THE SAME CORNER OF THE UNIVERSE WITHOUT TEARING EACH OTHER'S THROATS OUT, LET ALONE THE SHARE THE SAME ORBIT.
THE DIPLOMATIC UNDERTAKING AHEAD OF SARDATH AND THE THANAGARIAN HIGH COUNCIL IS GOING TO BE A LONG AND DELICATE PROCESS...
SURE. WHATEVER. LOOK, THE OTHERS ARE ALMOST READY, THEY SENT ME TO FIND YOU.
SURE--OF COURSE.
I-I JUST MET HER. KARA. I-I WONDER IF COMING BACK HERE CHANGED EVERYTHING. I WONDER IF IT CHANGED WHAT WILL HAPPEN BETWEEN US...

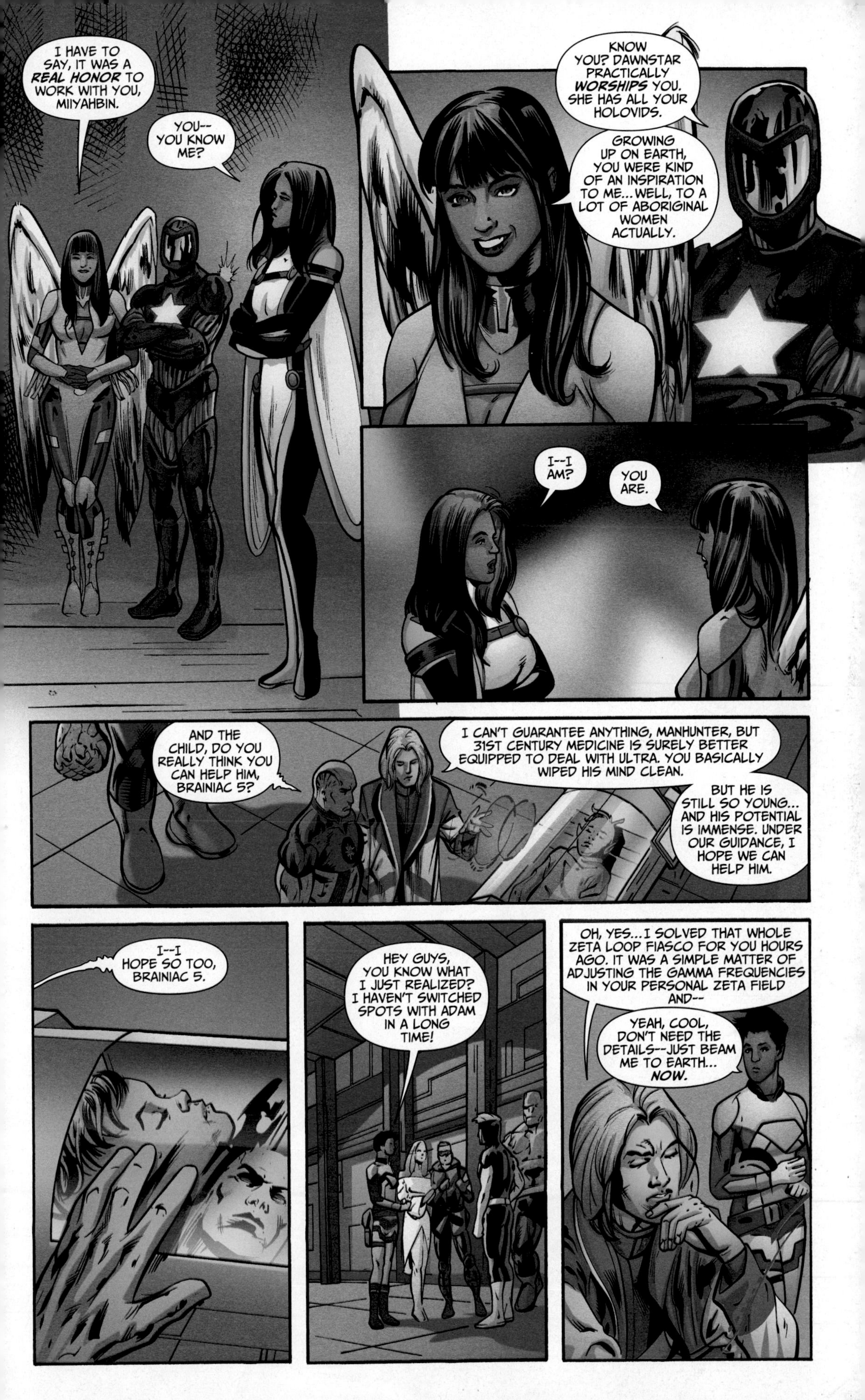
I HAVE TO SAY, IT WAS A REAL HONOR TO WORK WITH YOU, MIIYAHBIN.
YOU-- YOU KNOW ME?
KNOW YOU? DAWNSTAR PRACTICALLY WORSHIPS YOU. SHE HAS ALL YOUR HOLOVIDS.
GROWING UP ON EARTH, YOU WERE KIND OF AN INSPIRATION TO ME...WELL, TO A LOT OF ABORIGINAL WOMEN ACTUALLY.
I--I AM?
YOU ARE.
AND THE CHILD, DO YOU REALLY THINK YOU CAN HELP HIM, BRAINIAC 5?
I CAN'T GUARANTEE ANYTHING, MANHUNTER, BUT 31ST CENTURY MEDICINE IS SURELY BETTER EQUIPPED TO DEAL WITH ULTRA. YOU BASICALLY WIPED HIS MIND CLEAN.
BUT HE IS STILL SO YOUNG... AND HIS POTENTIAL IS IMMENSE. UNDER OUR GUIDANCE, I HOPE WE CAN HELP HIM.
I--I HOPE SO TOO, BRAINIAC 5.
HEY GUYS, YOU KNOW WHAT I JUST REALIZED? I HAVEN'T SWITCHED SPOTS WITH ADAM IN A LONG TIME!
OH, YES...I SOLVED THAT WHOLE ZETA LOOP FIASCO FOR YOU HOURS AGO. IT WAS A SIMPLE MATTER OF ADJUSTING THE GAMMA FREQUENCIES IN YOUR PERSONAL ZETA FIELD AND--
YEAH, COOL, DON'T NEED THE DETAILS--JUST BEAM ME TO EARTH... NOW.

WELL, THAT WAS FUN.

IT WAS?

IS HAWKMAN COMING?

HAWKMAN IS A DIPLOMAT?!

HE'S STAYING ON THANAGAR FOR A WHILE...HELPING WITH THE DIPLOMATIC DISCUSSIONS. BUT HE SAID HE'LL BE AROUND IF WE NEED HIM.

I KNOW, RIGHT?

SO...NOW WHAT?

NOW? NOW WE *GO HOME,* COURTNEY.

FWASH

UH...WE MAY WANT TO GIVE ALANNA AND ADAM SOME TIME ALONE.

WHY?

NEVER CHANGE, KID.

TO BE HONEST, I SHOULD PROBABLY GET BACK TO SEATTLE, SEE IF EVERYTHING IS COOL.

YEAH...I MISS ELLEN AND MAXINE. WANT ME TO FLY YOU HOME? WE CAN CATCH A TAILWIND IF WE LEAVE NOW.

⧽SIGH⧼, I REALLY NEED A JET PACK.

SO...UM...ARE WE--DONE? I MEAN IS THAT IT FOR OUR TEAM, OR...

I WAS THINKING WE SHOULD SET UP A REGULAR MONITOR DUTY SCHEDULE.

YES...AND I SUPPOSE I SHOULD CONTACT THE JUSTICE LEAGUE, LET THEM KNOW OF OUR AFFILIATION.

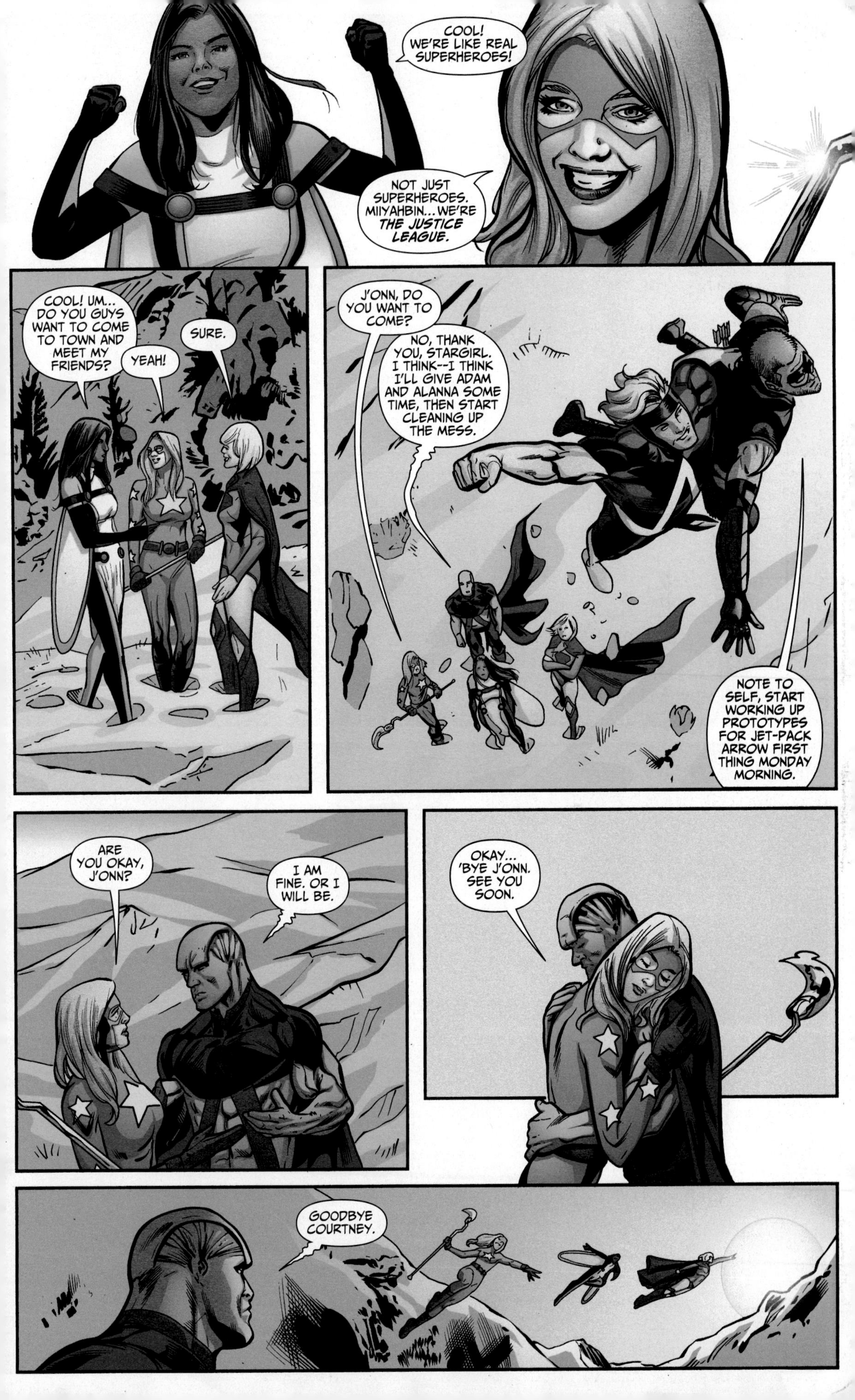
COOL! WE'RE LIKE REAL SUPERHEROES!
NOT JUST SUPERHEROES. MIIYAHBIN...WE'RE *THE JUSTICE LEAGUE.*
COOL! UM... DO YOU GUYS WANT TO COME TO TOWN AND MEET MY FRIENDS?
YEAH!
SURE.
J'ONN, DO YOU WANT TO COME?
NO, THANK YOU, STARGIRL. I THINK--I THINK I'LL GIVE ADAM AND ALANNA SOME TIME, THEN START CLEANING UP THE MESS.
NOTE TO SELF, START WORKING UP PROTOTYPES FOR JET-PACK ARROW FIRST THING MONDAY MORNING.
ARE YOU OKAY, J'ONN?
I AM FINE. OR I WILL BE.
OKAY... 'BYE J'ONN. SEE YOU SOON.
GOODBYE COURTNEY.

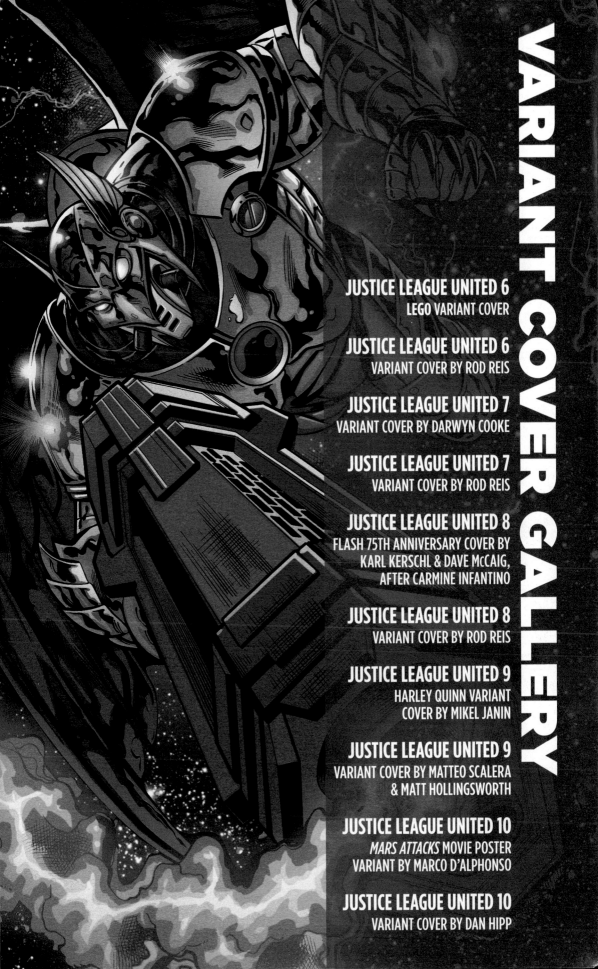

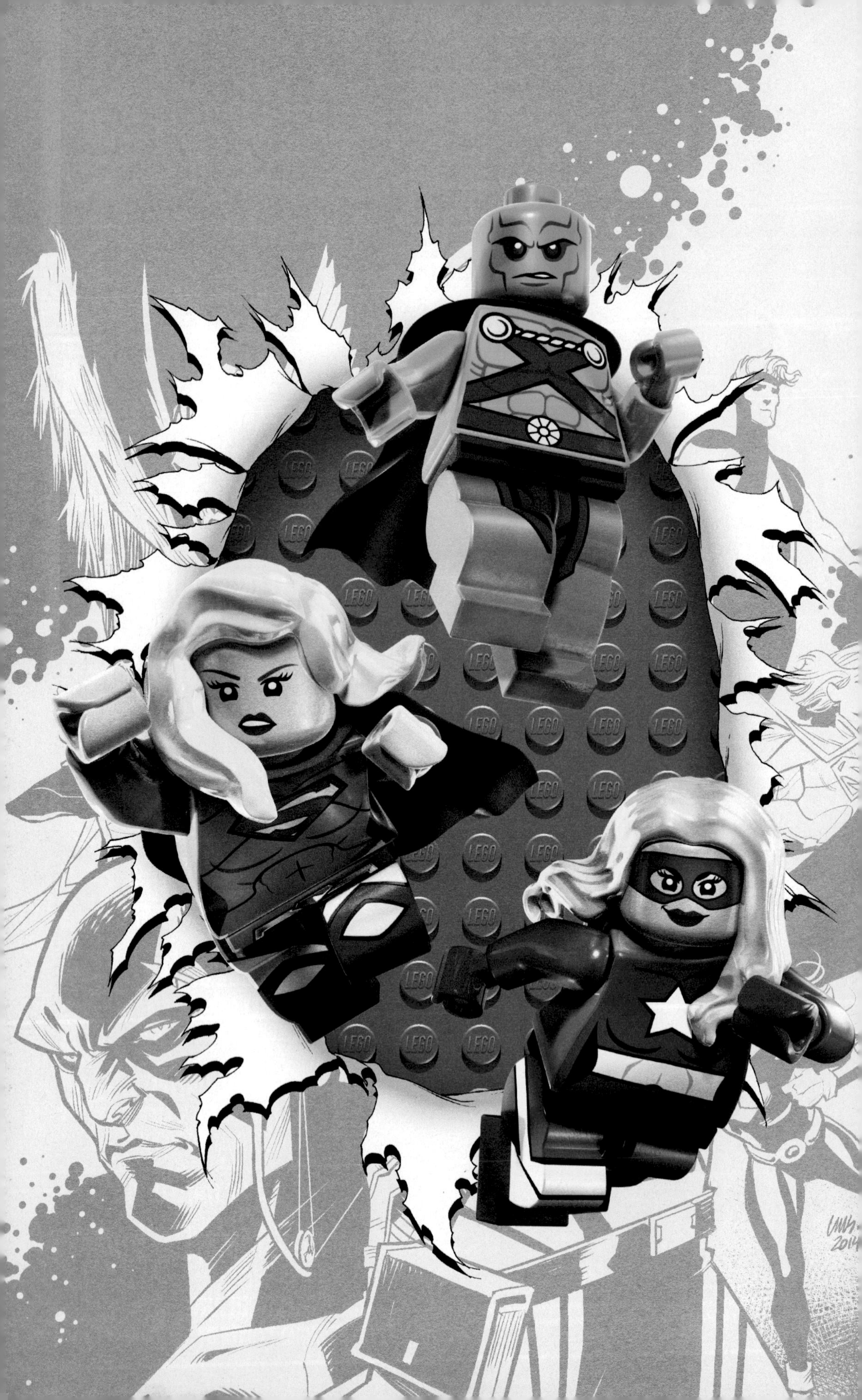

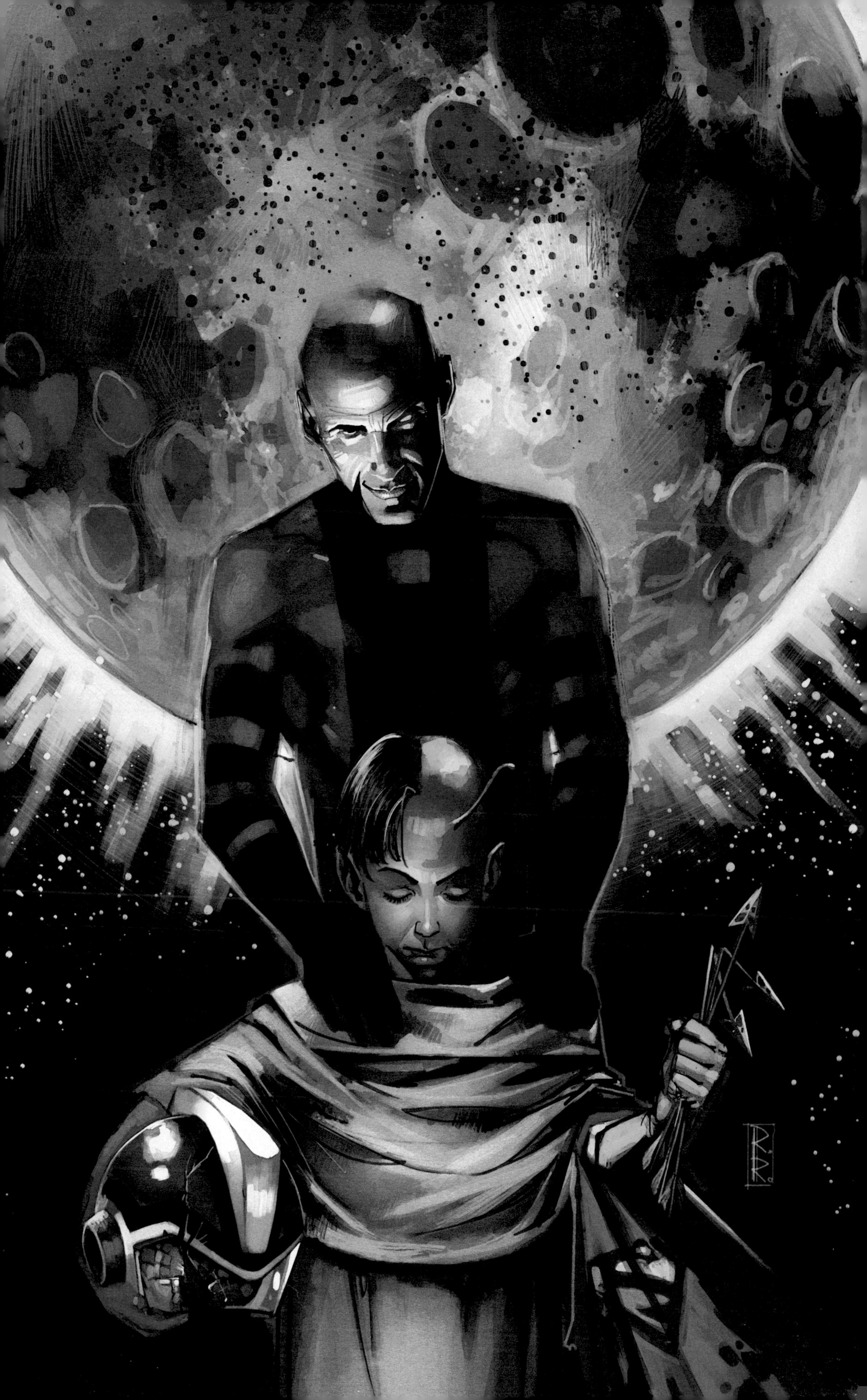

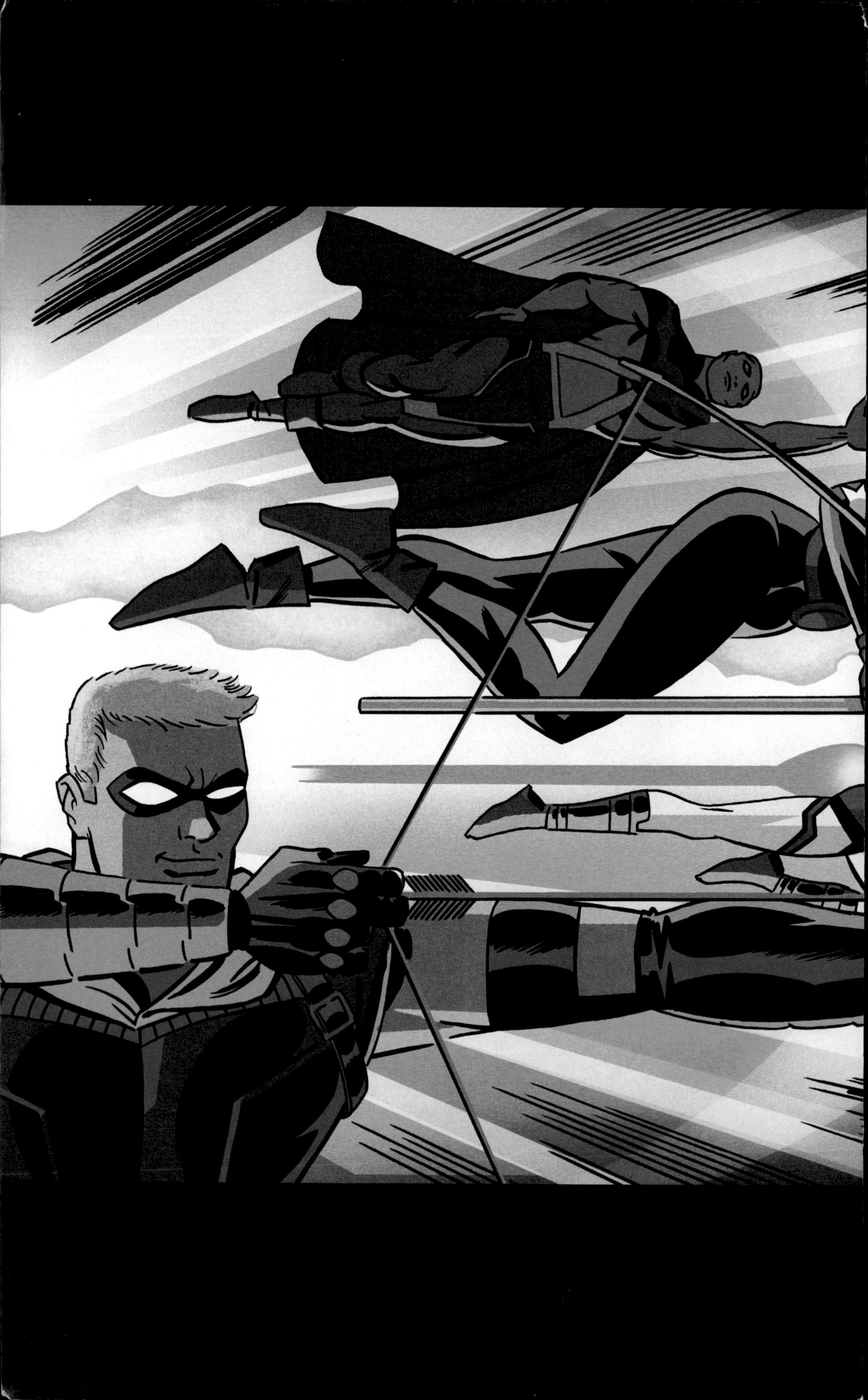

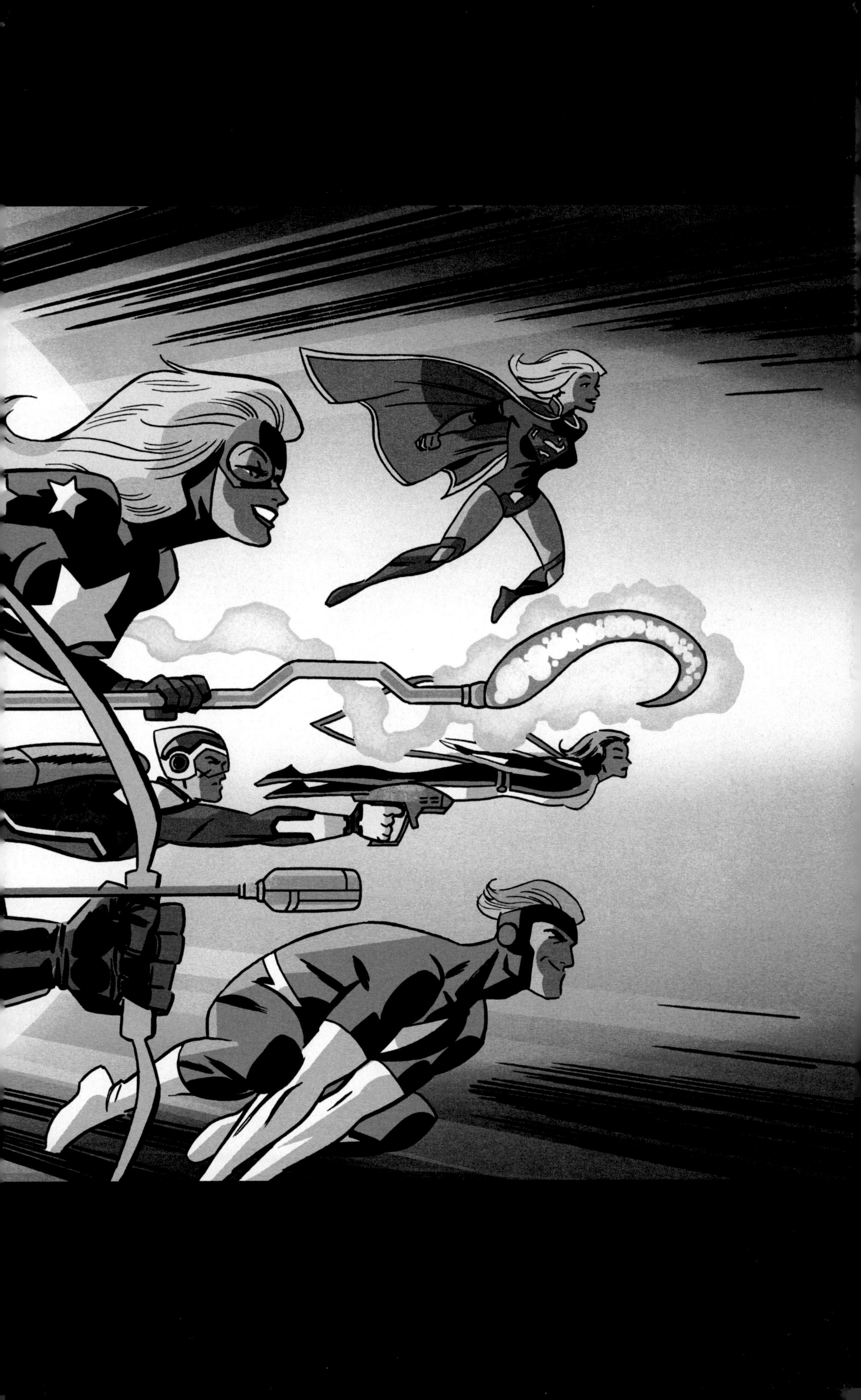

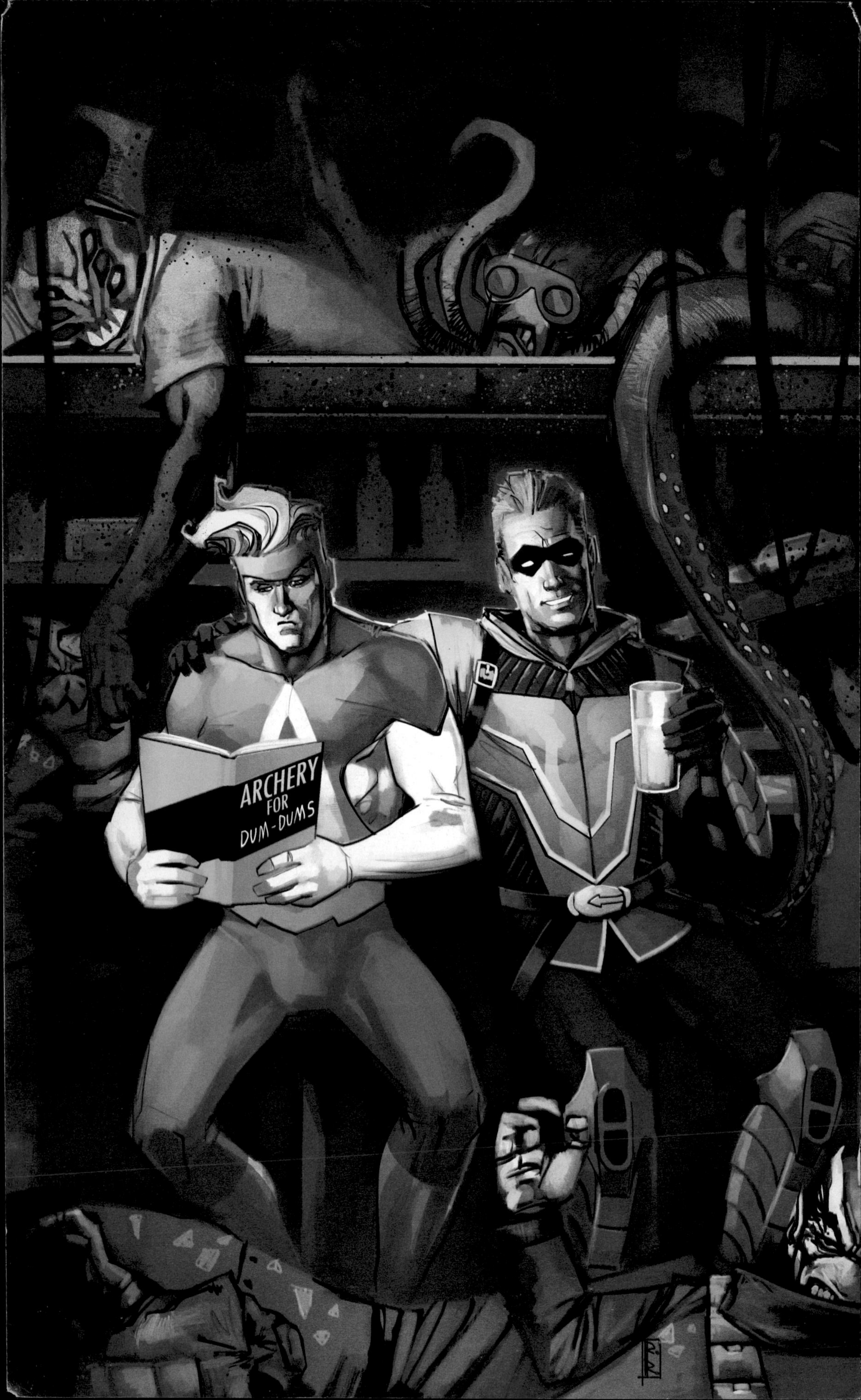
ARCHERY
FOR
DUM-DUMS

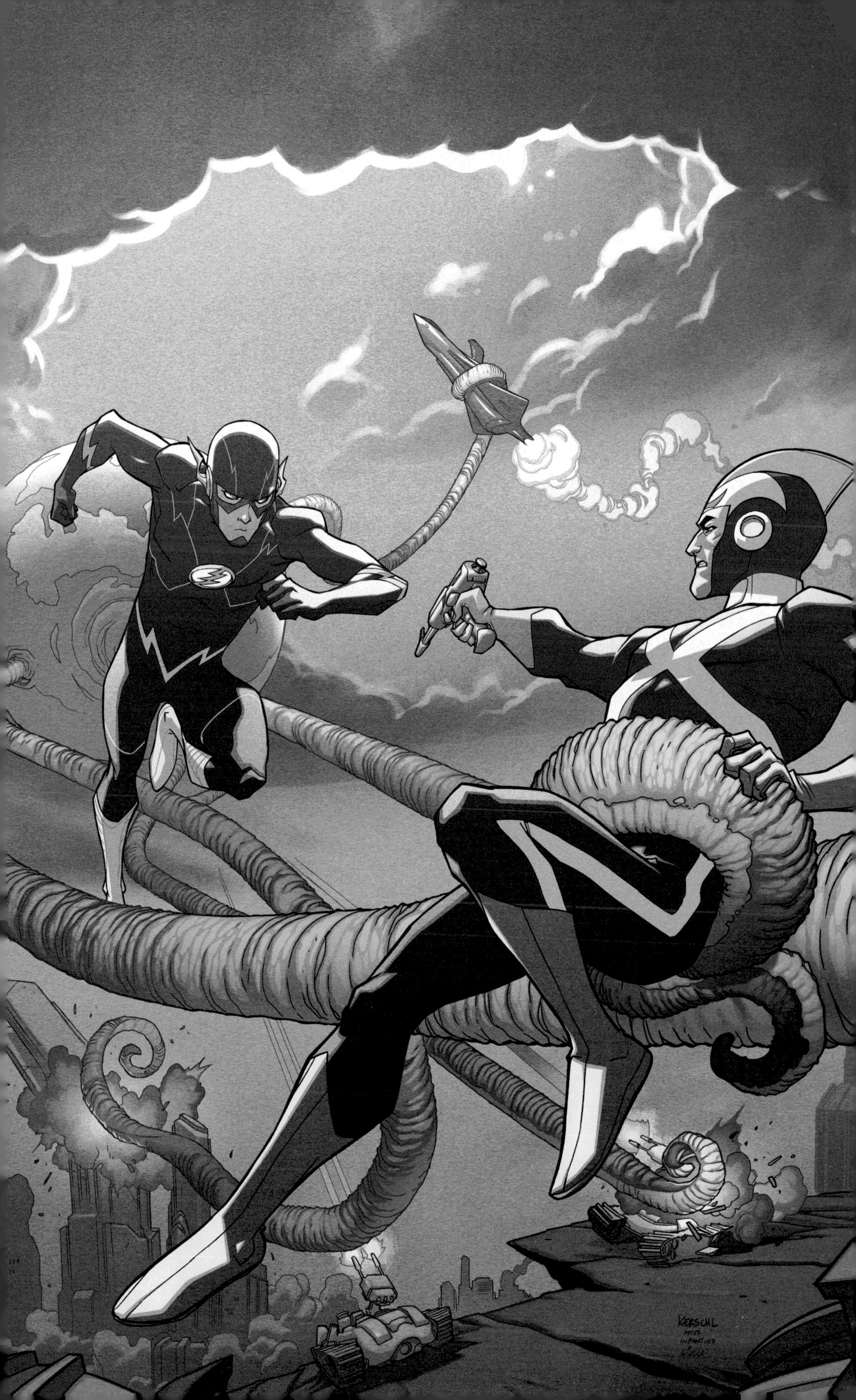
KERSCHL
AFTER
INFANTINO

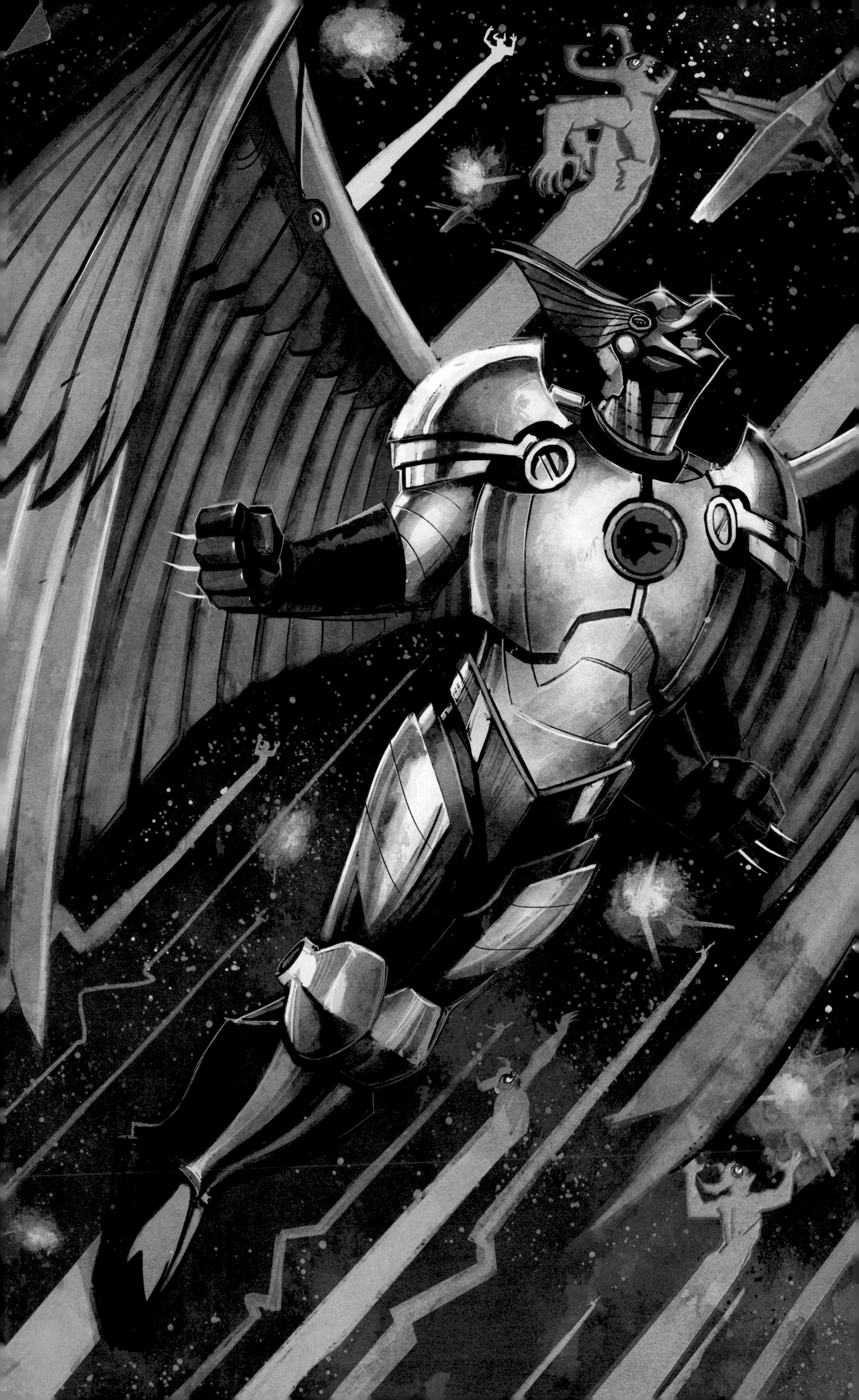

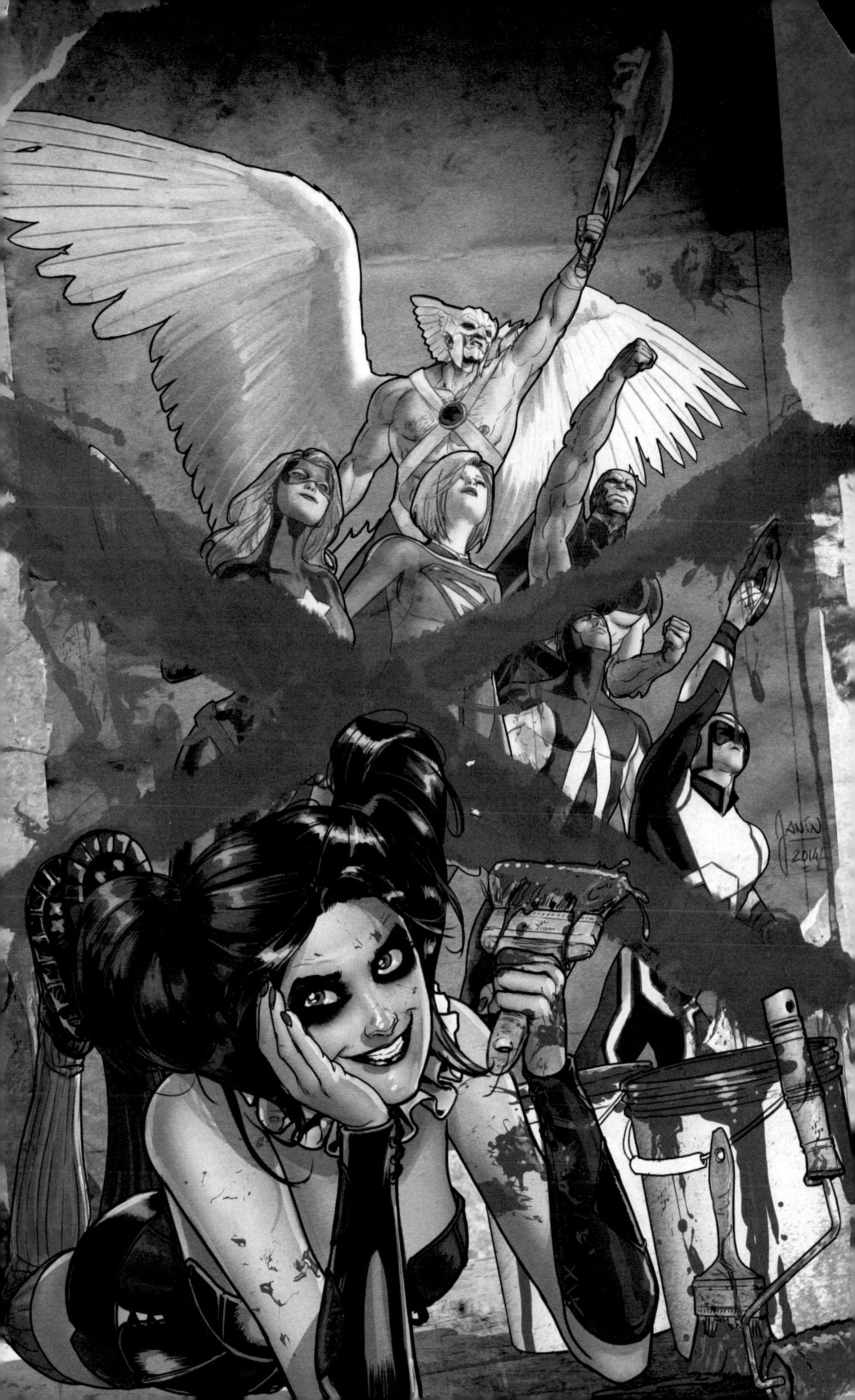
JANIN 2014

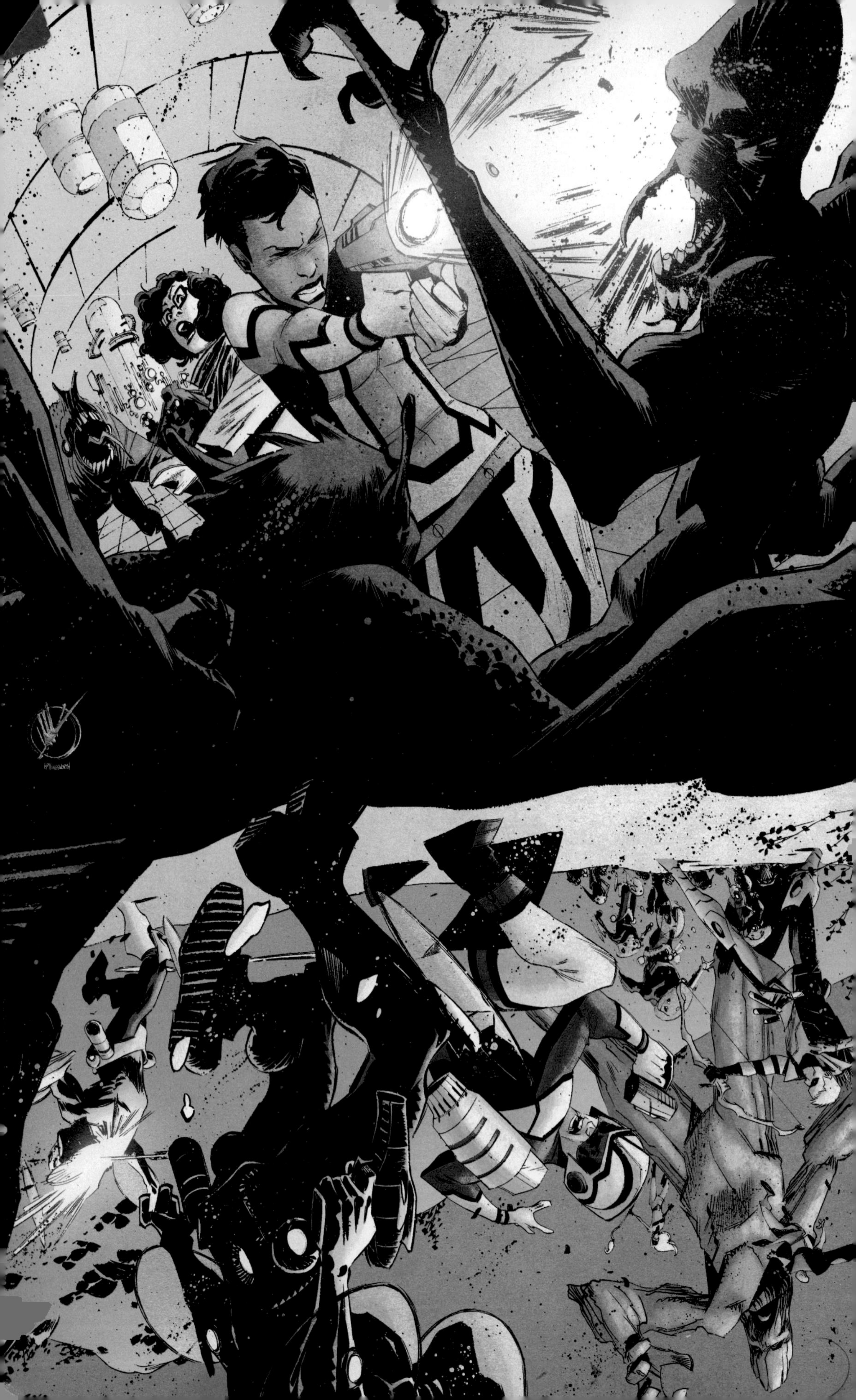

JEFF LEMIRE NEIL EDWARDS JAY LEISTEN JEROMY COX

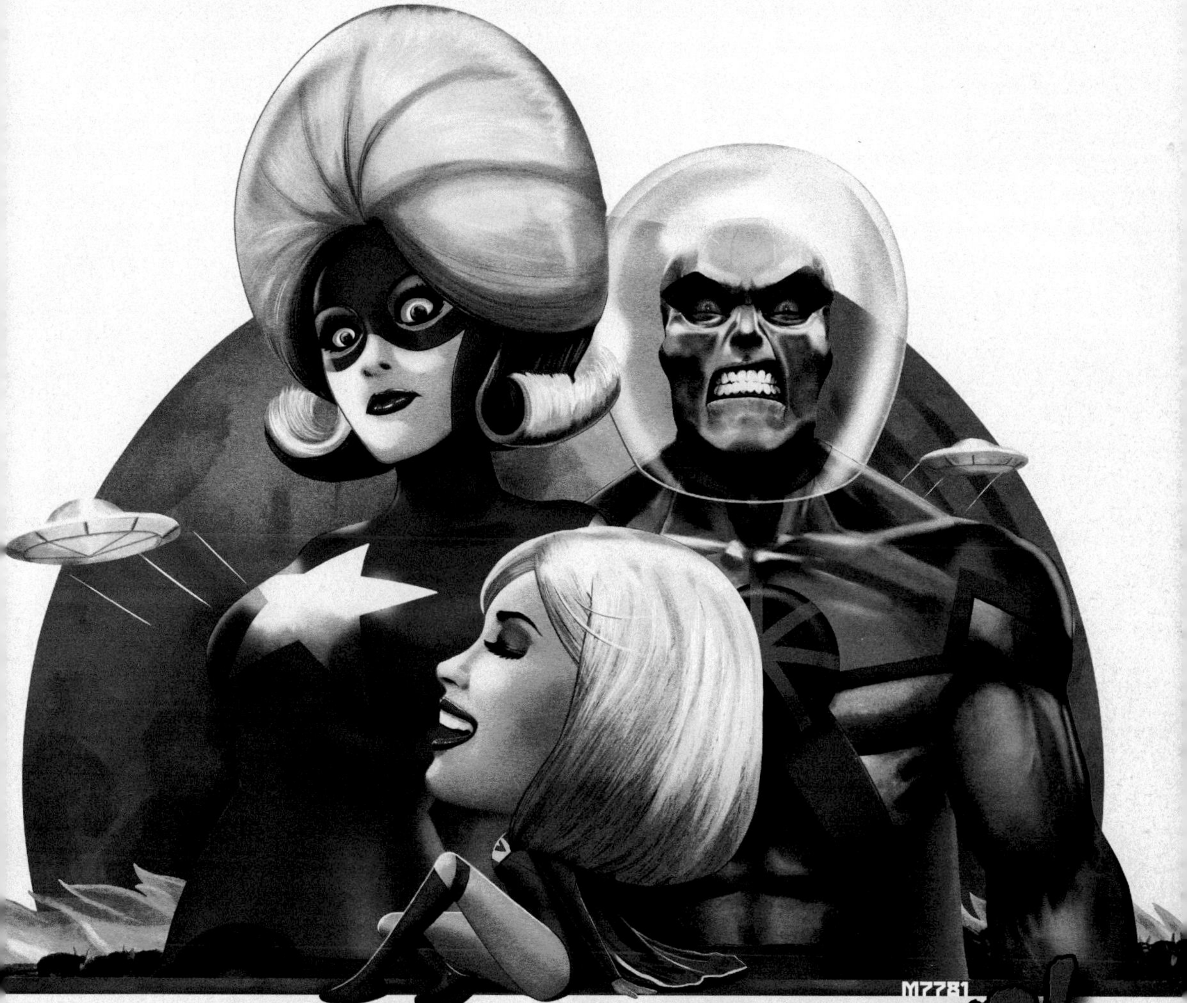

JUSTICE LEAGUE UNITED!™

NICE PLANET. WE'LL TAKE IT!

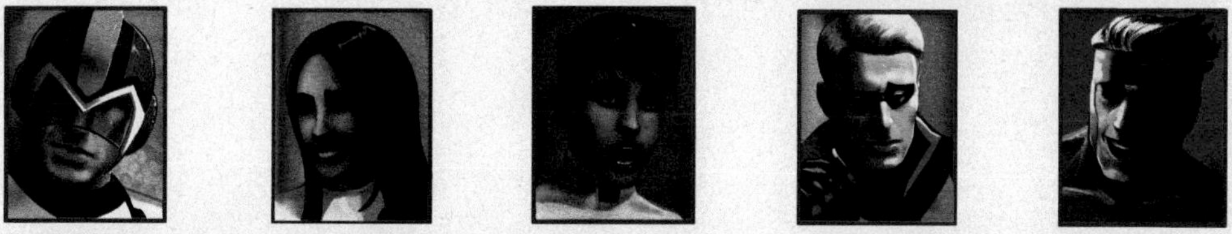

JUSTICE LEAGUE UNITED ISSUE TEN JEFF LEMIRE WRITER NEIL EDWARDS PENCILLER JAY LEISTEN INKER JEROMY COX COLORIST
TRAVIS LANHAM LETTERER MARCO D'ALFONSO MOVIE POSTER VARIANT COVER AMEDEO TURTURRO ASSISTANT EDITOR BRIAN CUNNINGHAM GROUP EDITOR
BOB HARRAS SENIOR VP — EDITOR-IN-CHIEF, DC COMICS DAN DIDIO AND JIM LEE CO-PUBLISHERS
RATED T TEEN GEOFF JOHNS CHIEF CREATIVE OFFICER DIANE NELSON PRESIDENT DC COMICS

MAY 2015

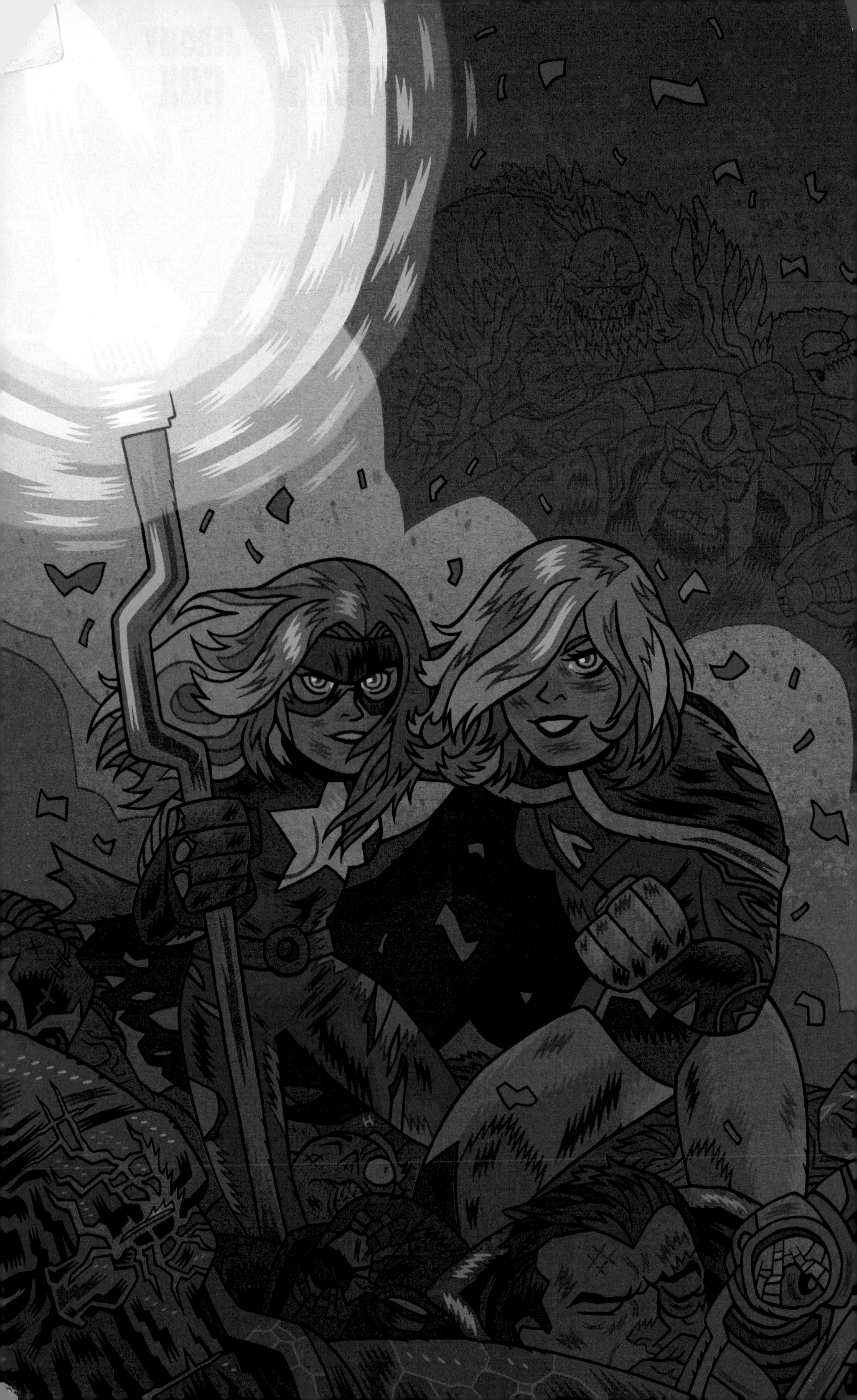

"Writer Geoff Johns and artist Jim Lee toss you–and their heroes–into the action from the very start and don't put on the brakes. DC's über-creative team craft an inviting world for those who are trying out a comic for the first time. Lee's art is stunning."—USA TODAY

"A fun ride."—IGN

START AT THE BEGINNING!
JUSTICE LEAGUE
VOLUME 1: ORIGIN
GEOFF JOHNS and JIM LEE

JUSTICE LEAGUE VOL. 2: THE VILLAIN'S JOURNEY

JUSTICE LEAGUE VOL. 3: THRONE OF ATLANTIS

JUSTICE LEAGUE OF AMERICA VOL. 1: WORLD'S MOST DANGEROUS

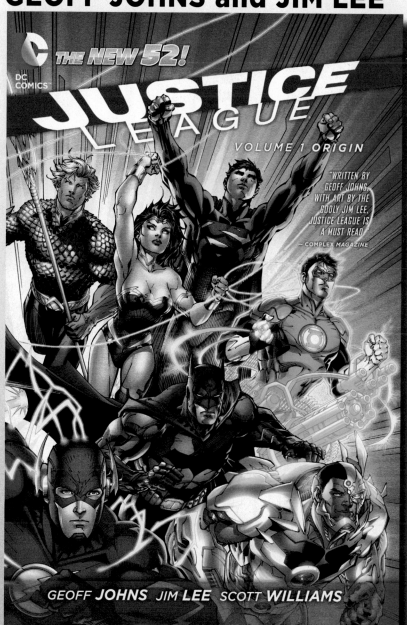

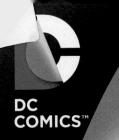

DC COMICS™

"[A] comic legend." —ROLLING STONE

"[Grant Morrison is] comics' high shaman."
—WASHINGTON POST

"[Grant Morrison] is probably my favorite writer. That guy has more ideas in his pinky than most people do in a lifetime."
—Gerard Way from MY CHEMICAL ROMANCE

FROM THE WRITER OF *ALL-STAR SUPERMAN* AND *BATMAN & ROBIN*

GRANT MORRISON

with HOWARD PORTER

JLA VOL. 2

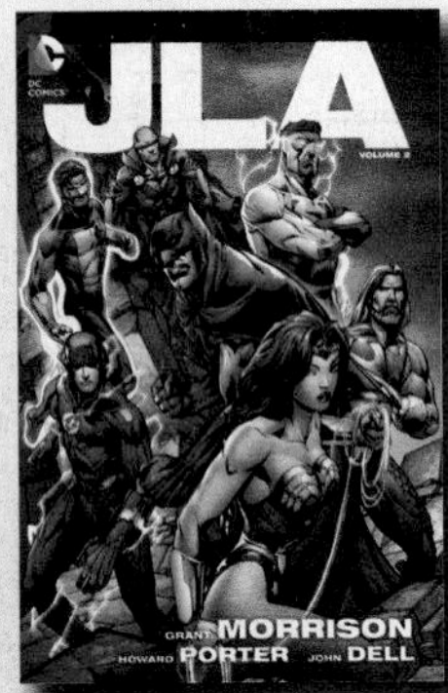
JLA
GRANT MORRISON
HOWARD PORTER JOHN DELL

with HOWARD PORTER

JLA VOL. 3

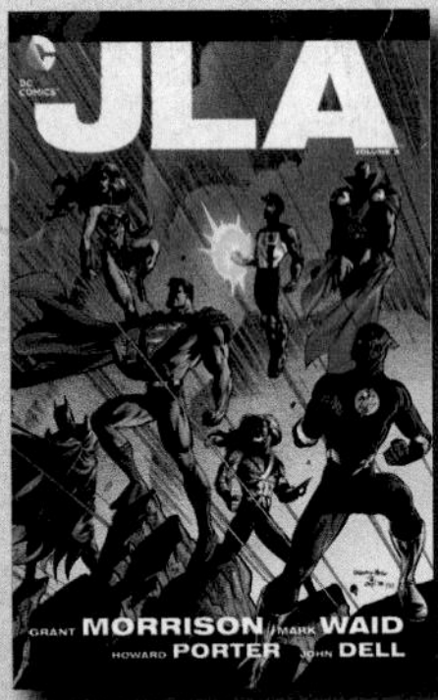
JLA
GRANT MORRISON MARK WAID
HOWARD PORTER JOHN DELL

with HOWARD PORTER

JLA VOL. 4

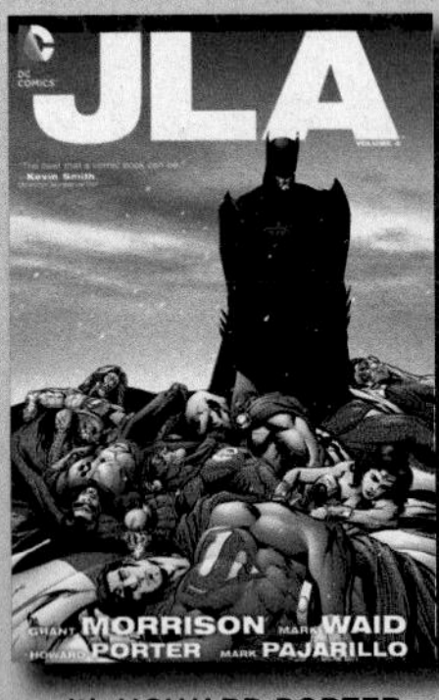
JLA
GRANT MORRISON MARK WAID
HOWARD PORTER MARK PAJARILLO

with HOWARD PORTER, MARK WAID, and MARK PAJARILLO

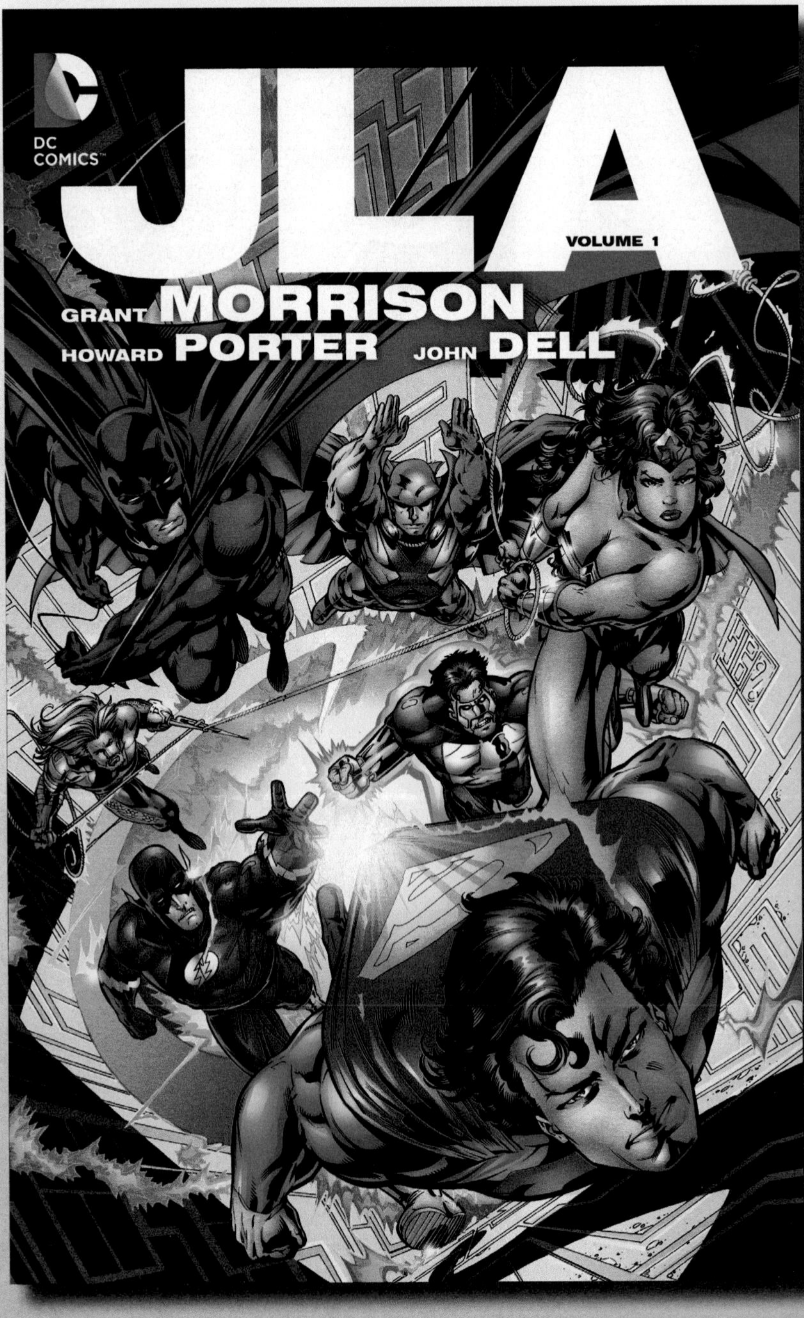
DC COMICS
JLA
VOLUME 1
GRANT MORRISON
HOWARD PORTER JOHN DELL

LEGION OF SUPER-
HEROES VOLUME 1:
HOSTILE WORLD

LEGION LOST
VOLUME 1: RUN FROM
TOMORROW

STATIC SHOCK
VOLUME 1:
SUPERCHARGED

START AT THE BEGINNING!

TEEN TITANS
VOLUME 1: IT'S
OUR RIGHT TO FIGHT

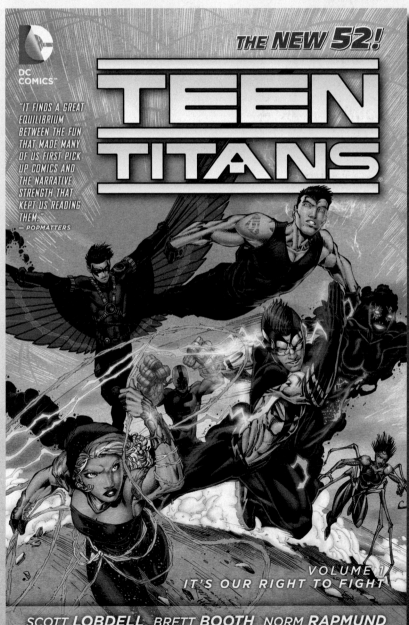

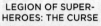